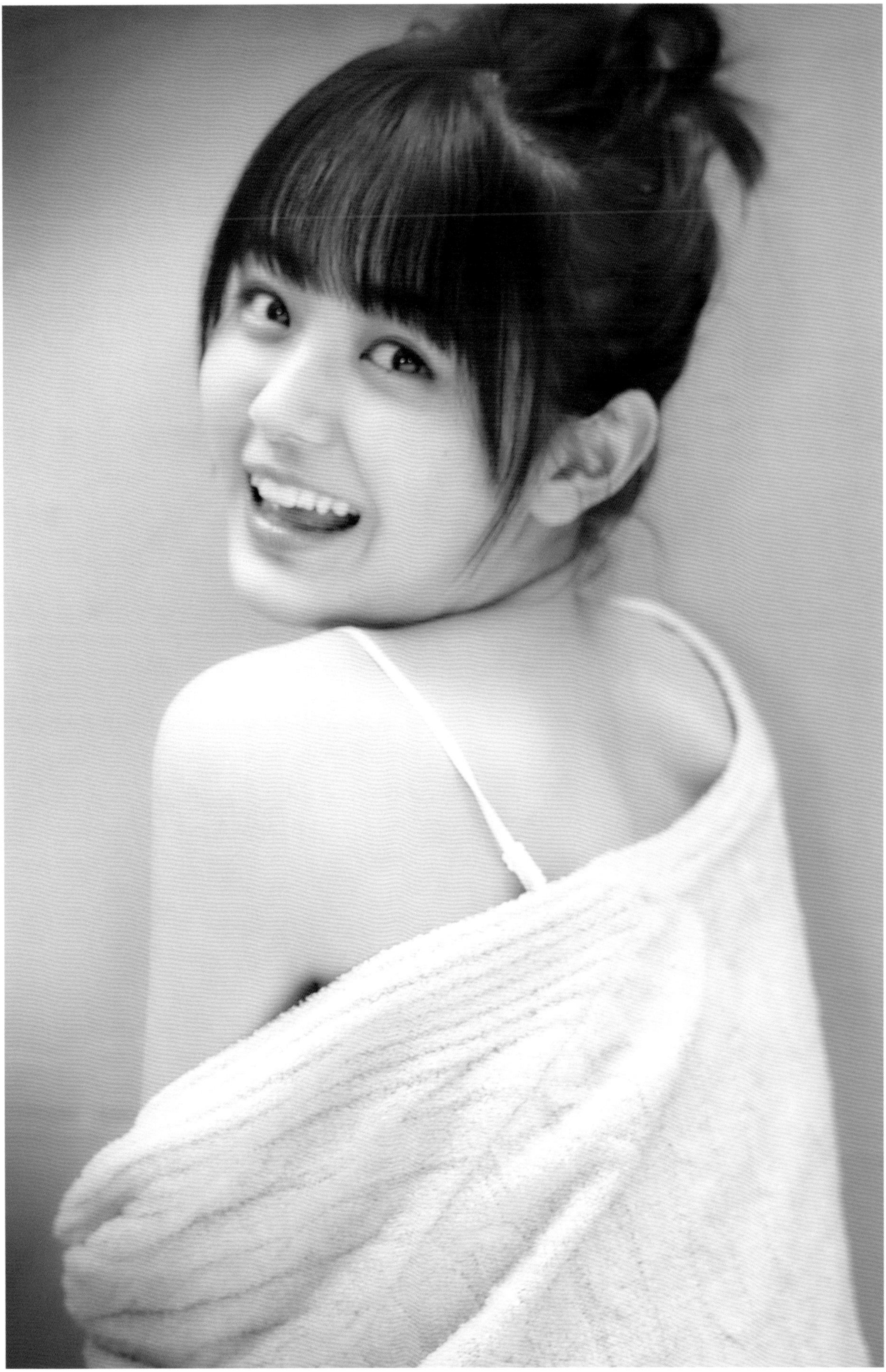

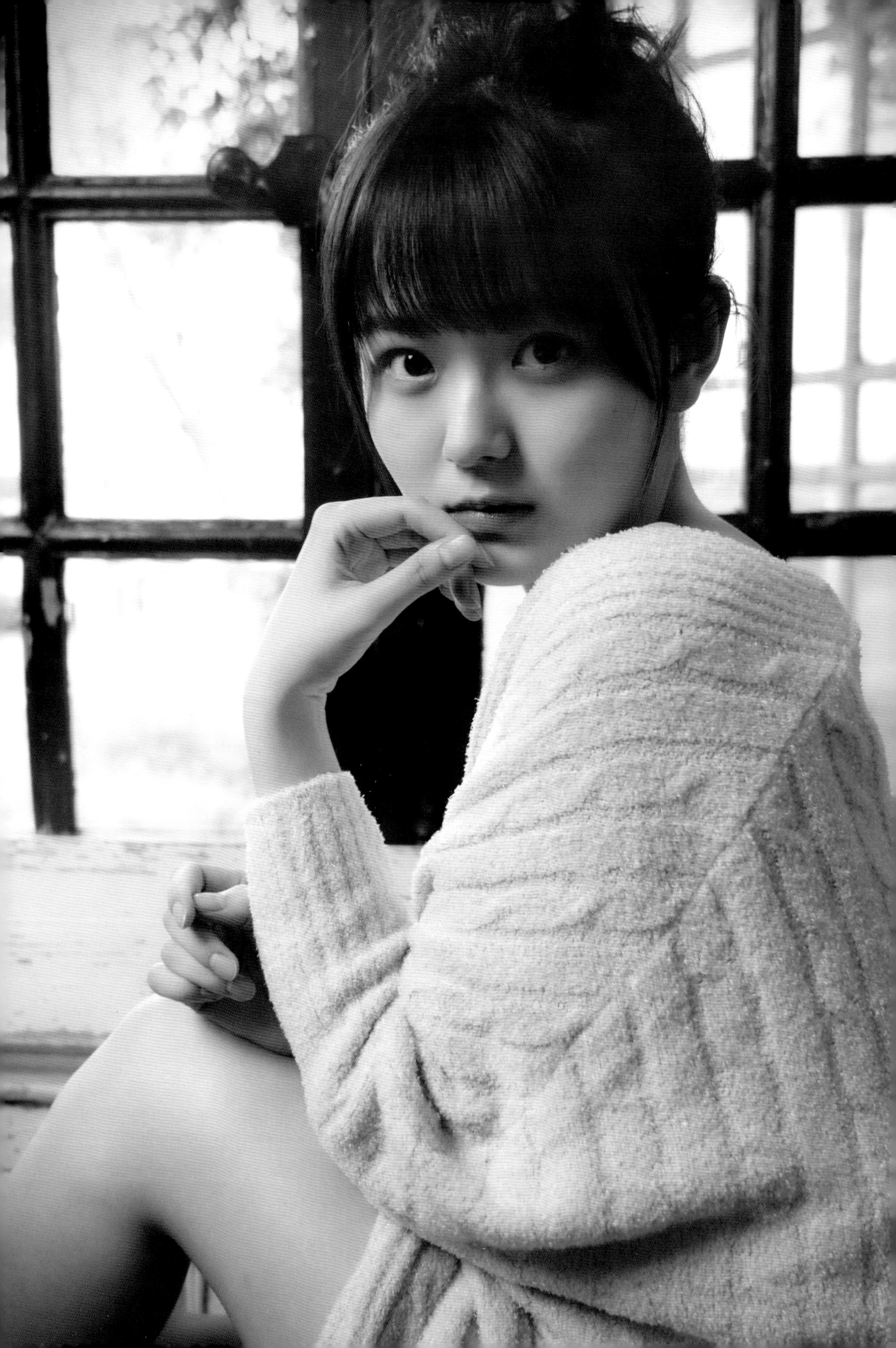

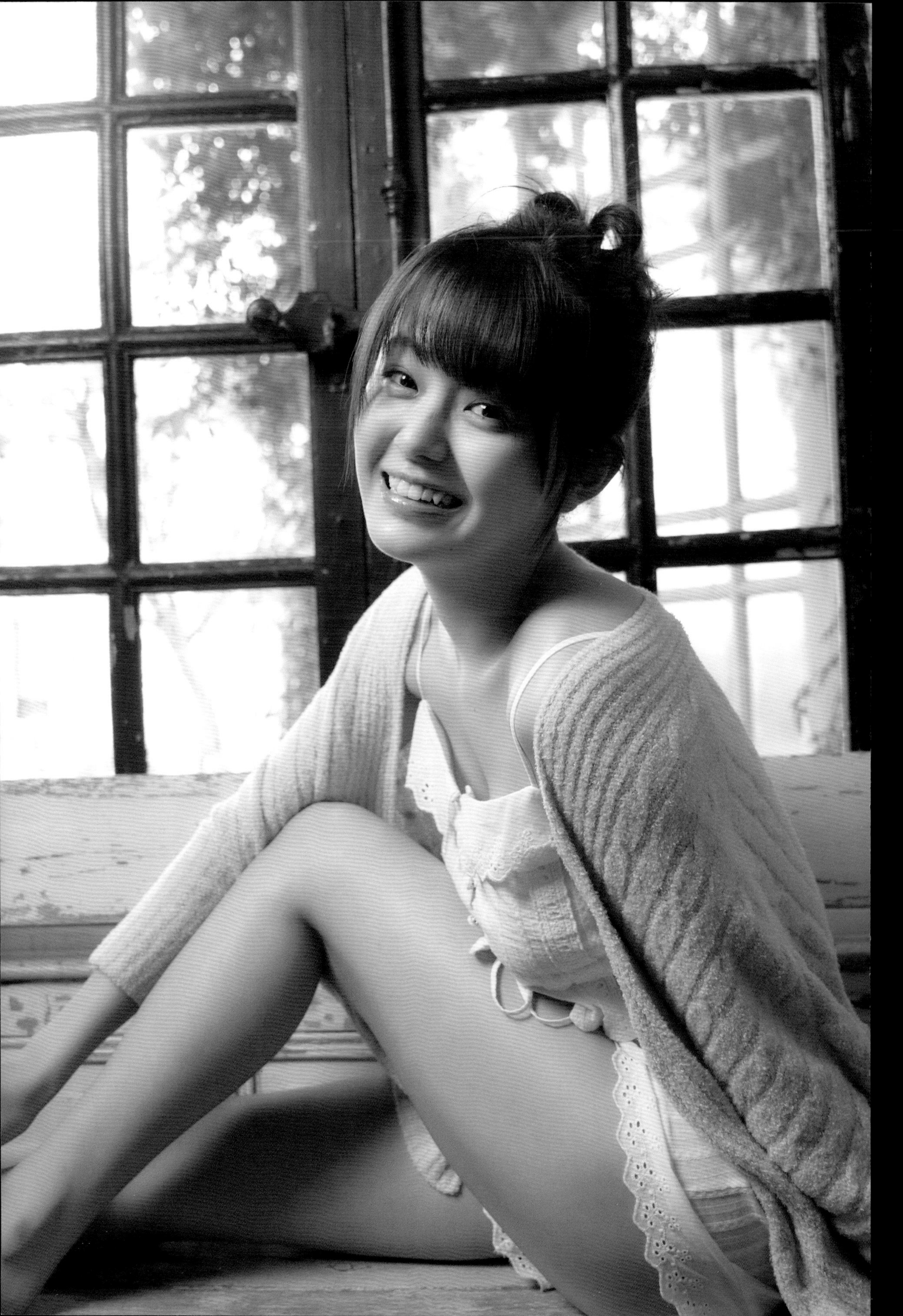

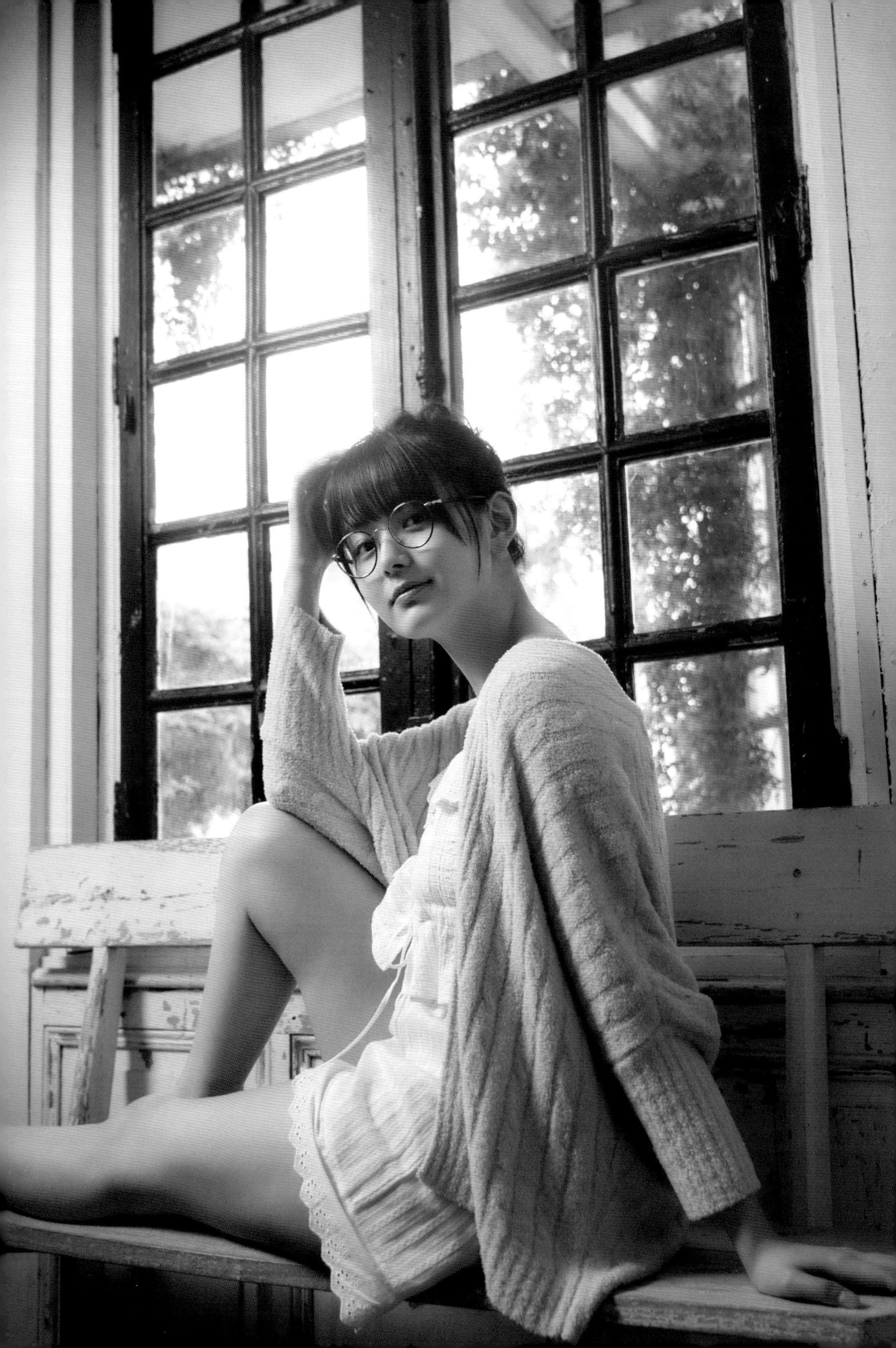

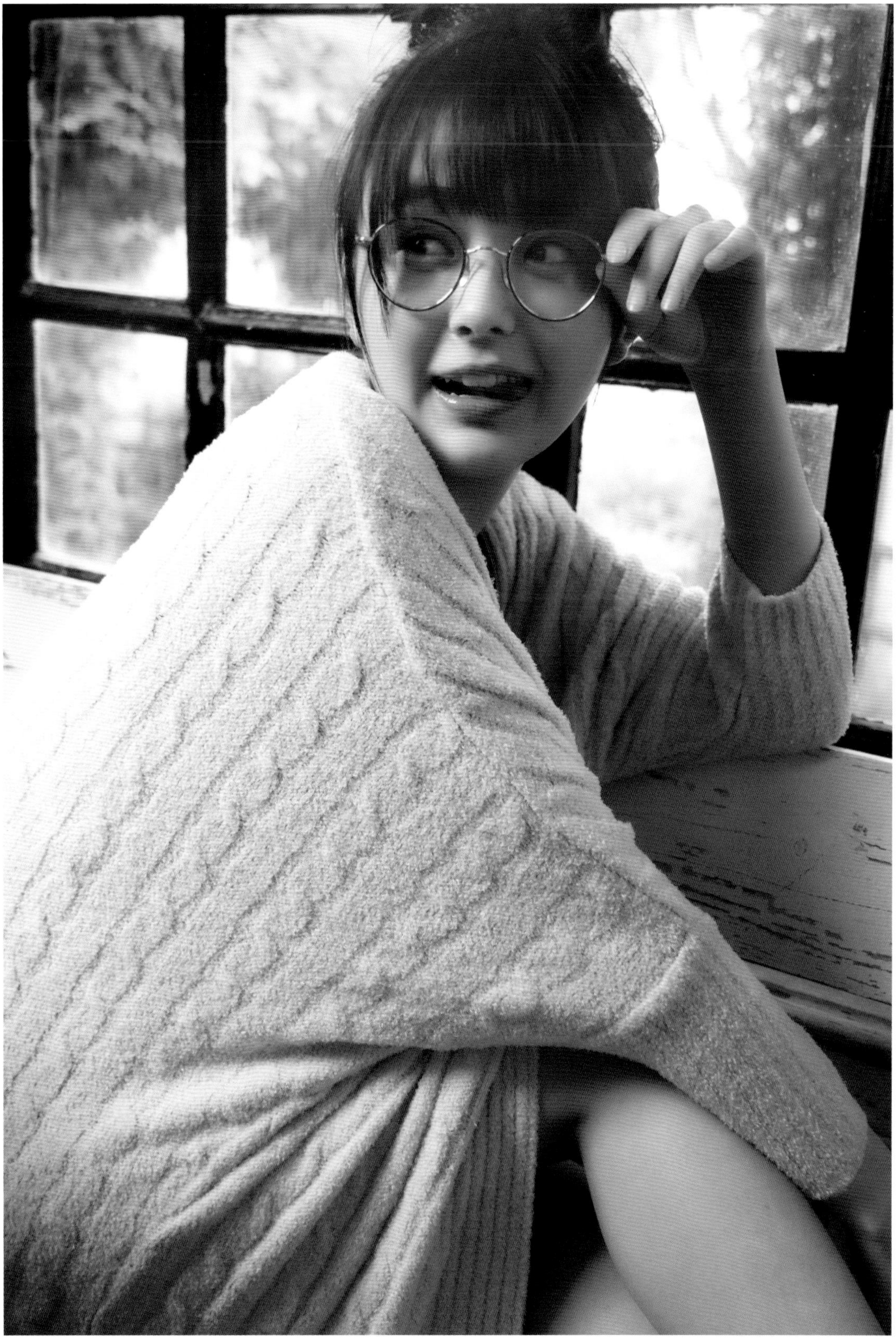

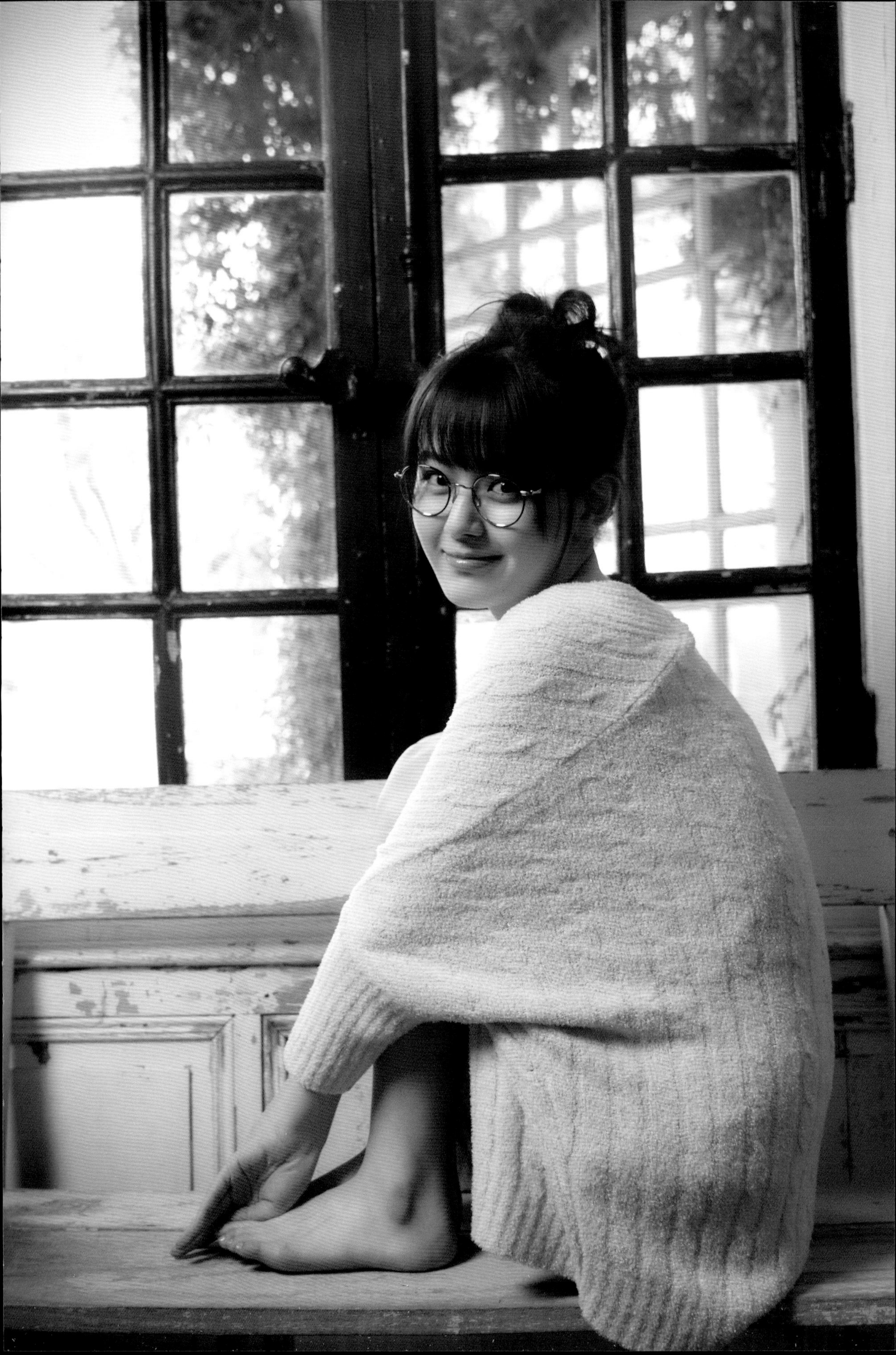

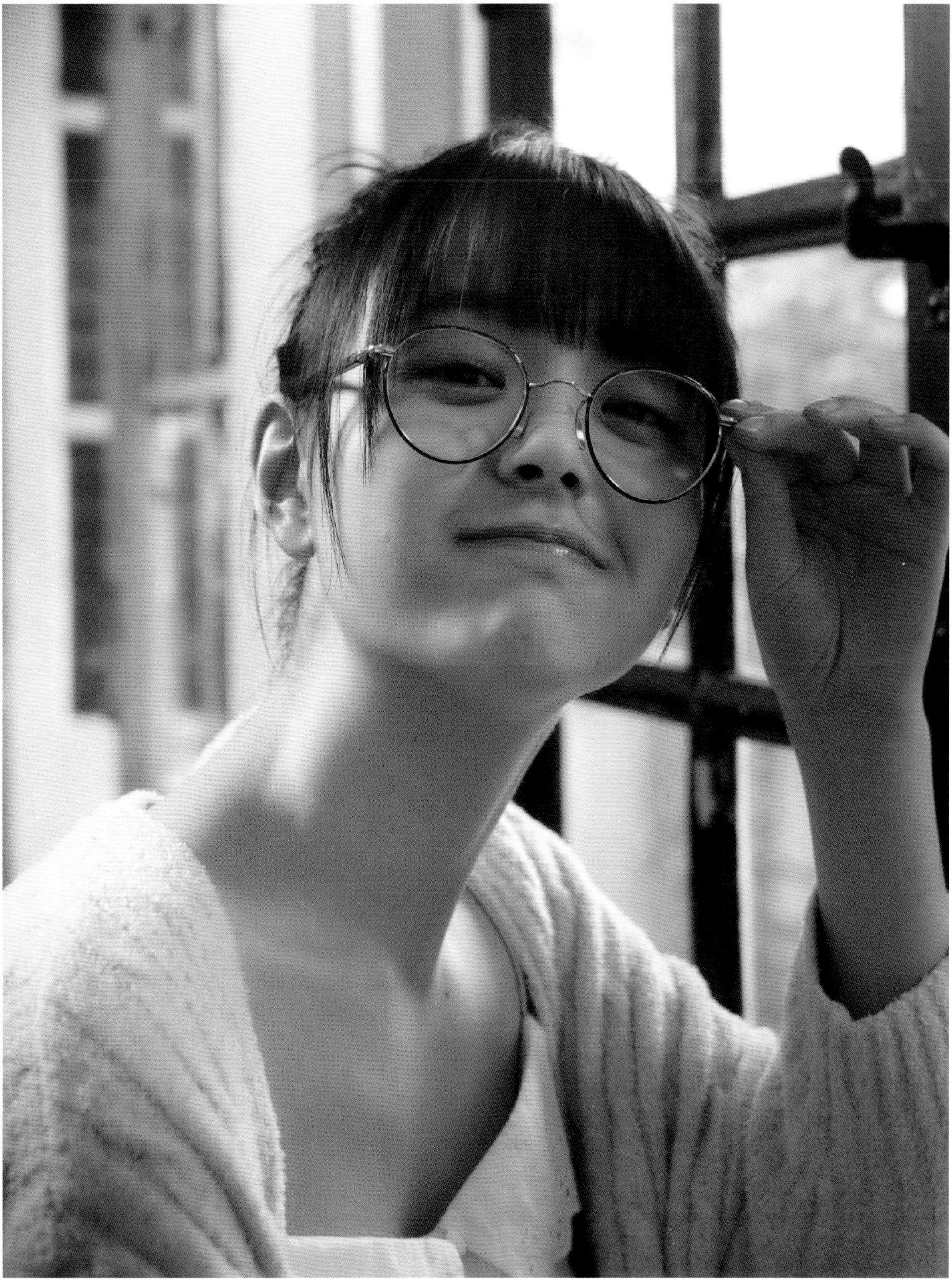

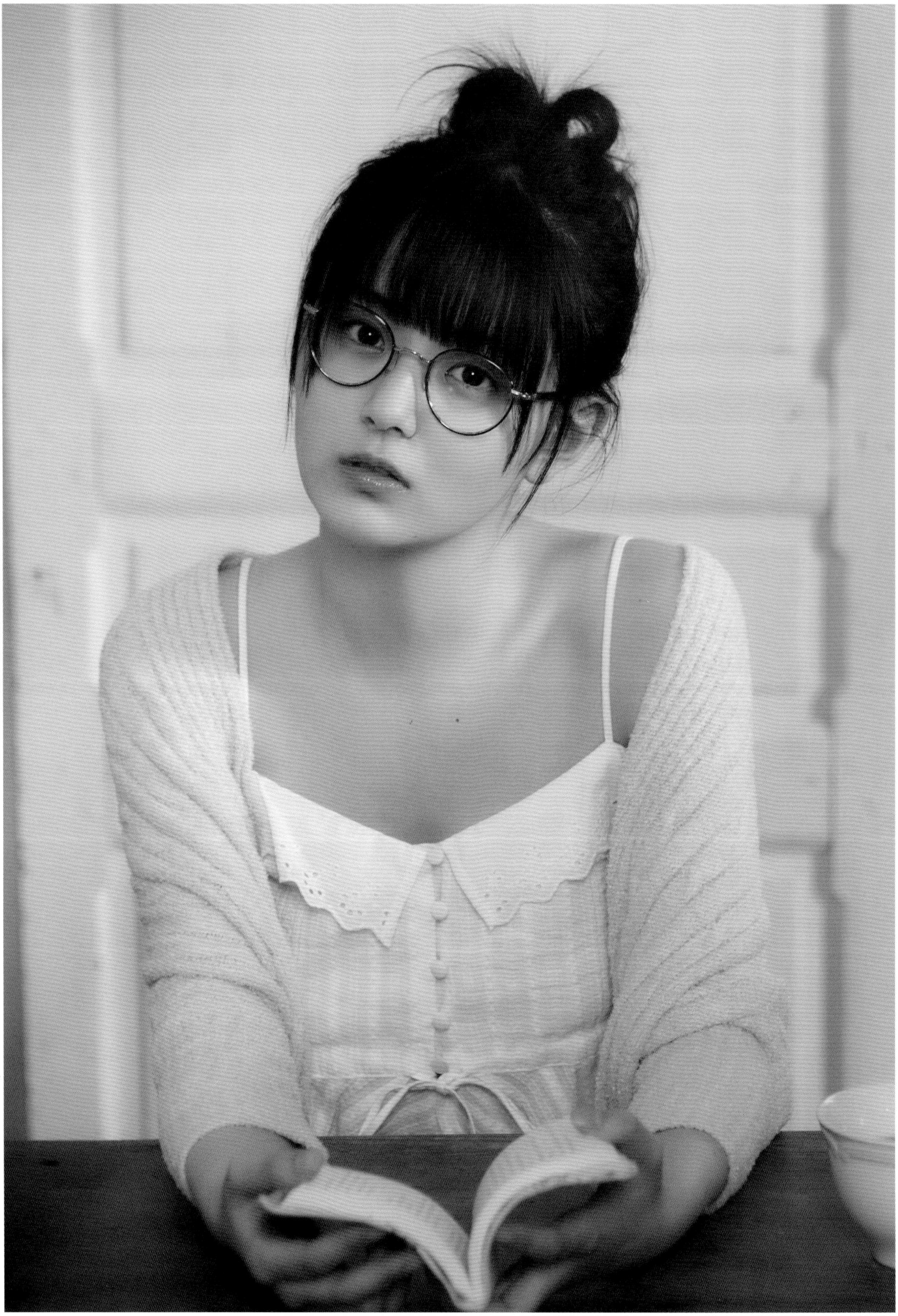

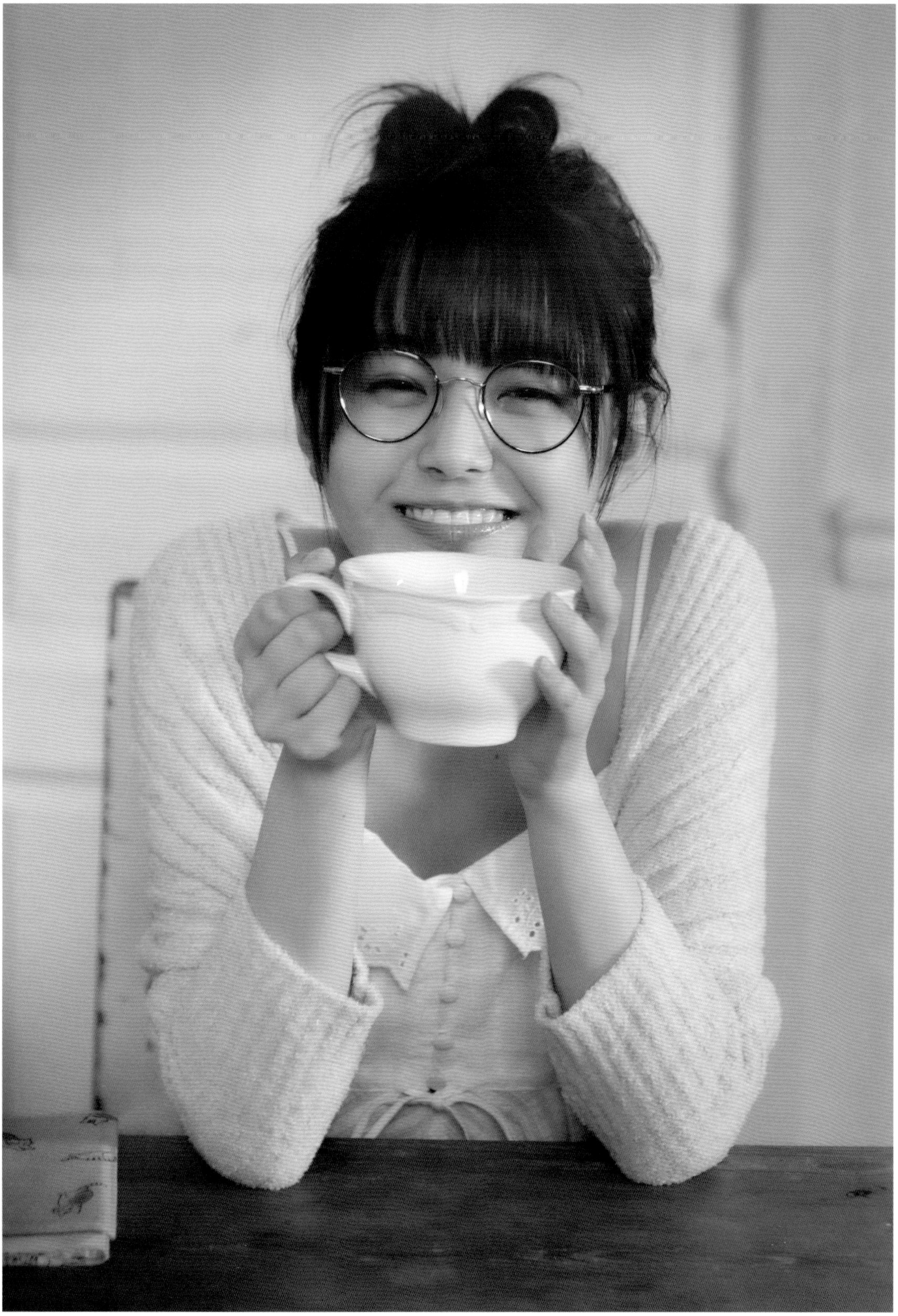

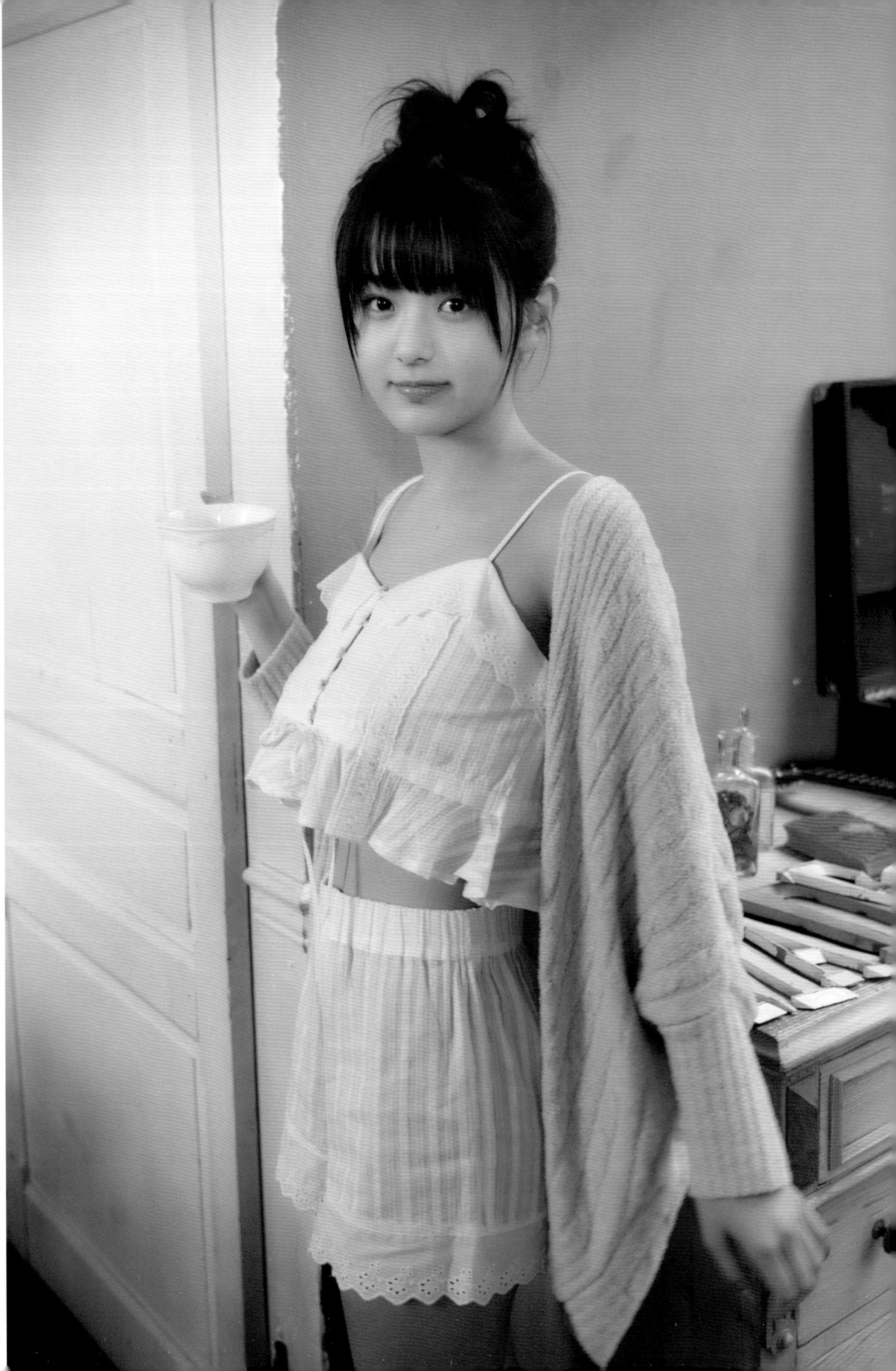

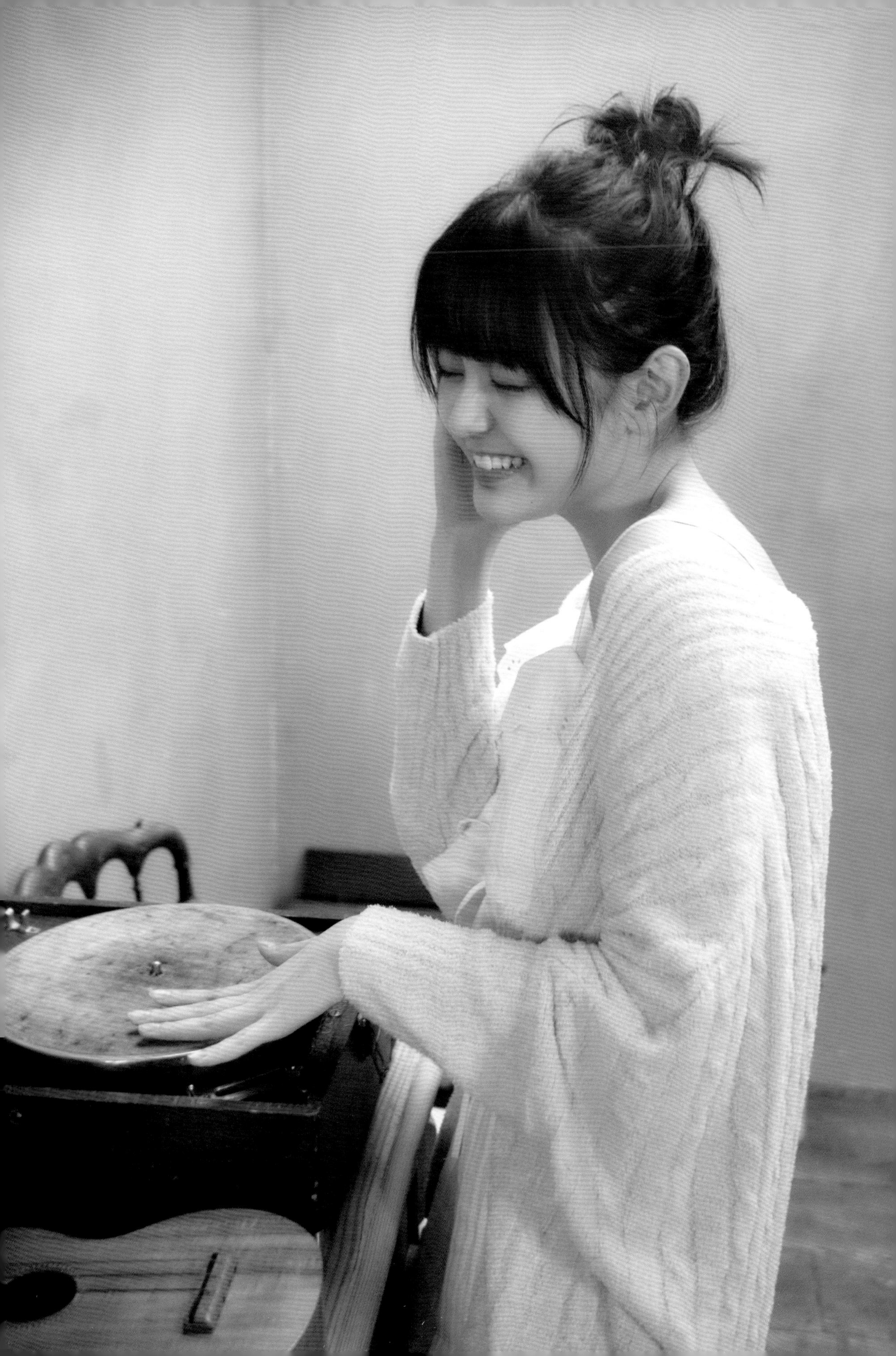

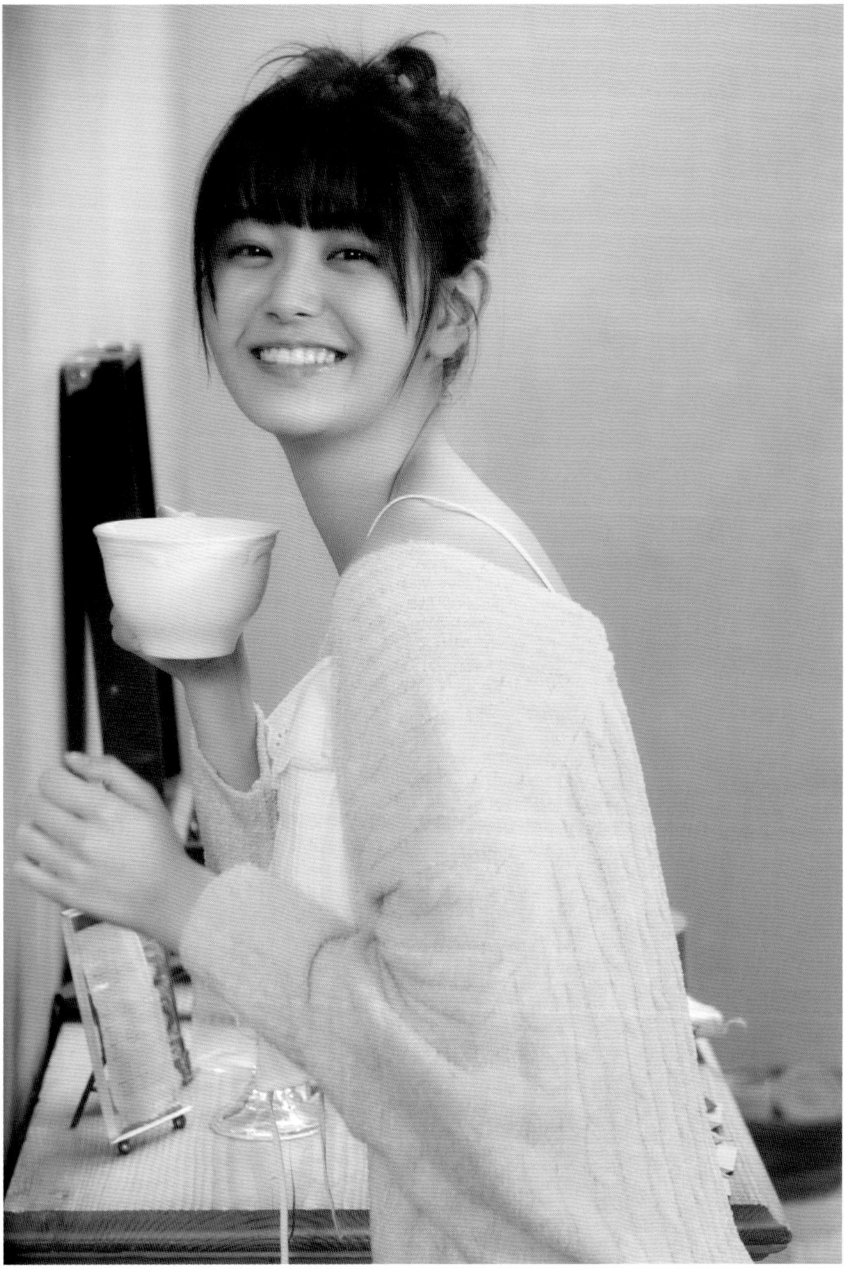

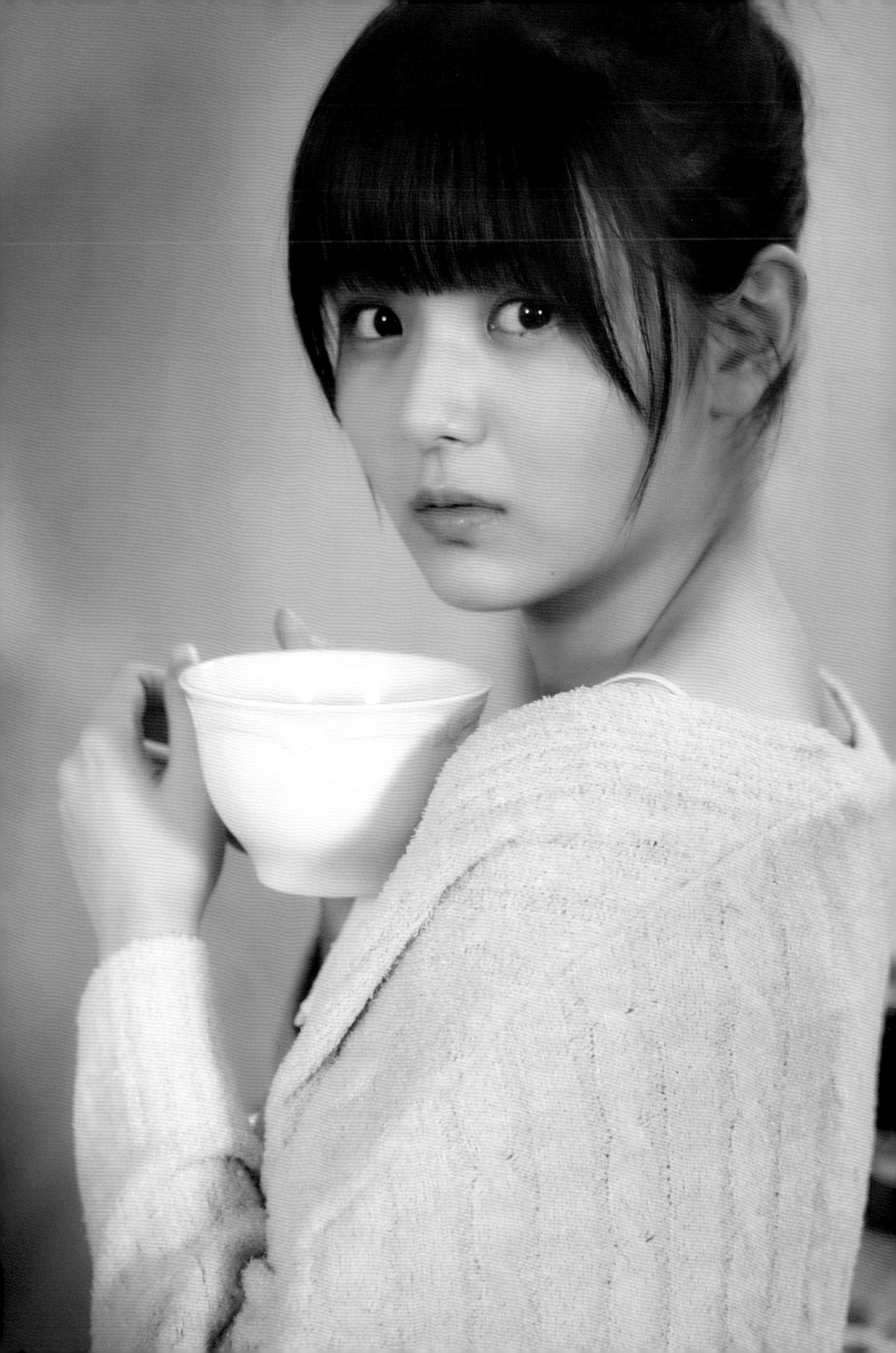

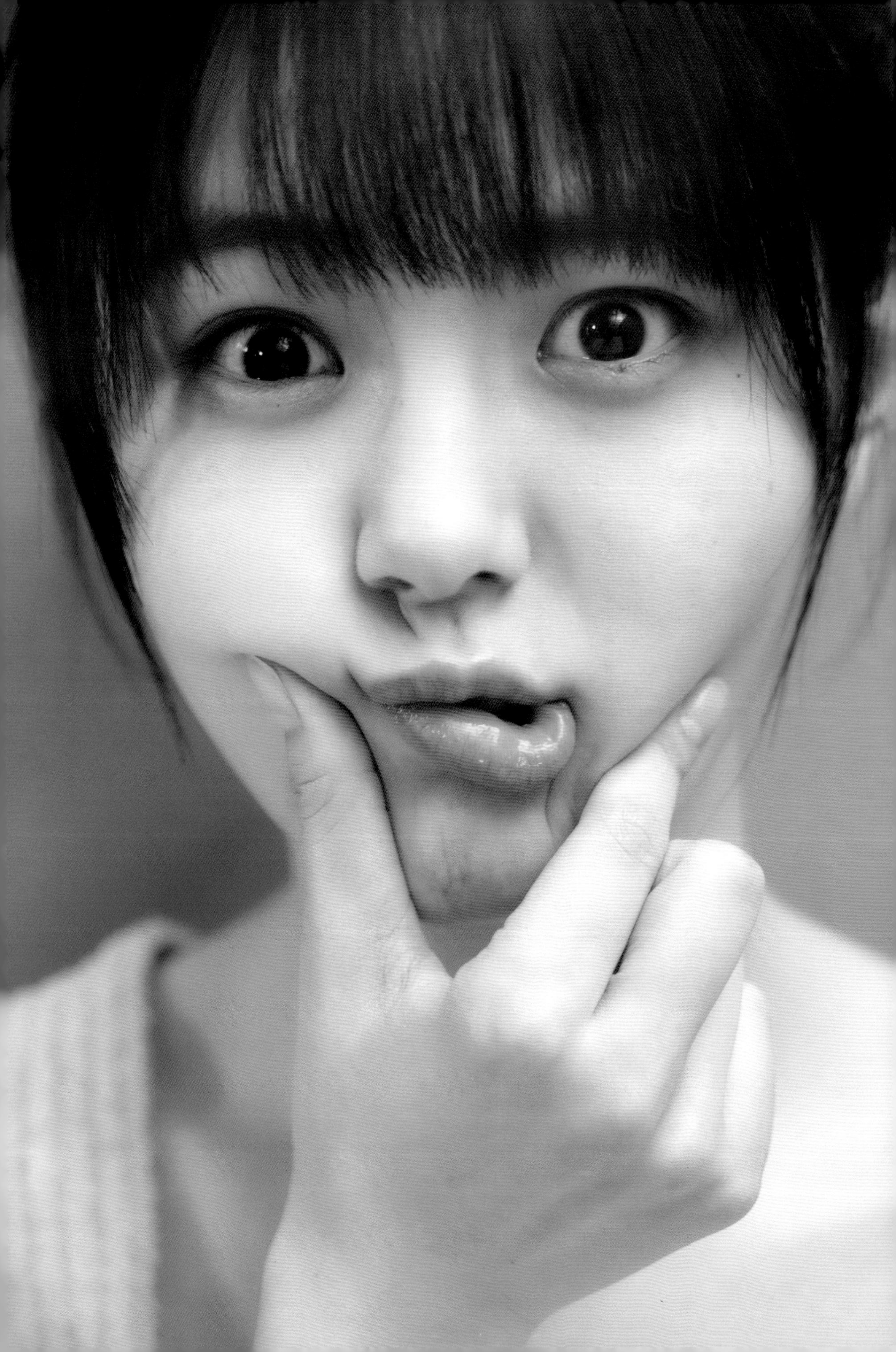

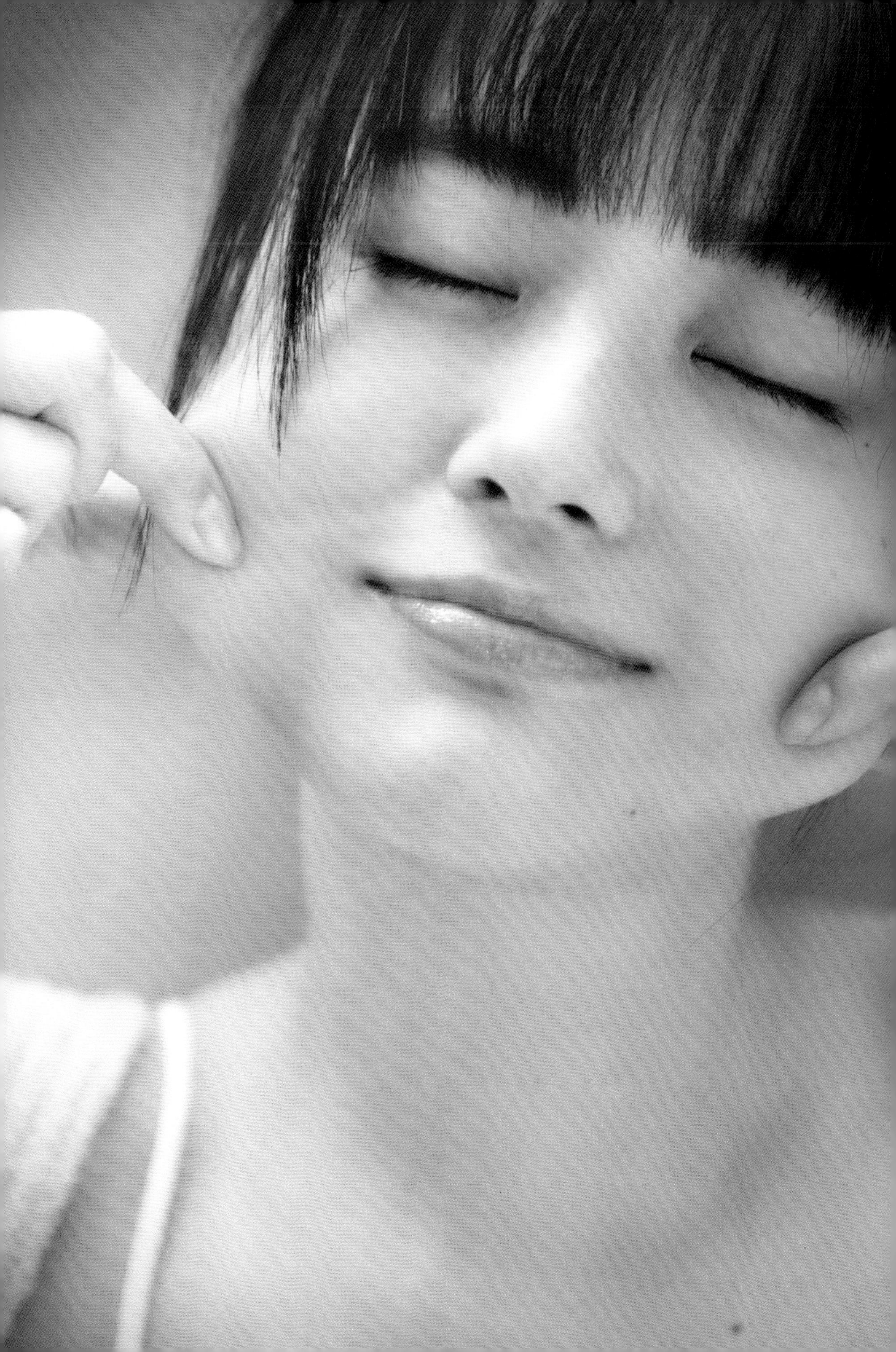

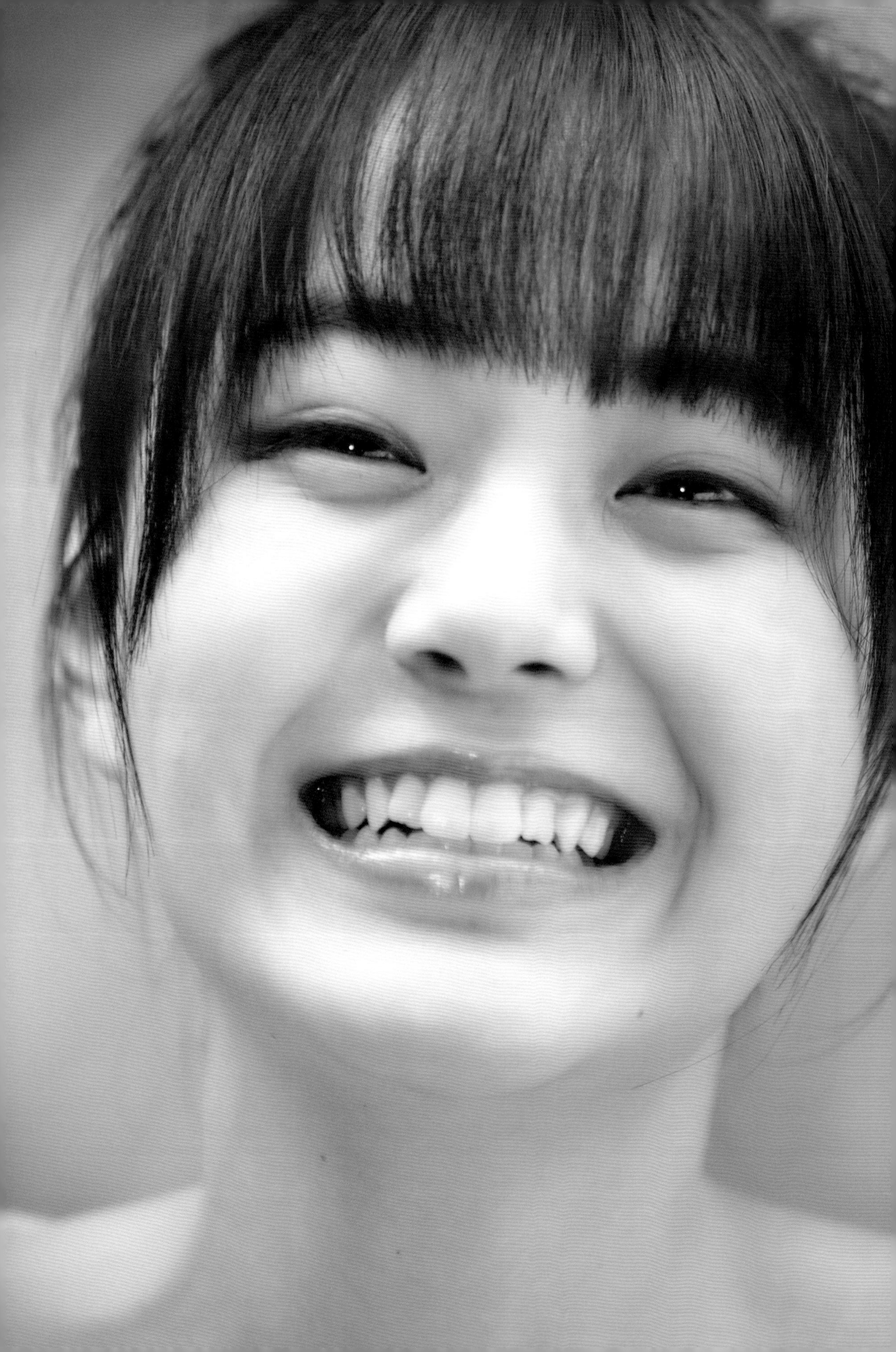

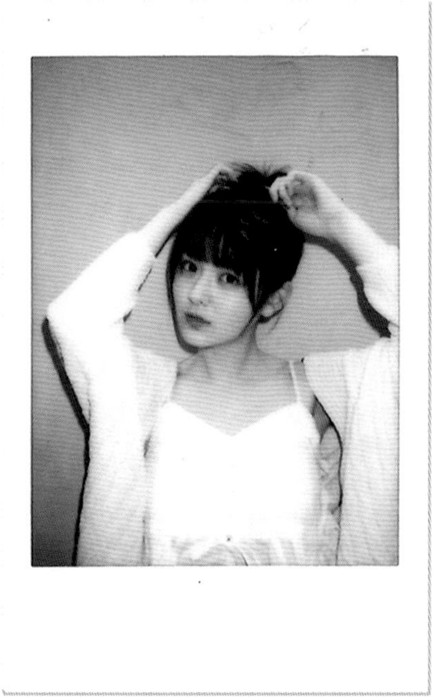
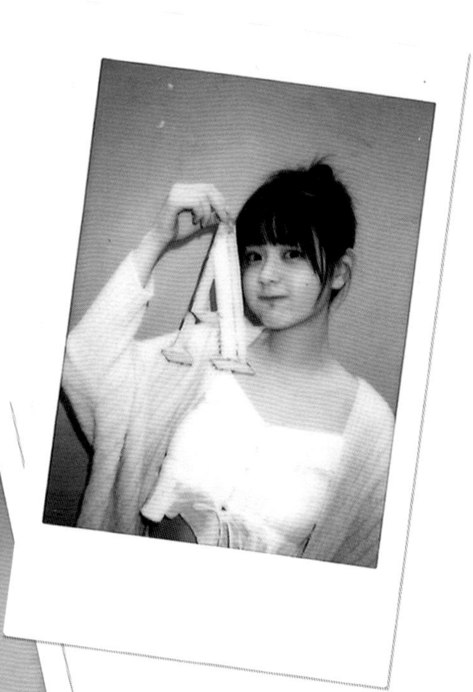
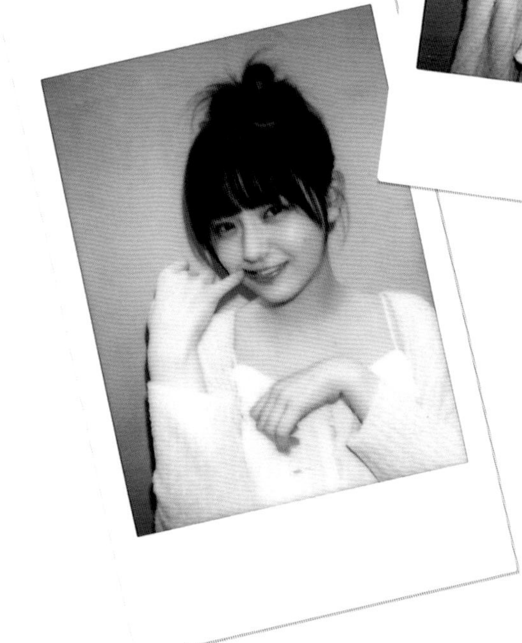
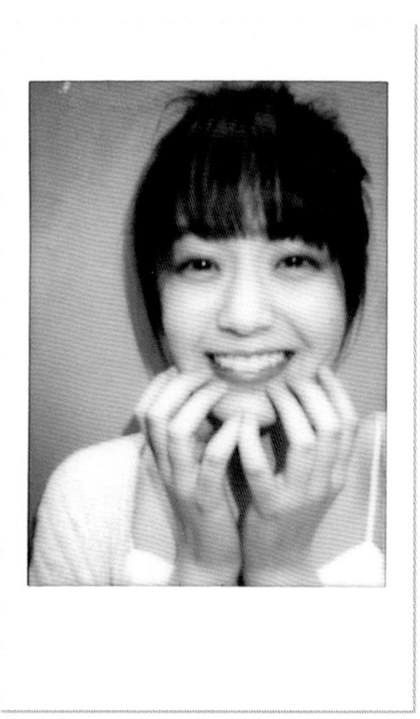

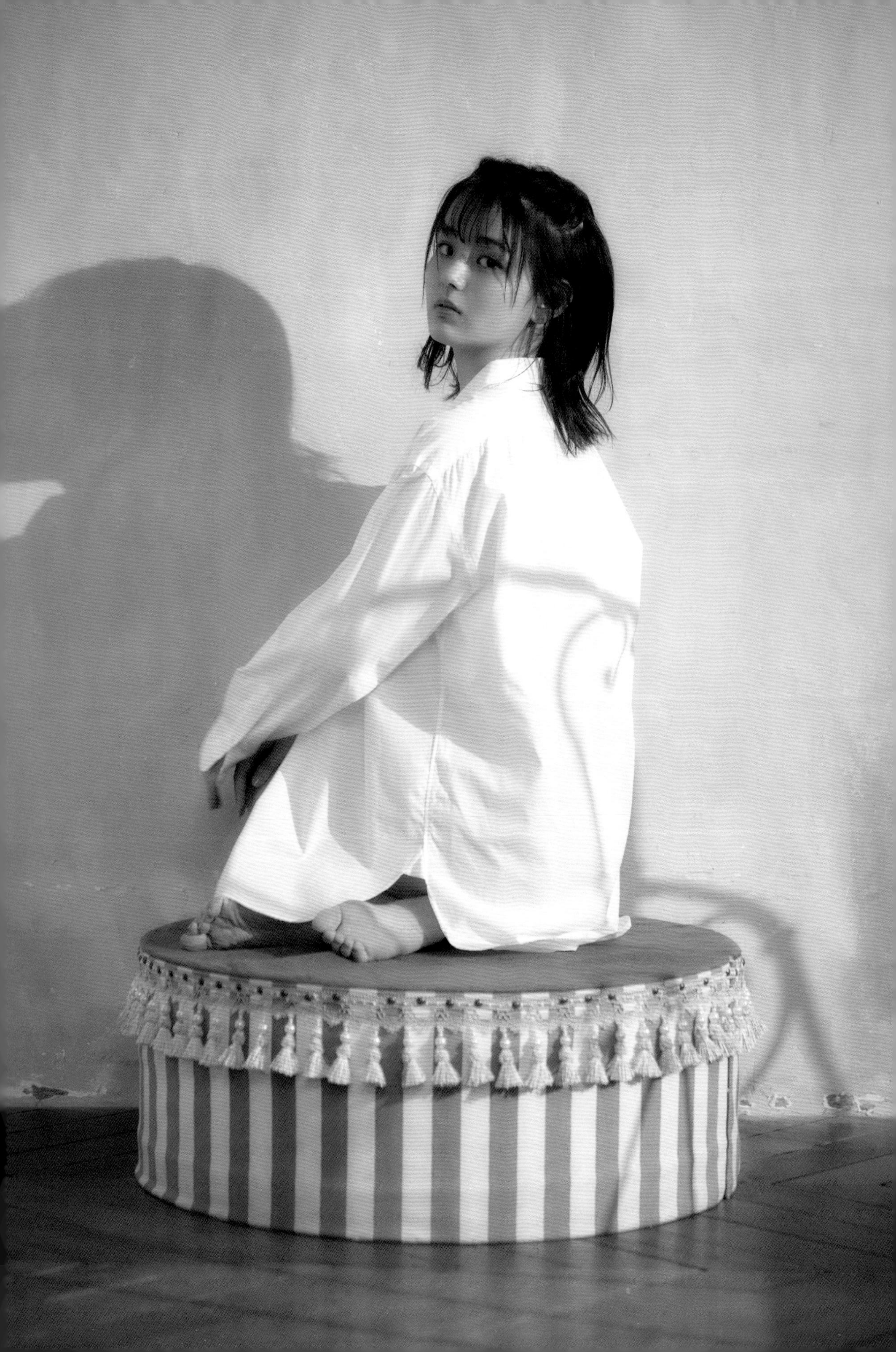

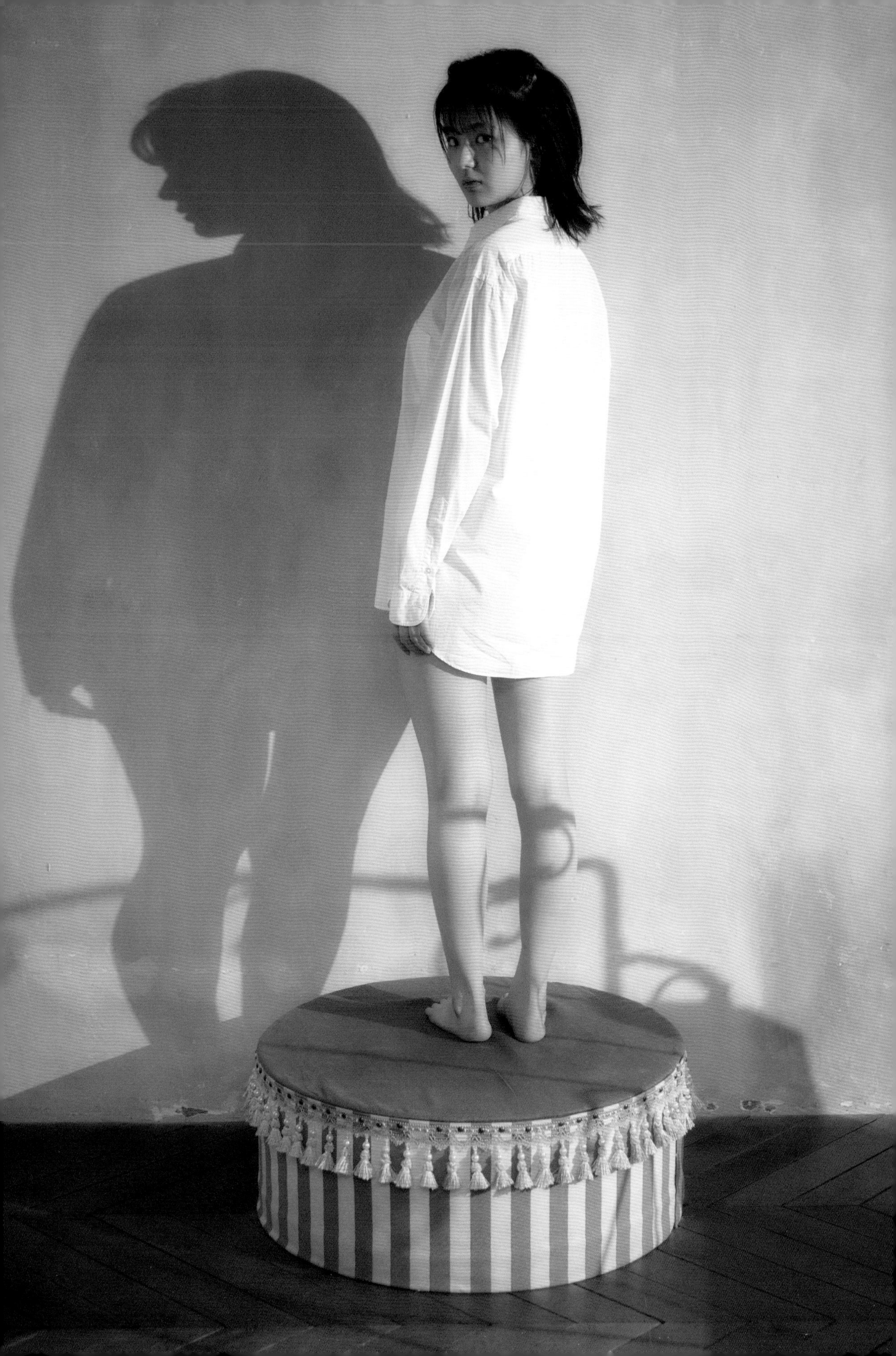

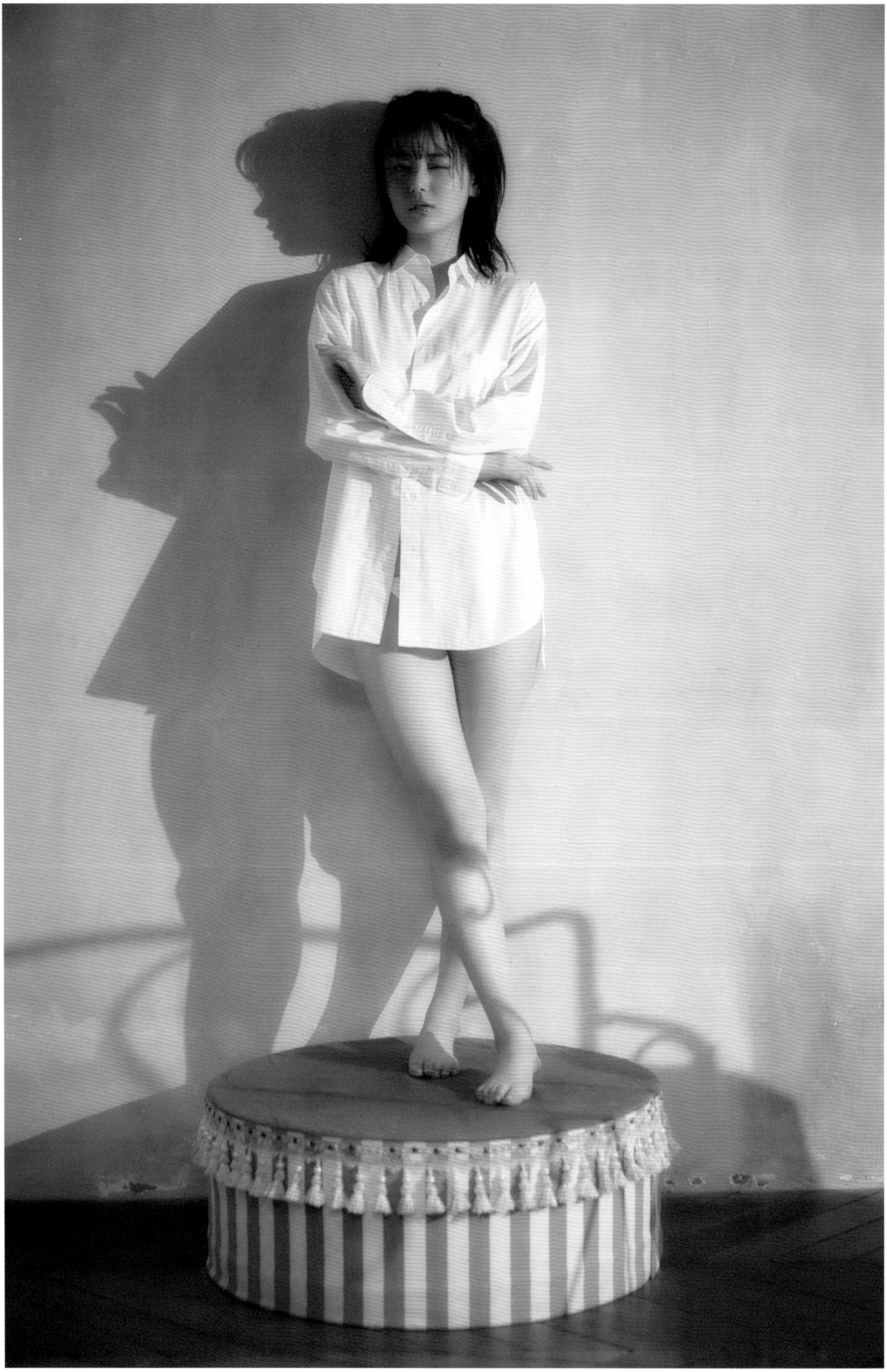

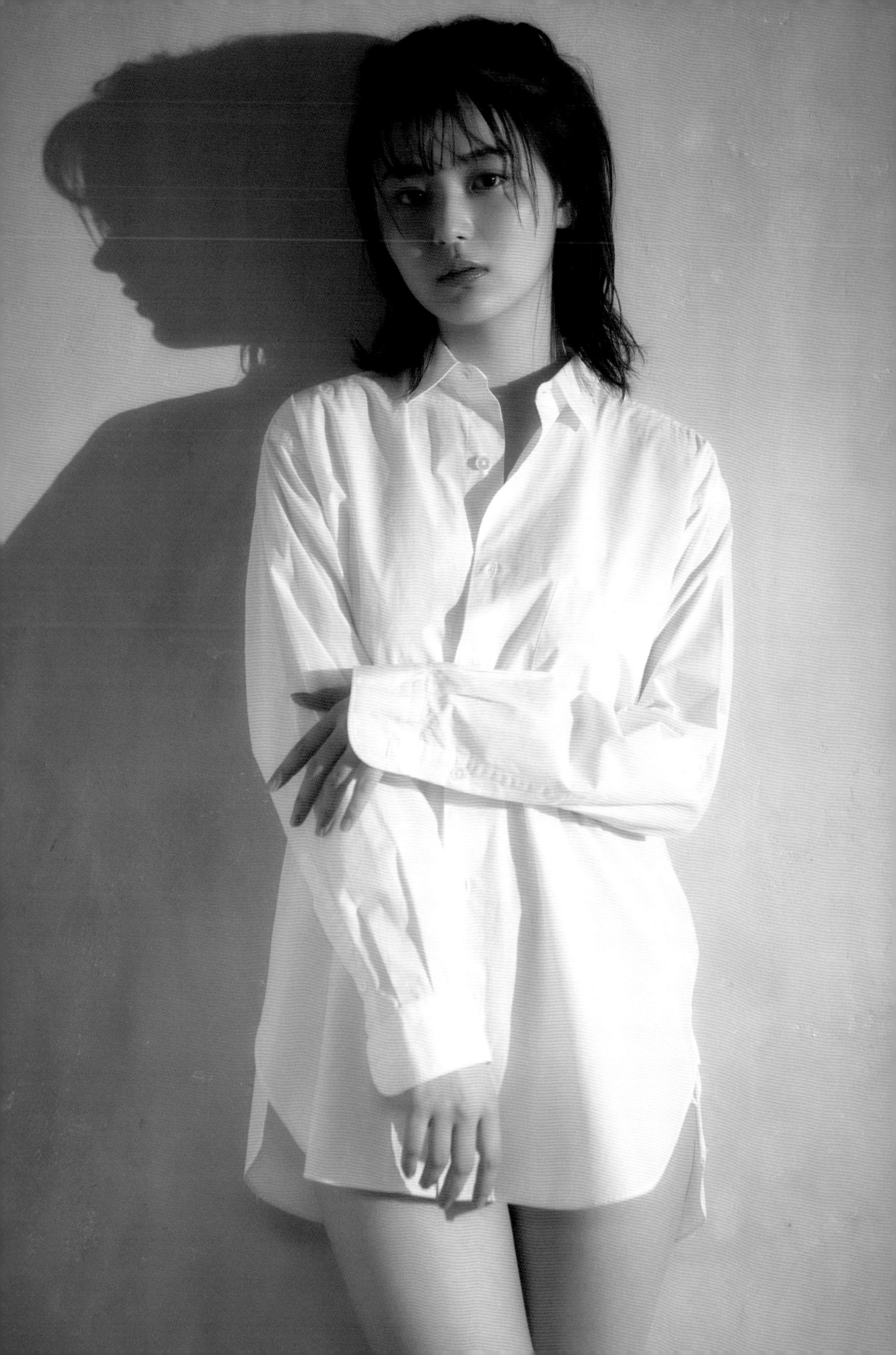

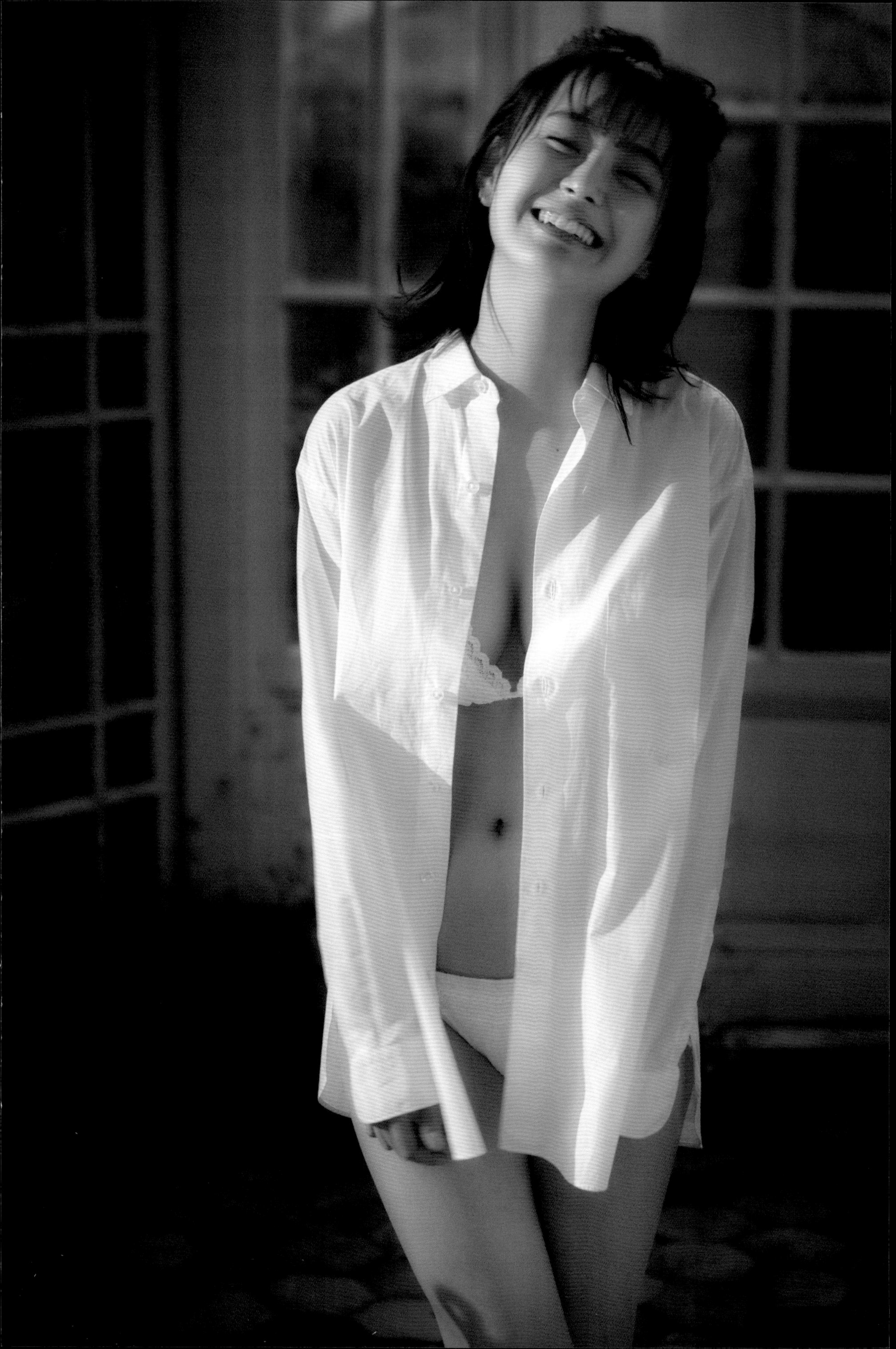

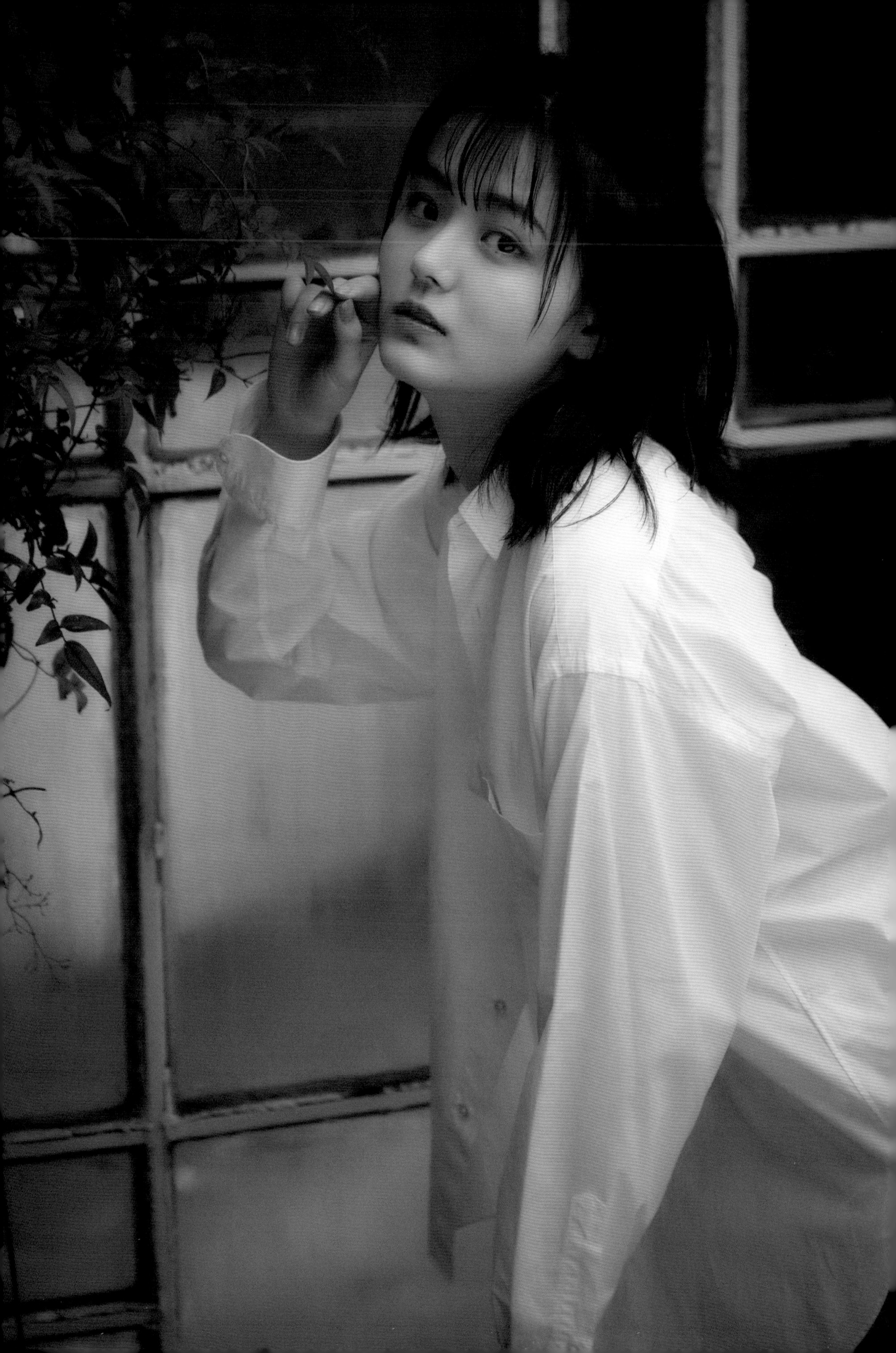

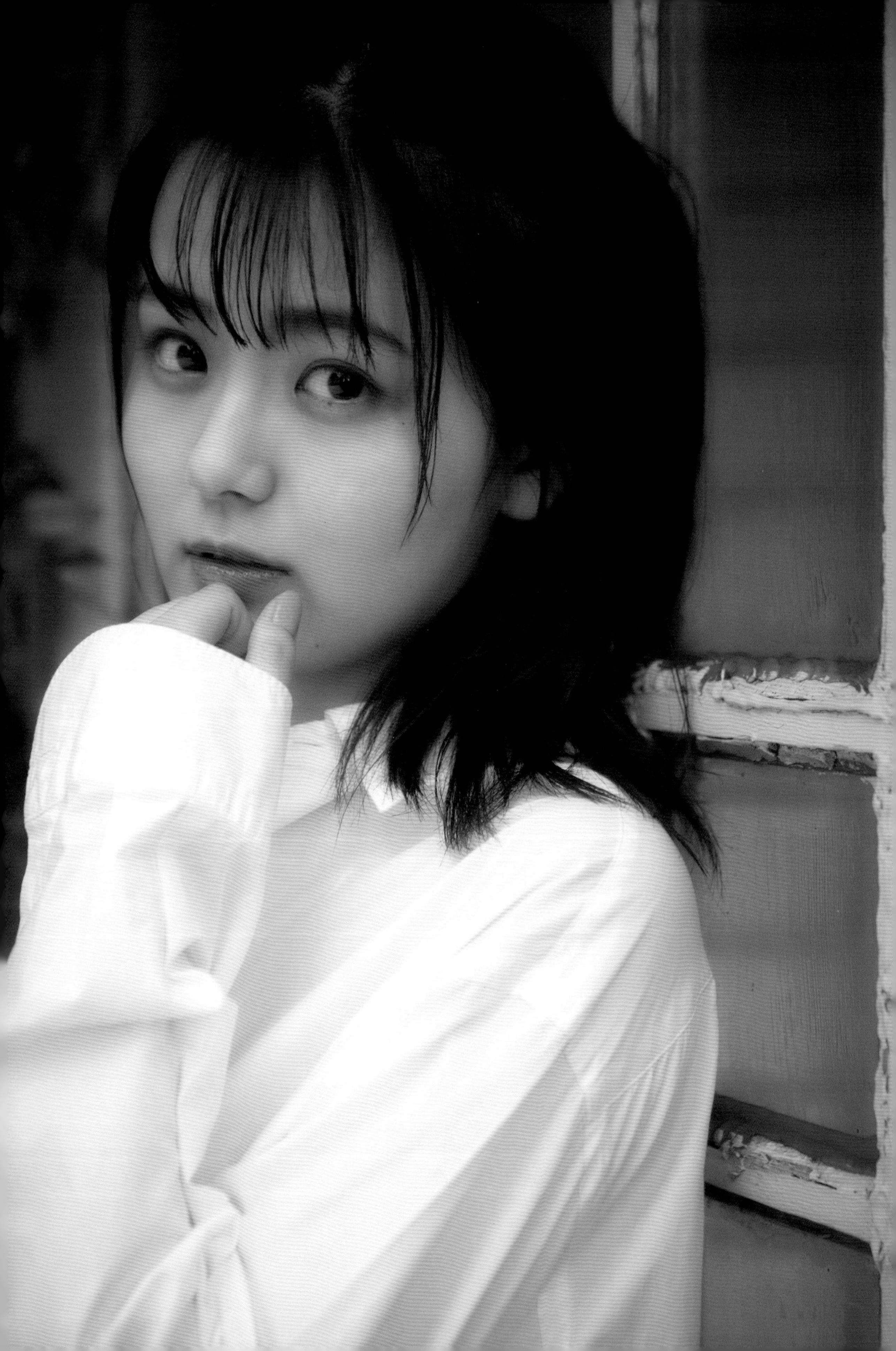

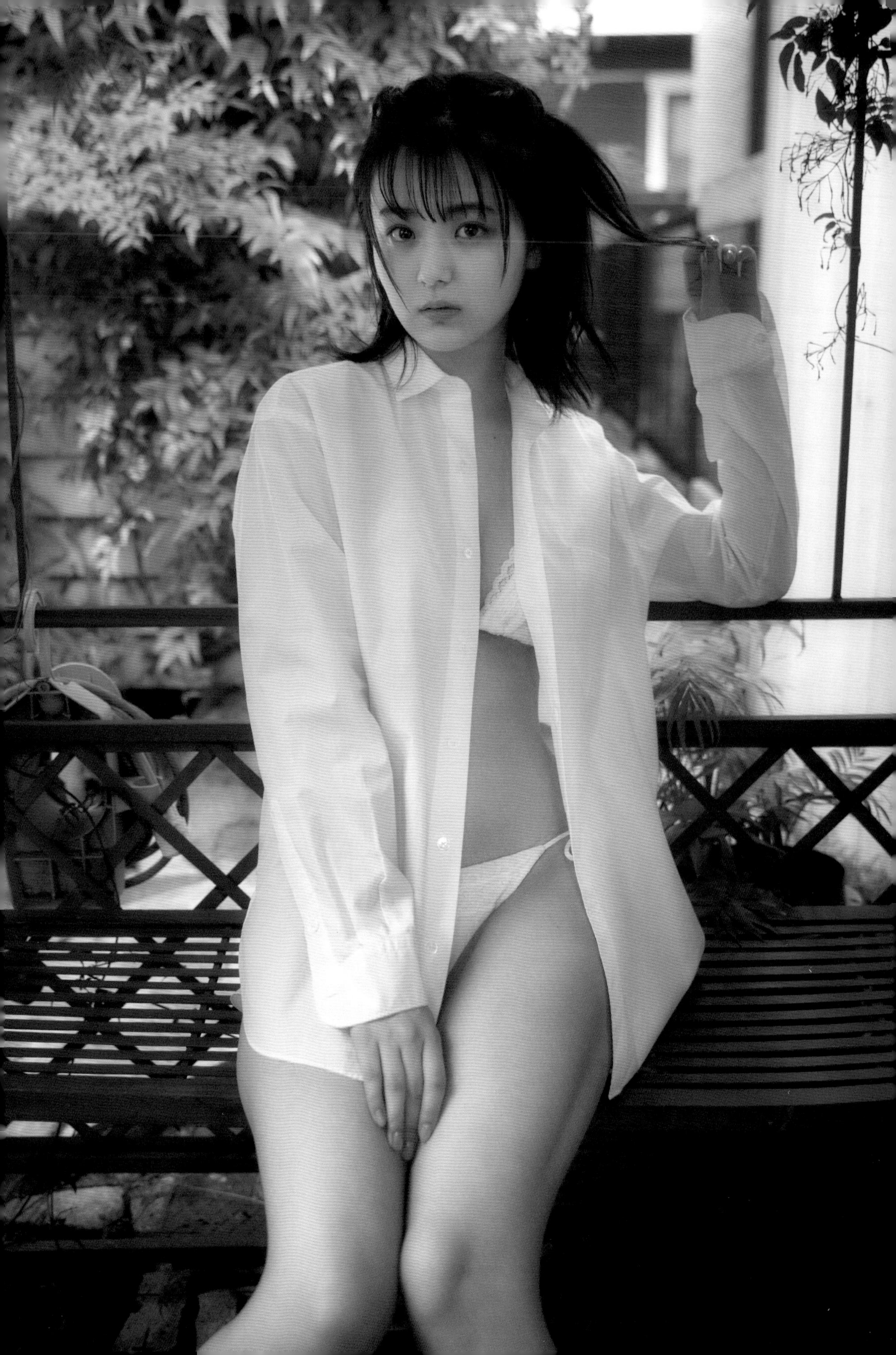

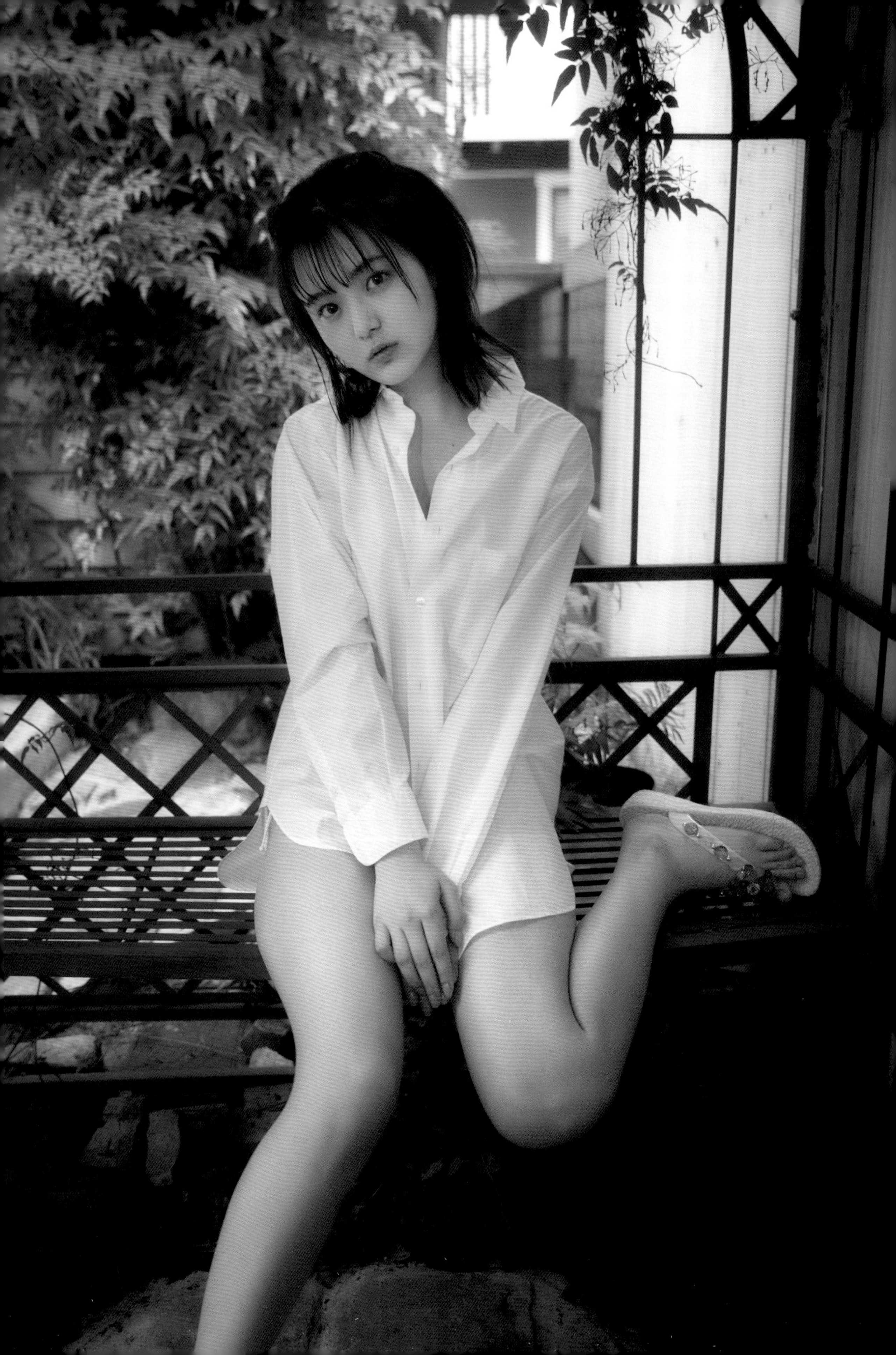

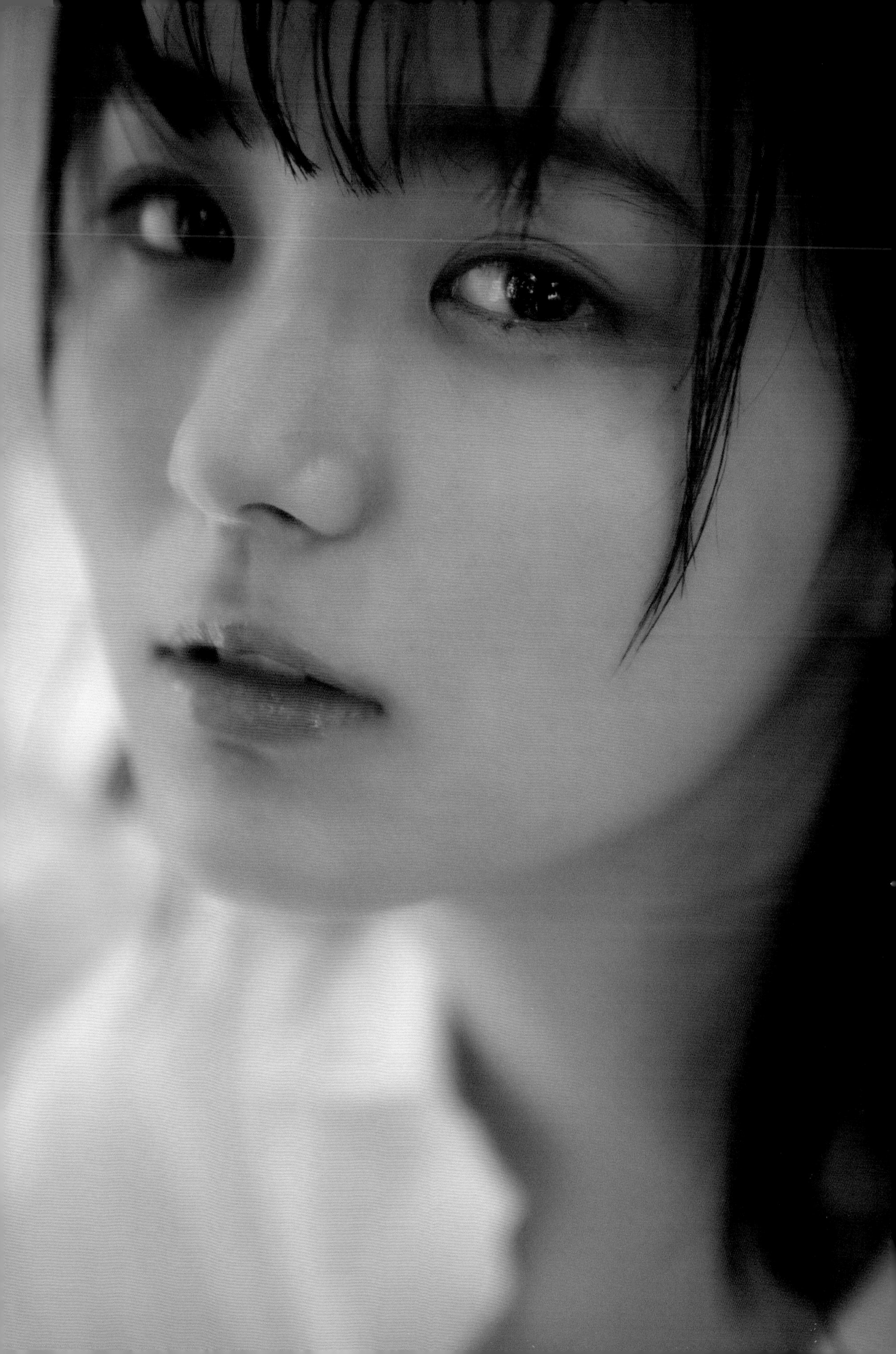

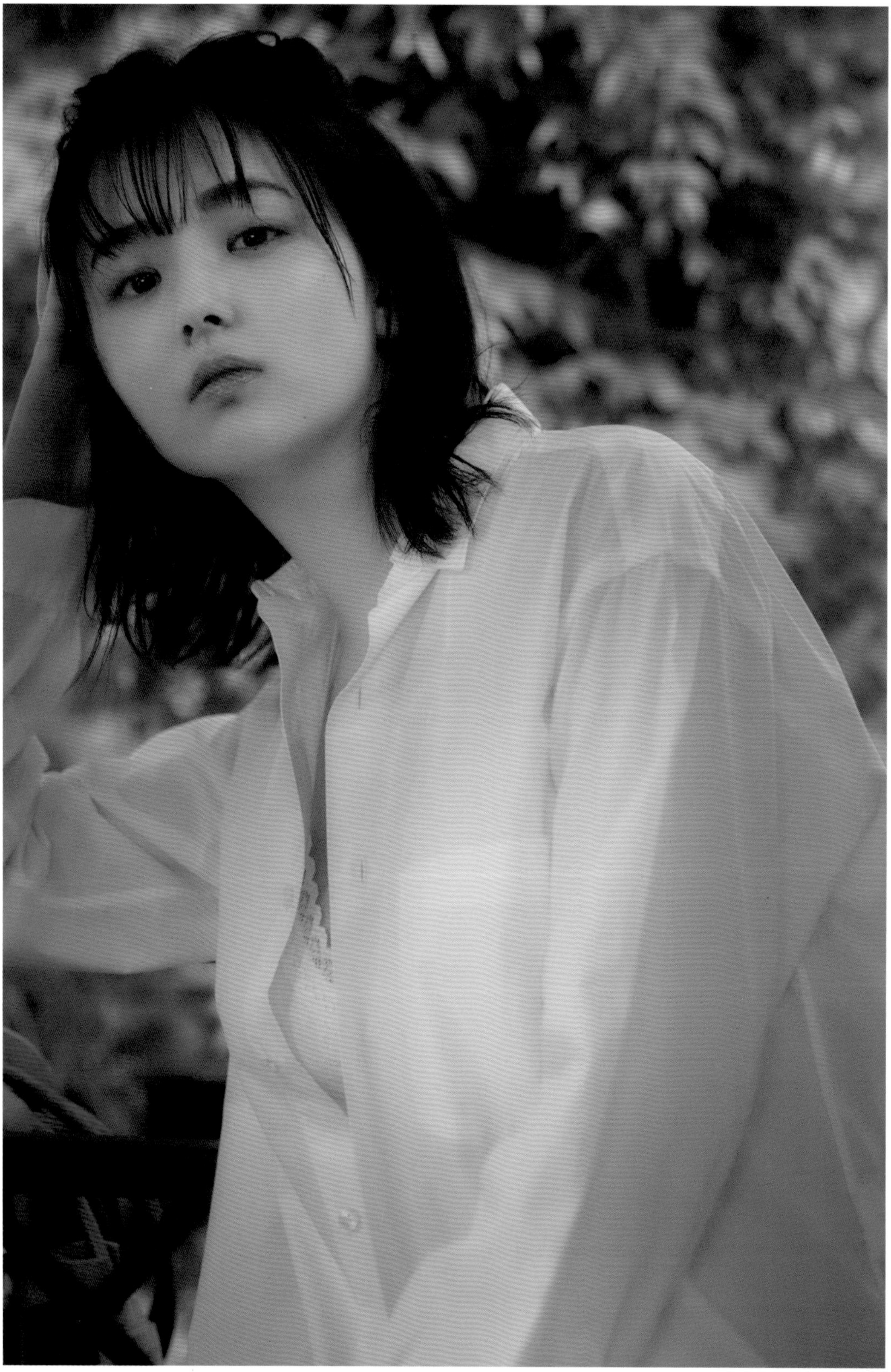

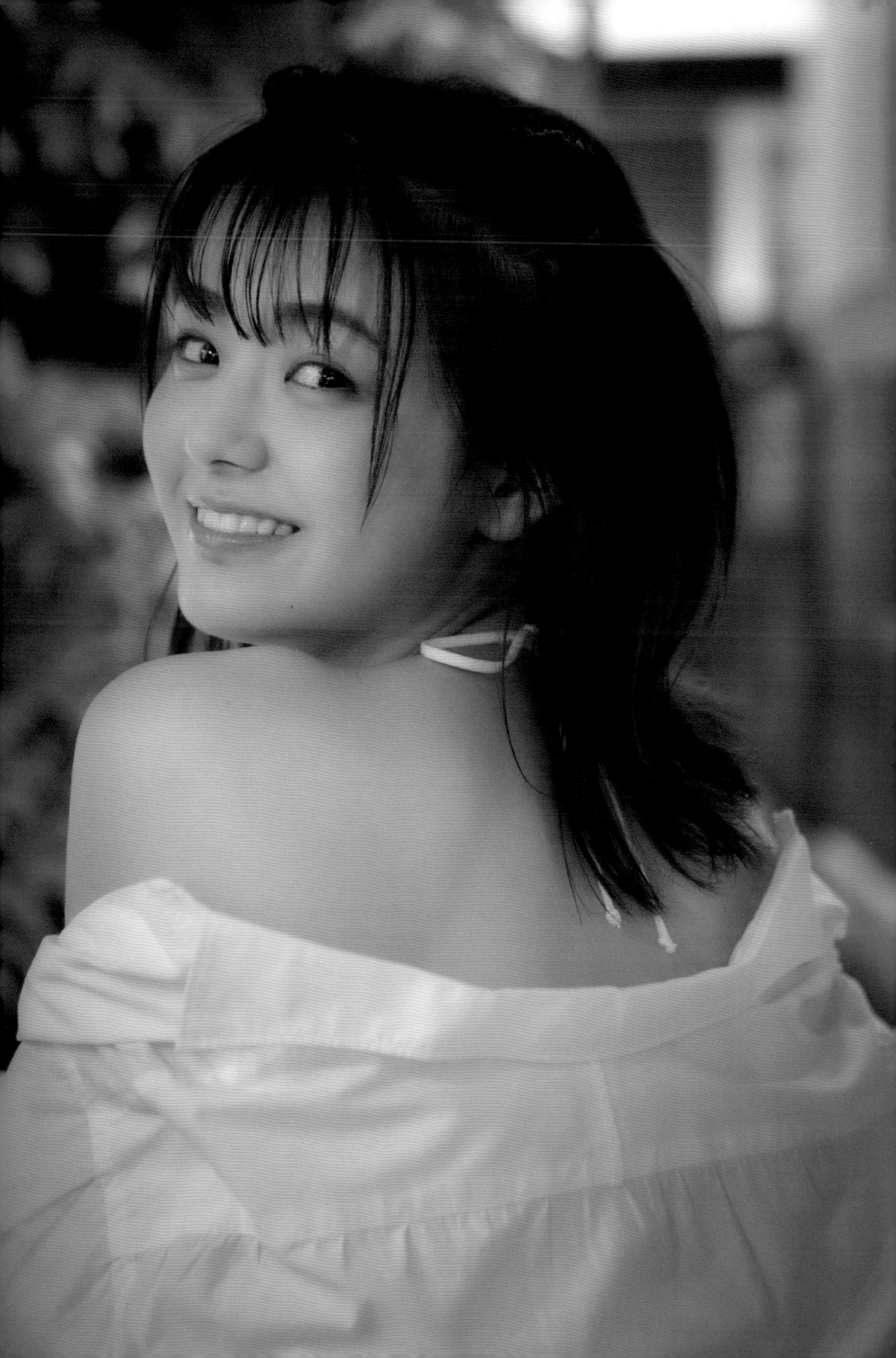

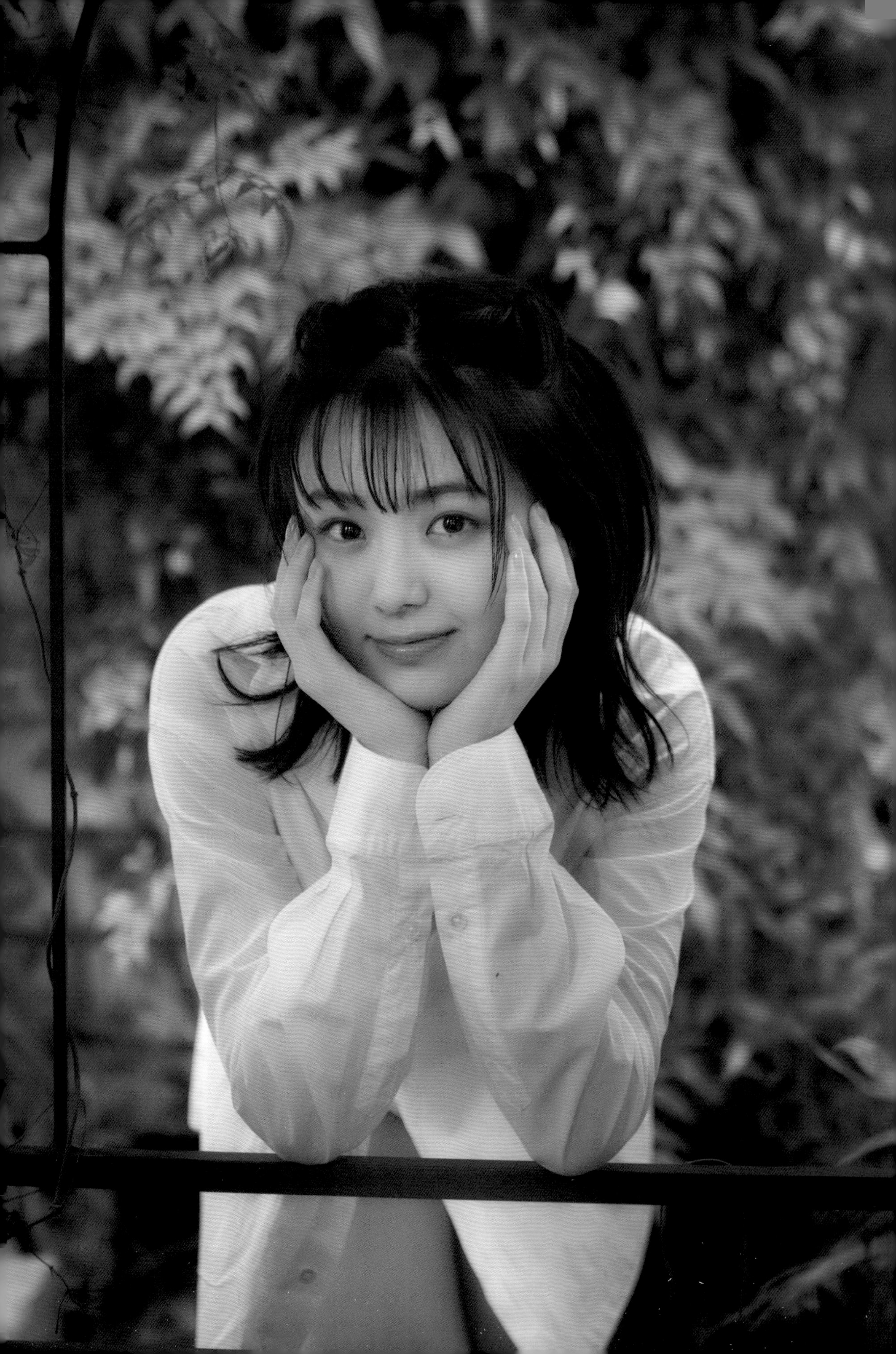

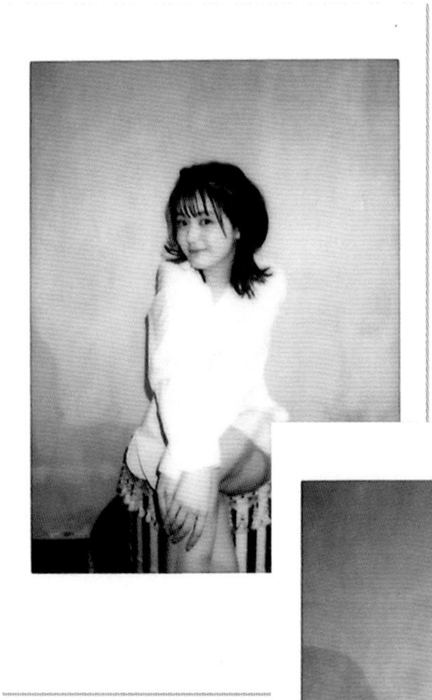
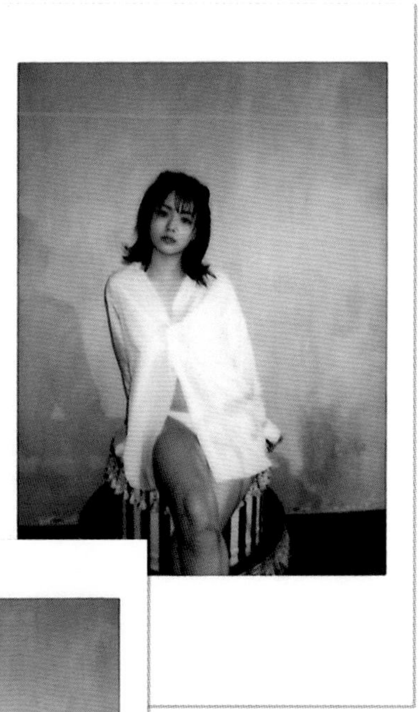
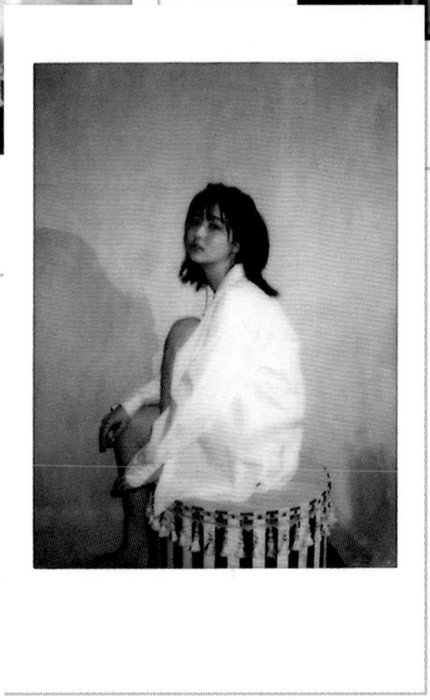
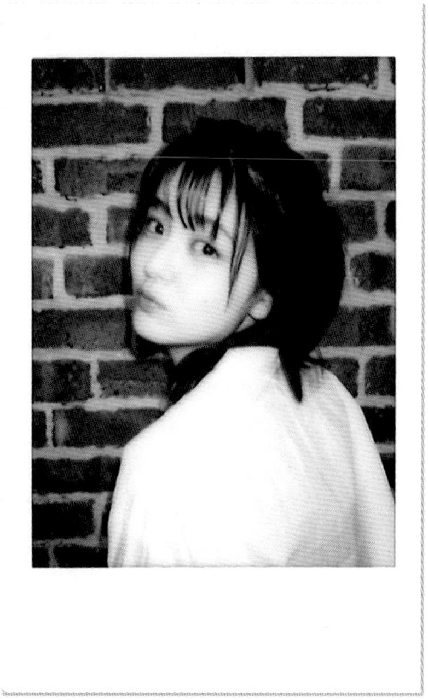

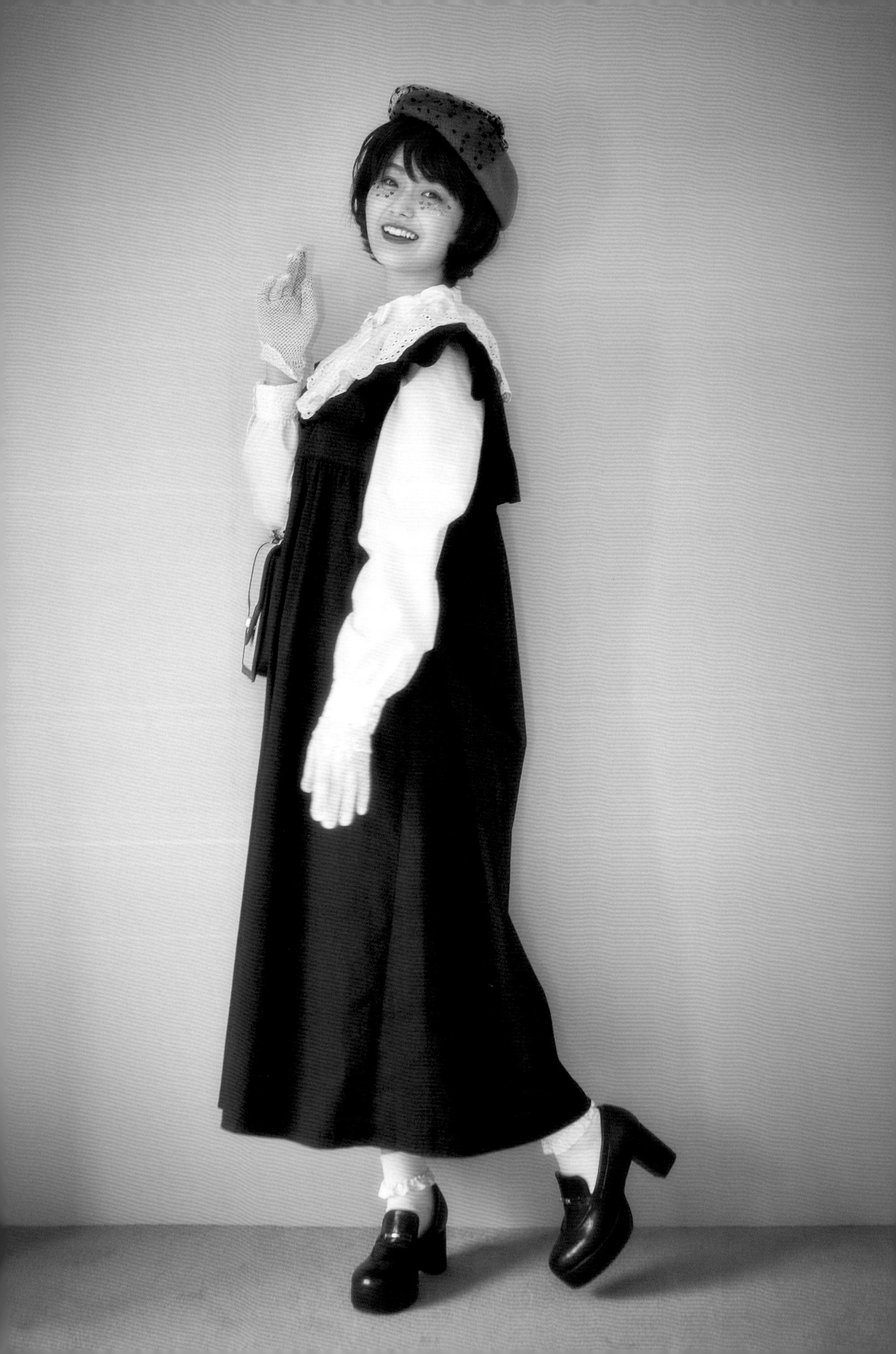

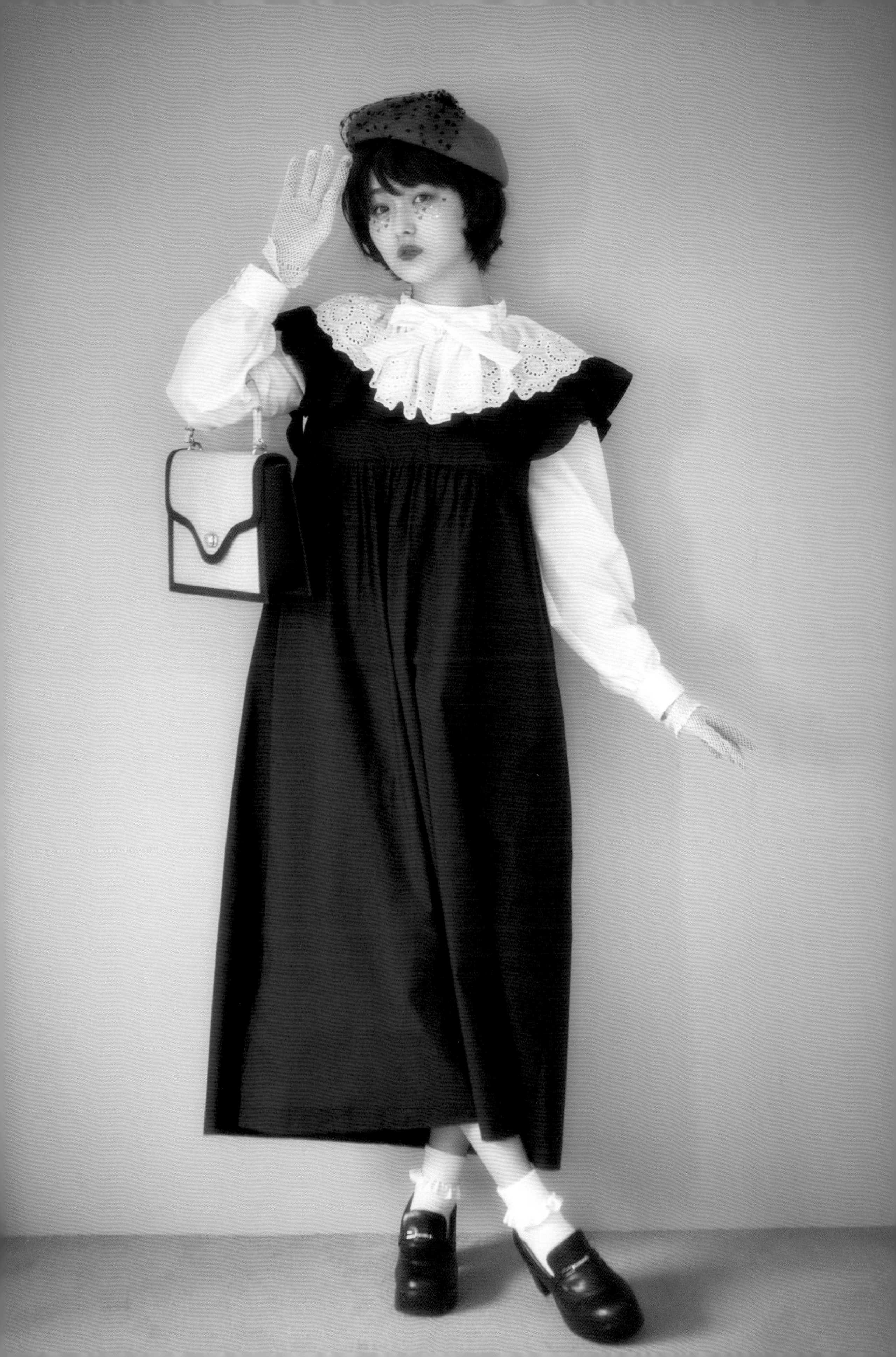

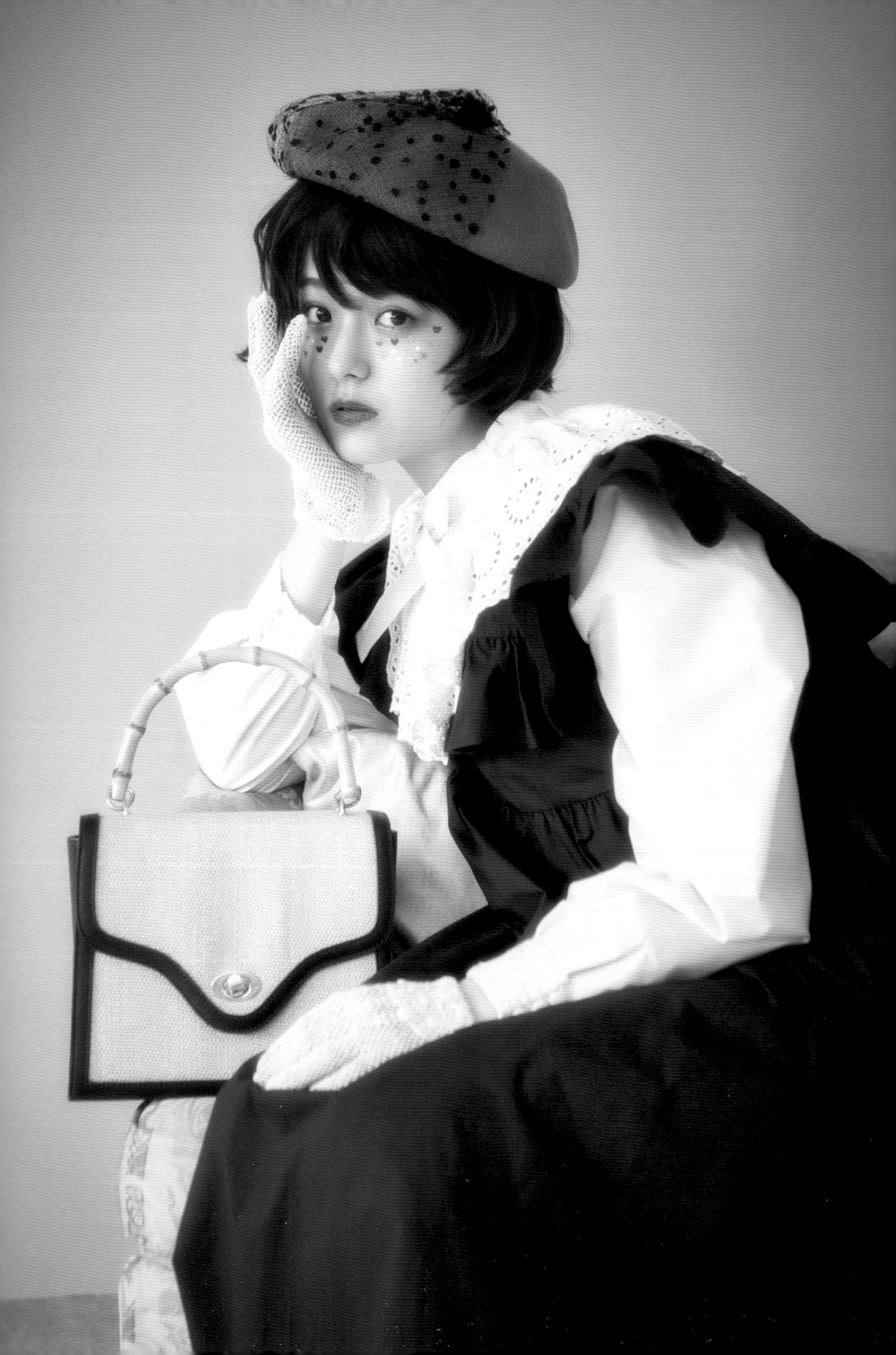

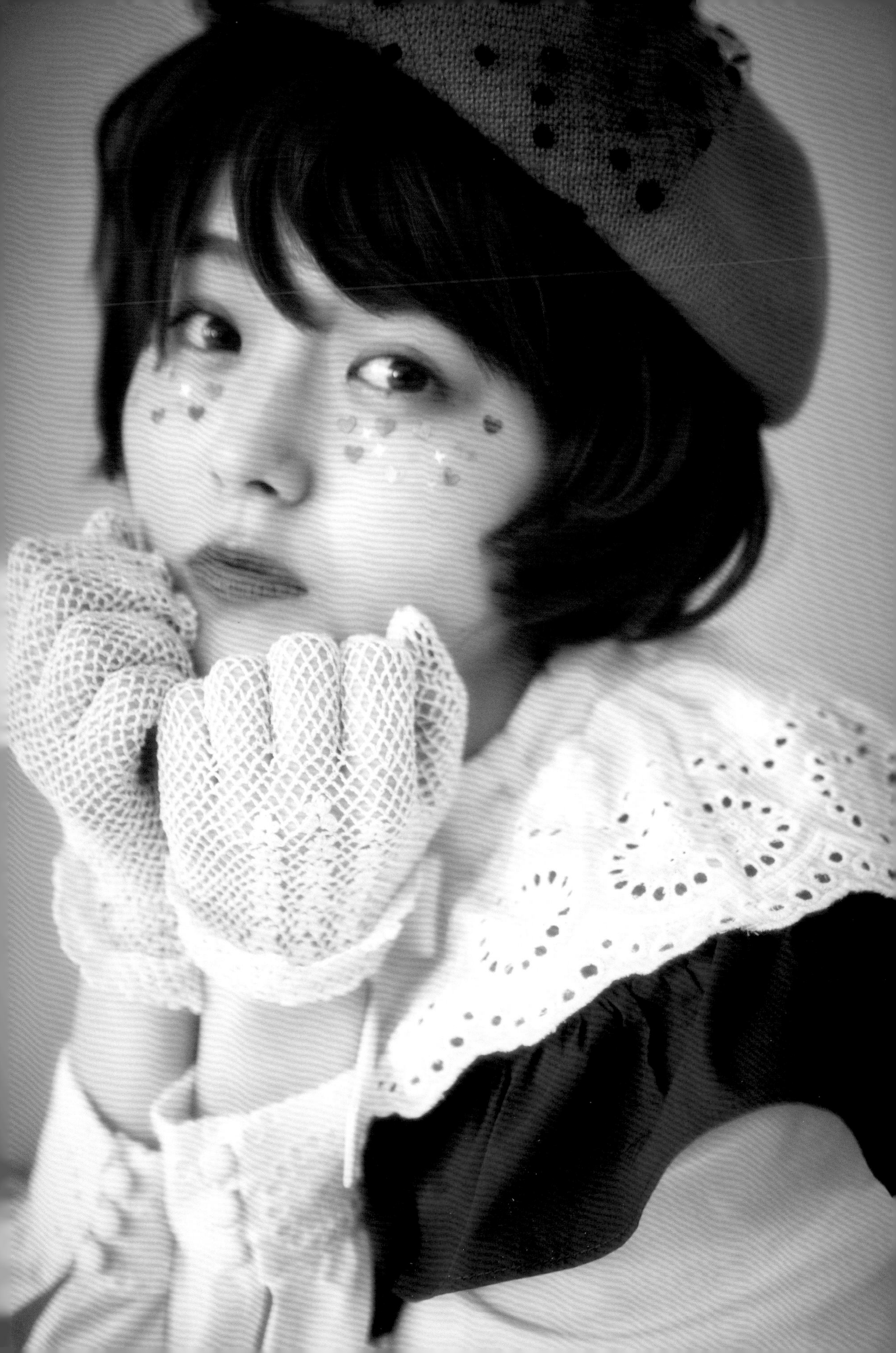

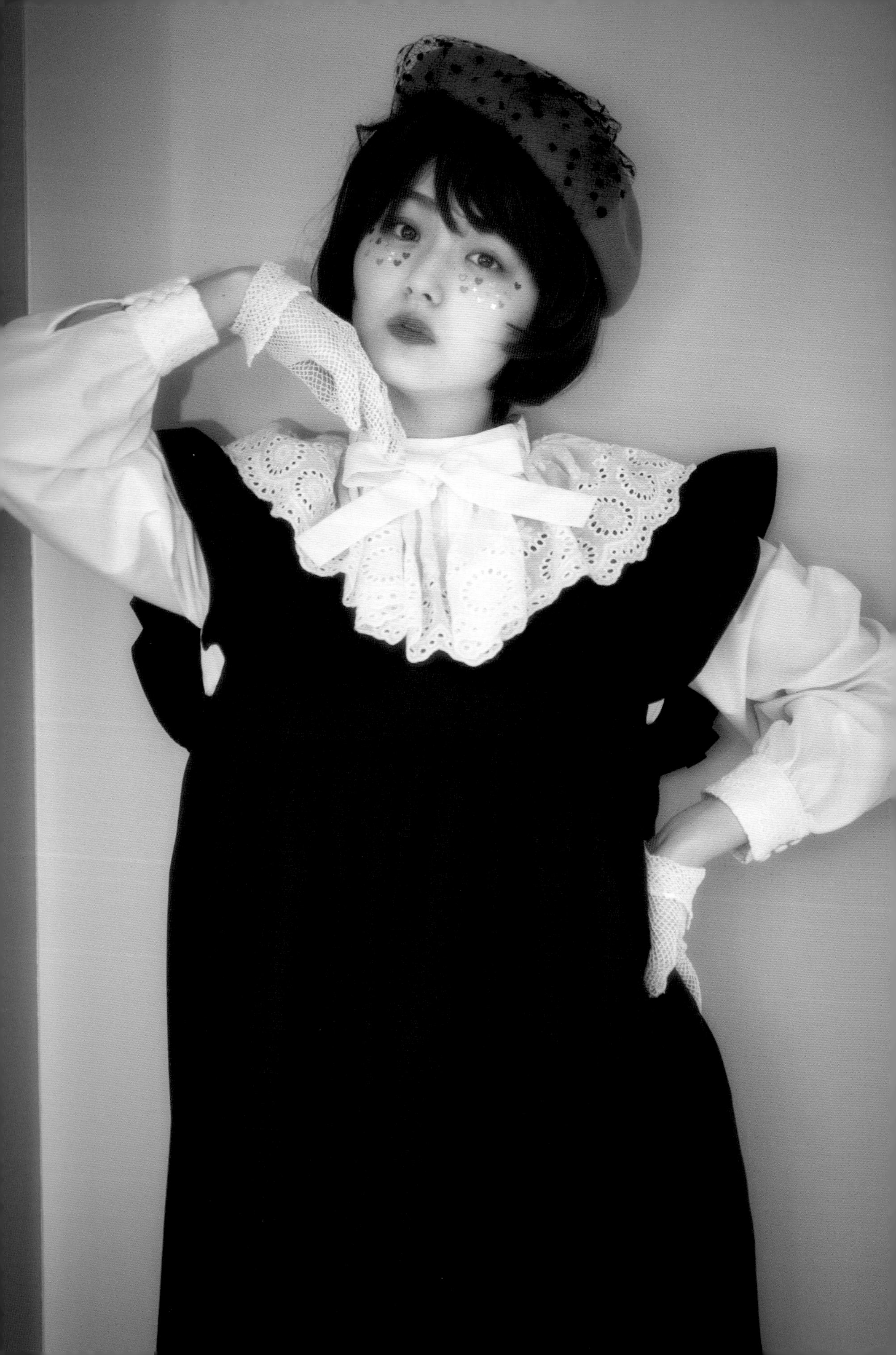

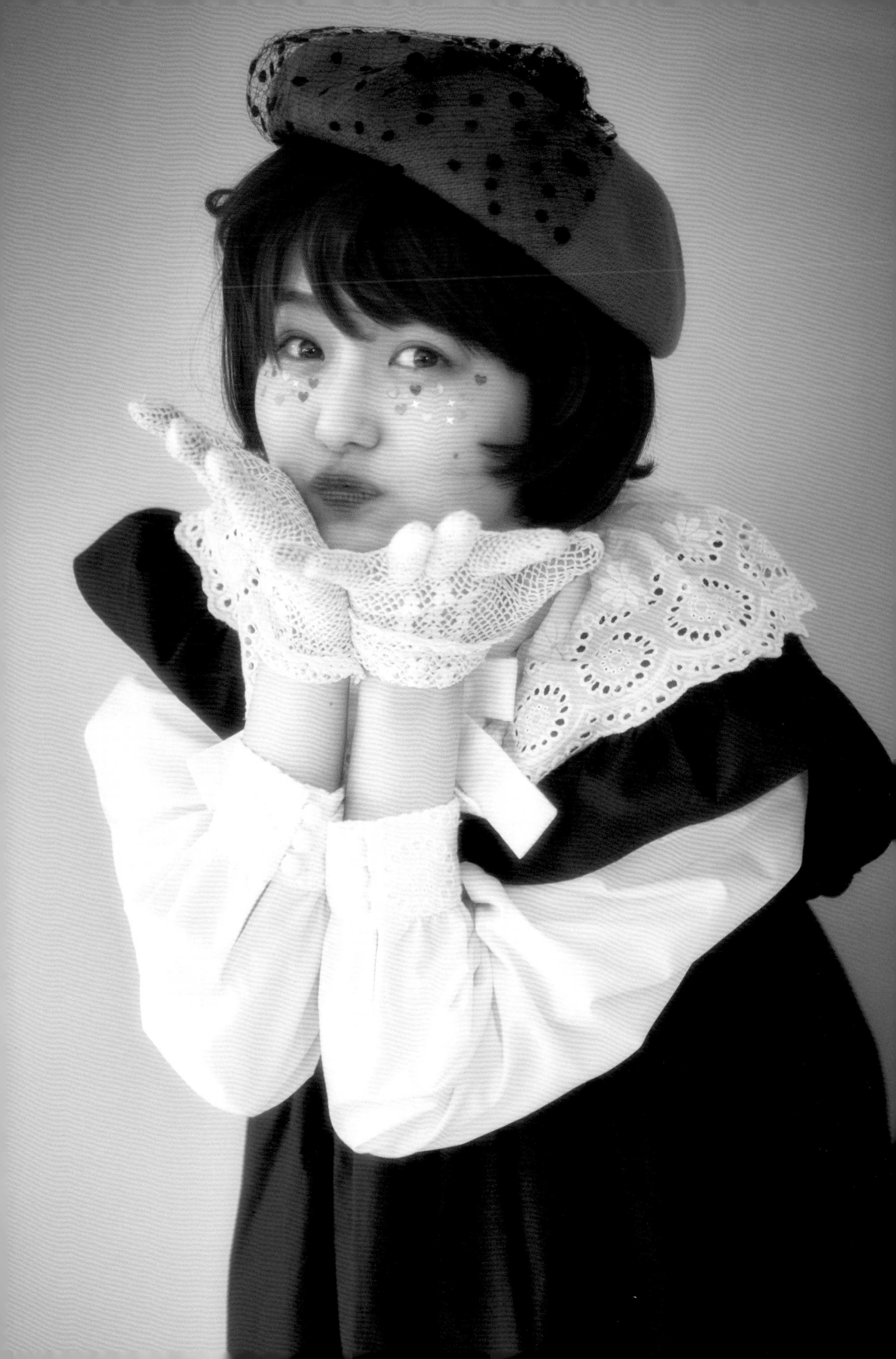

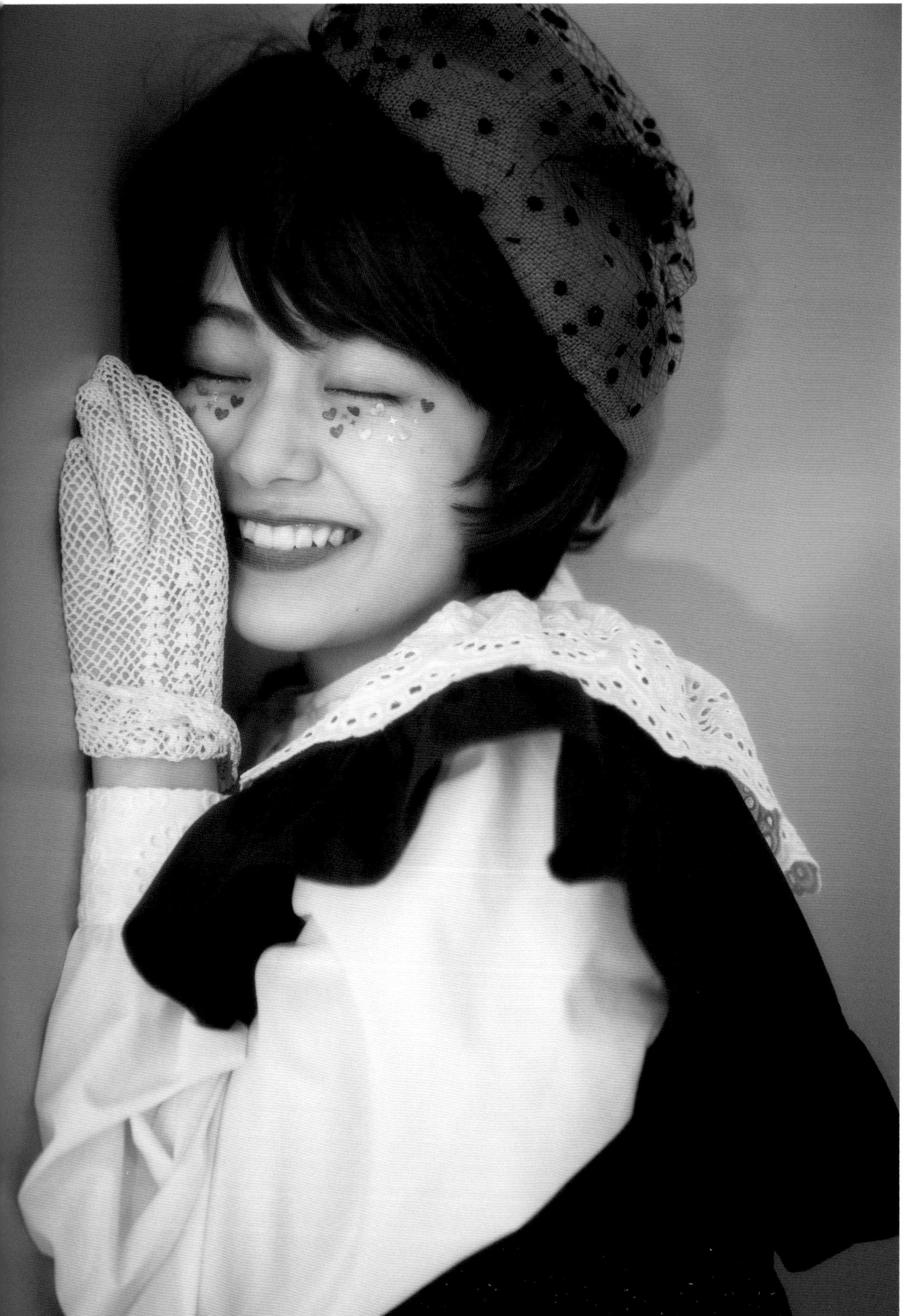

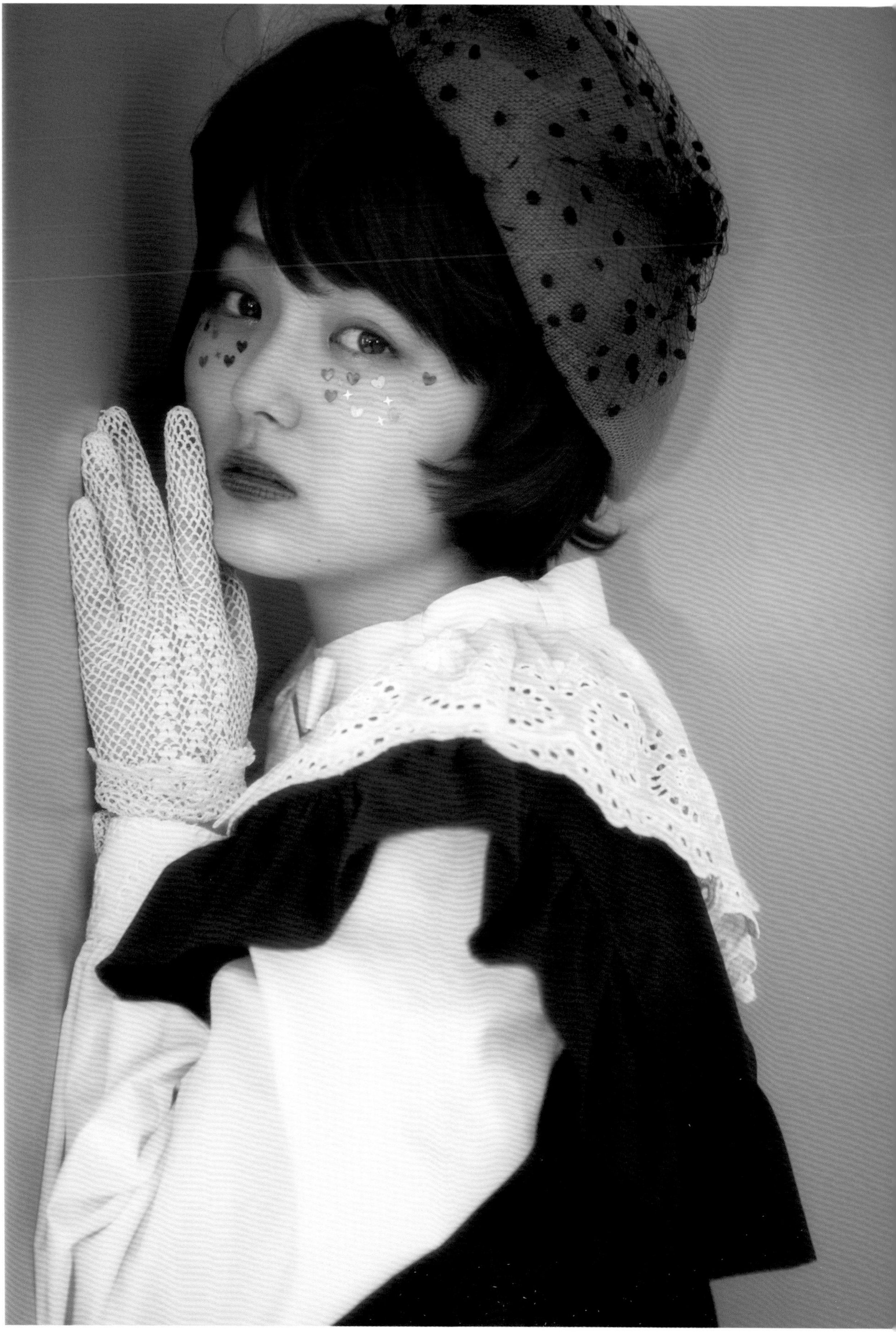

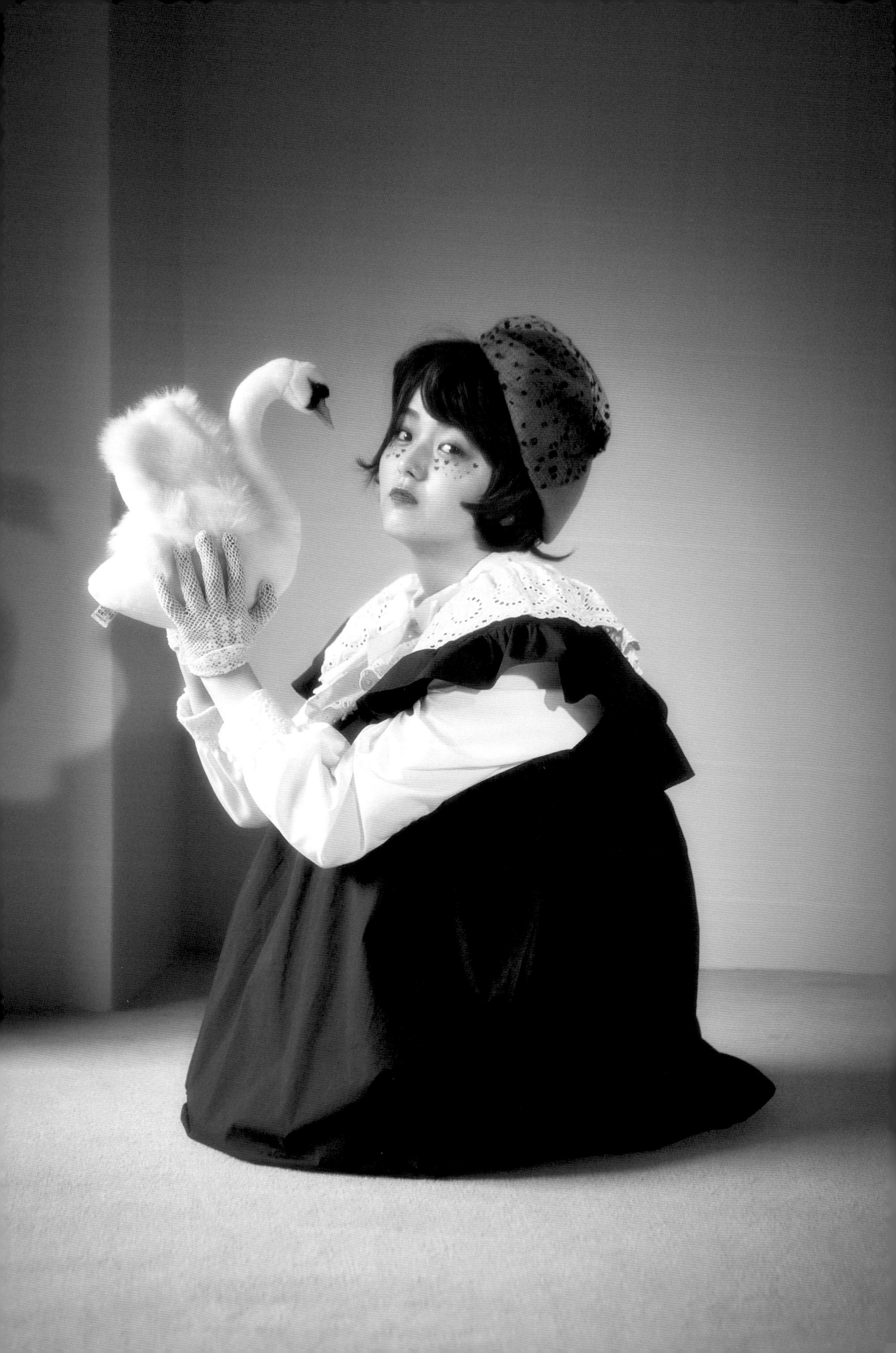

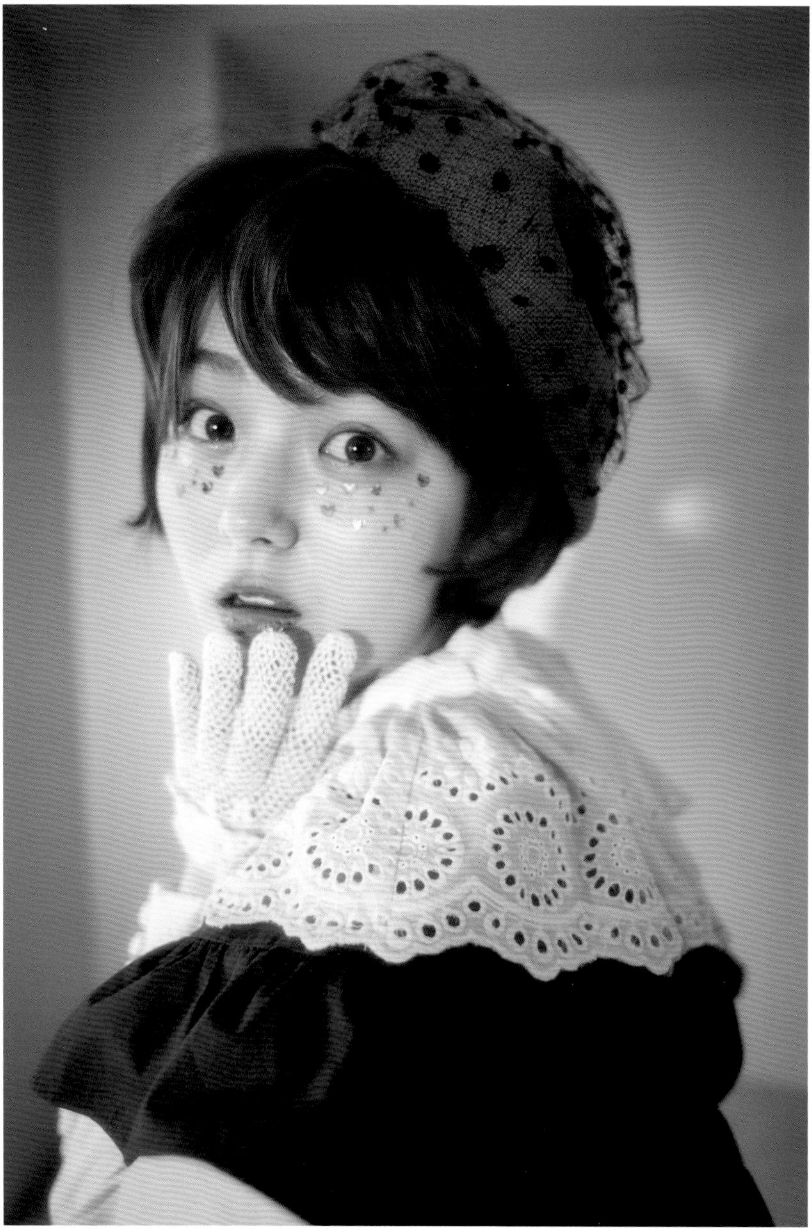

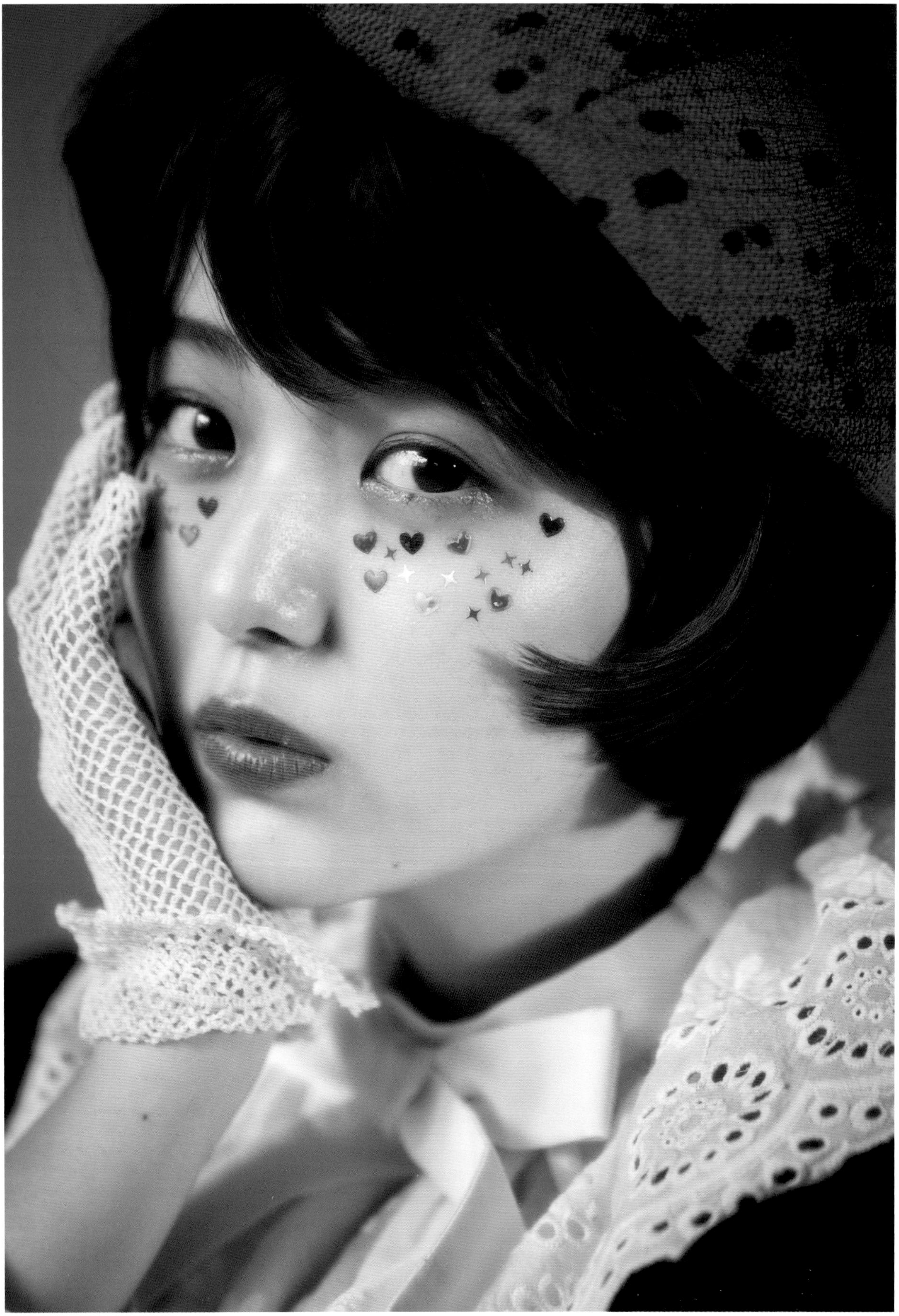

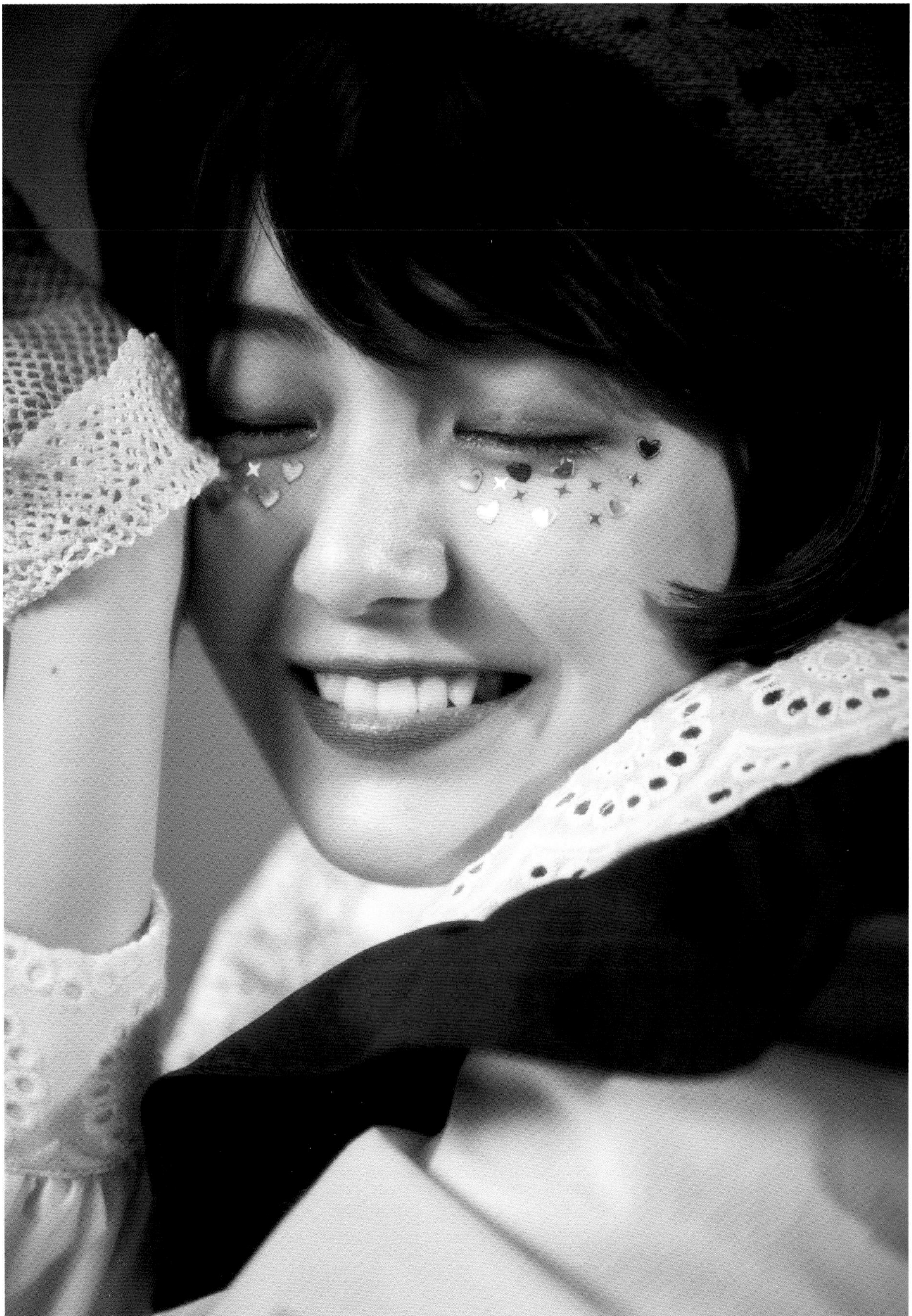

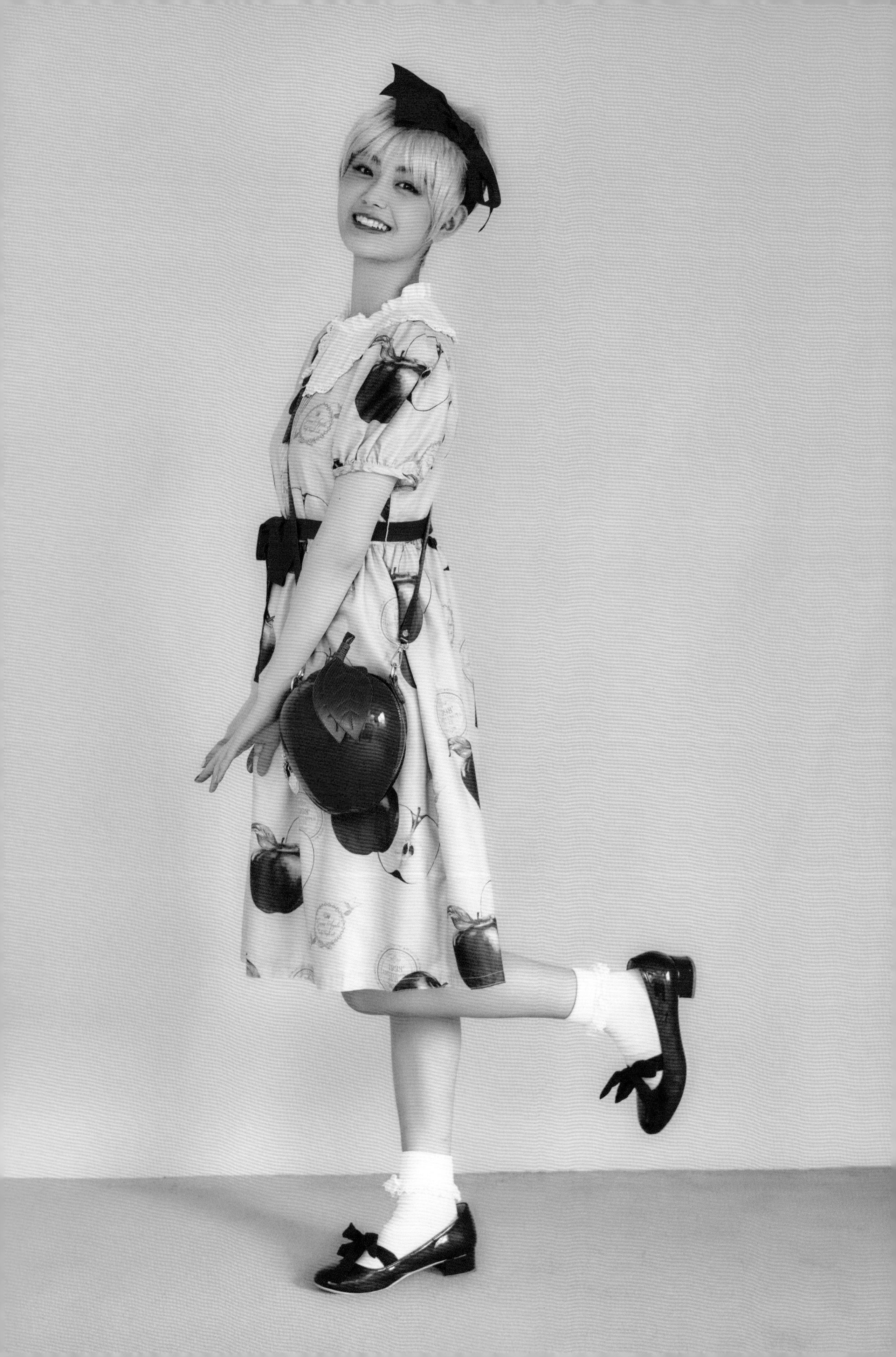

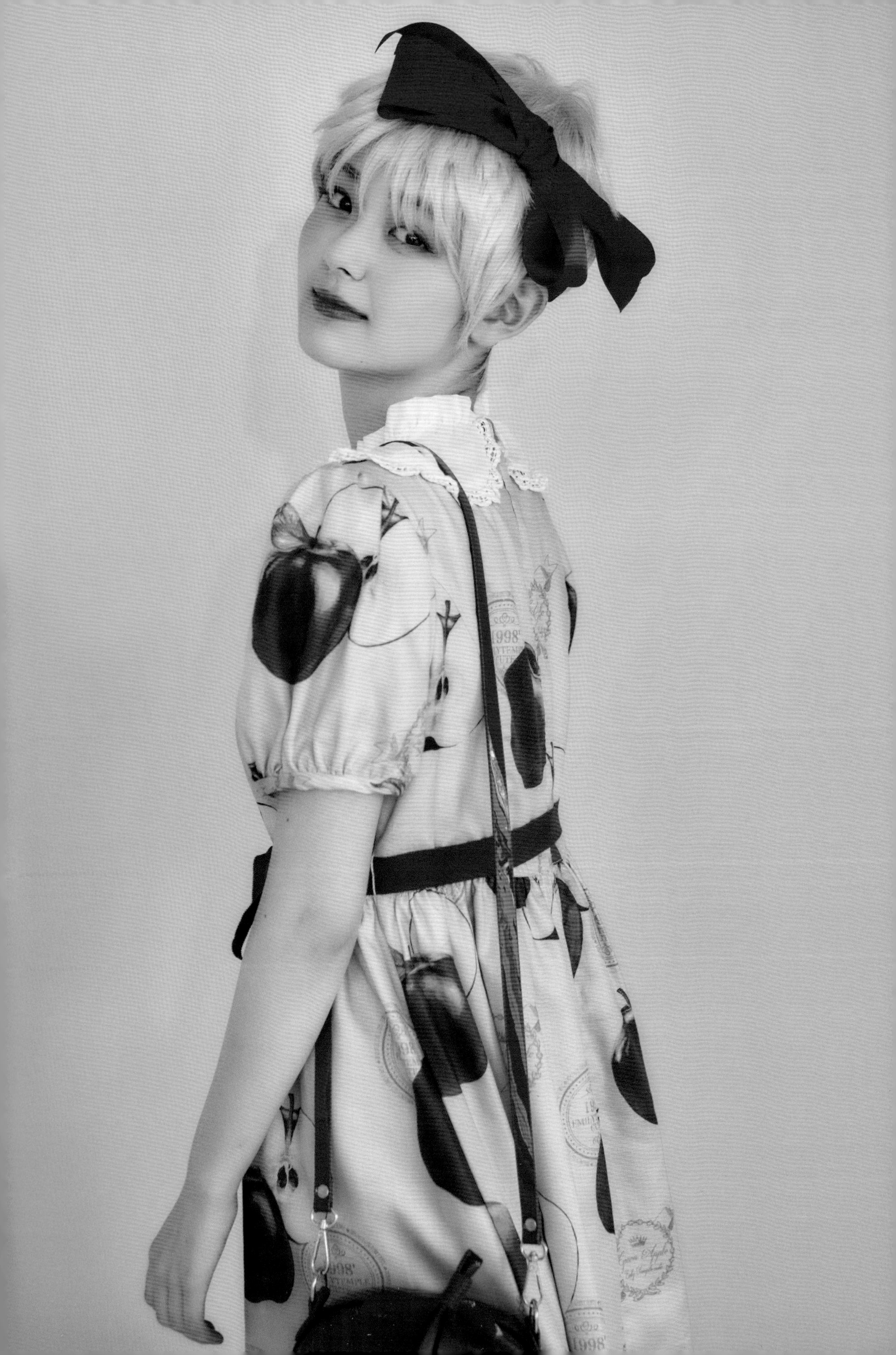

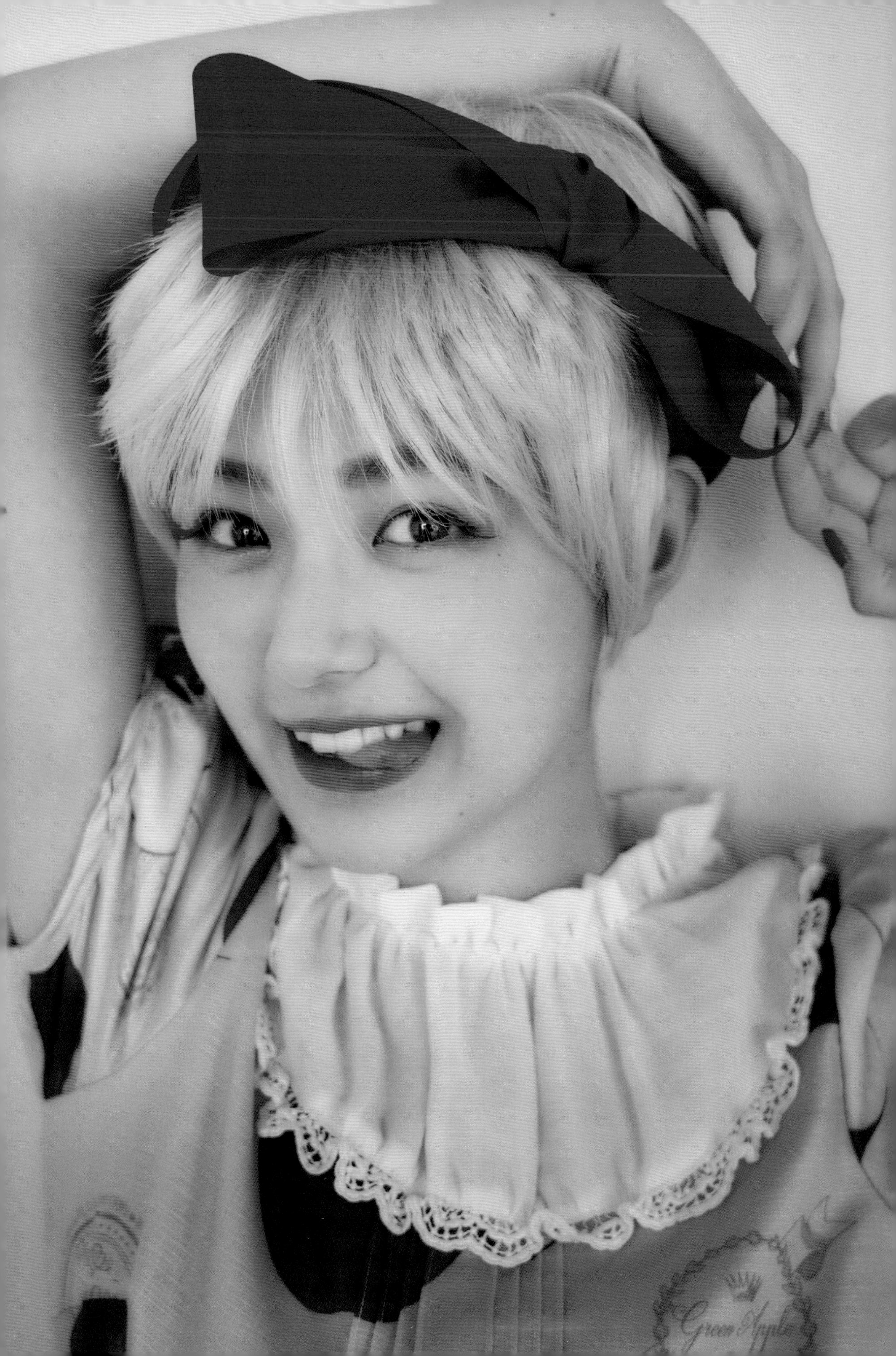
Green Apple

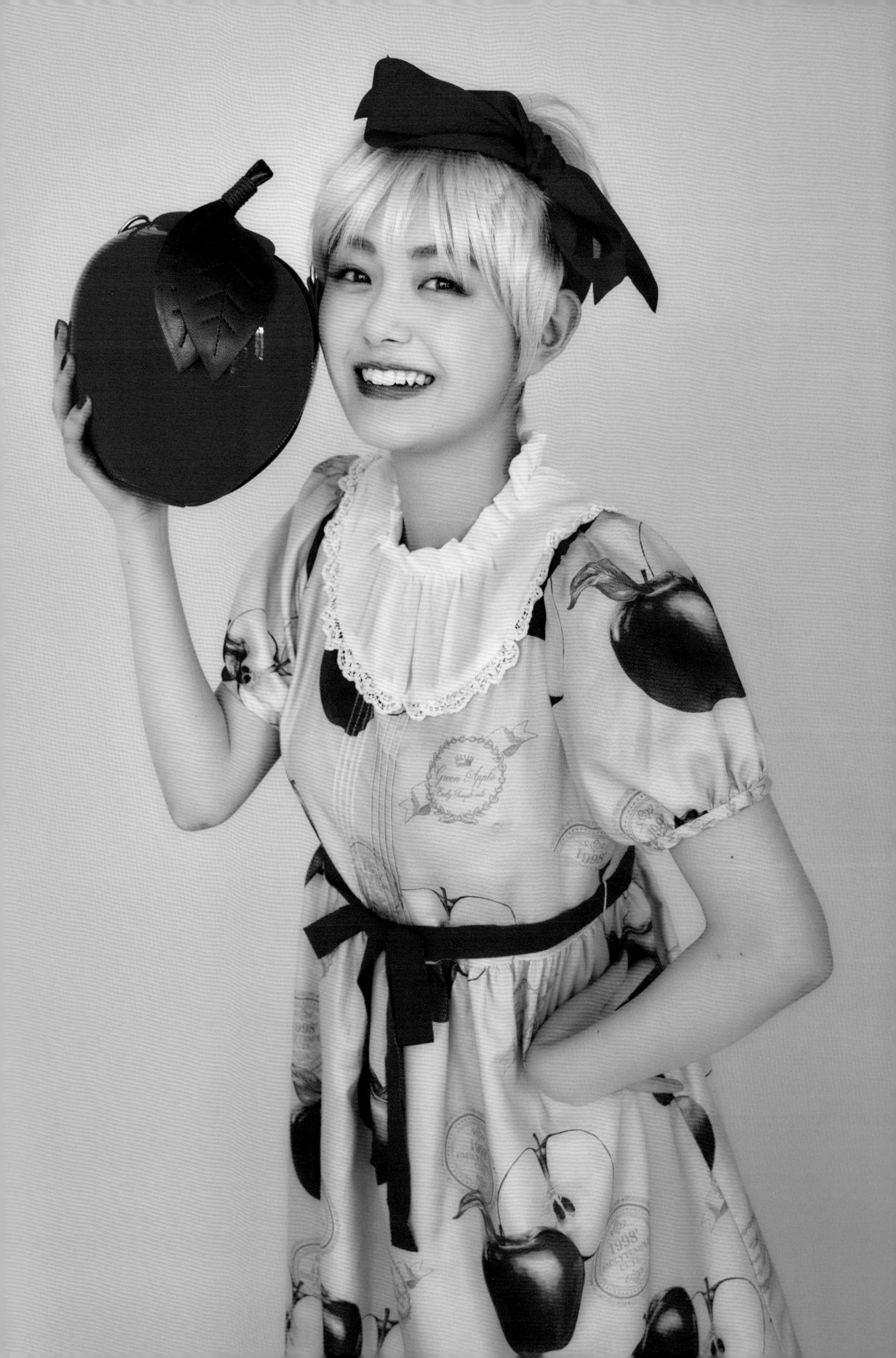
Green Apple
1998'

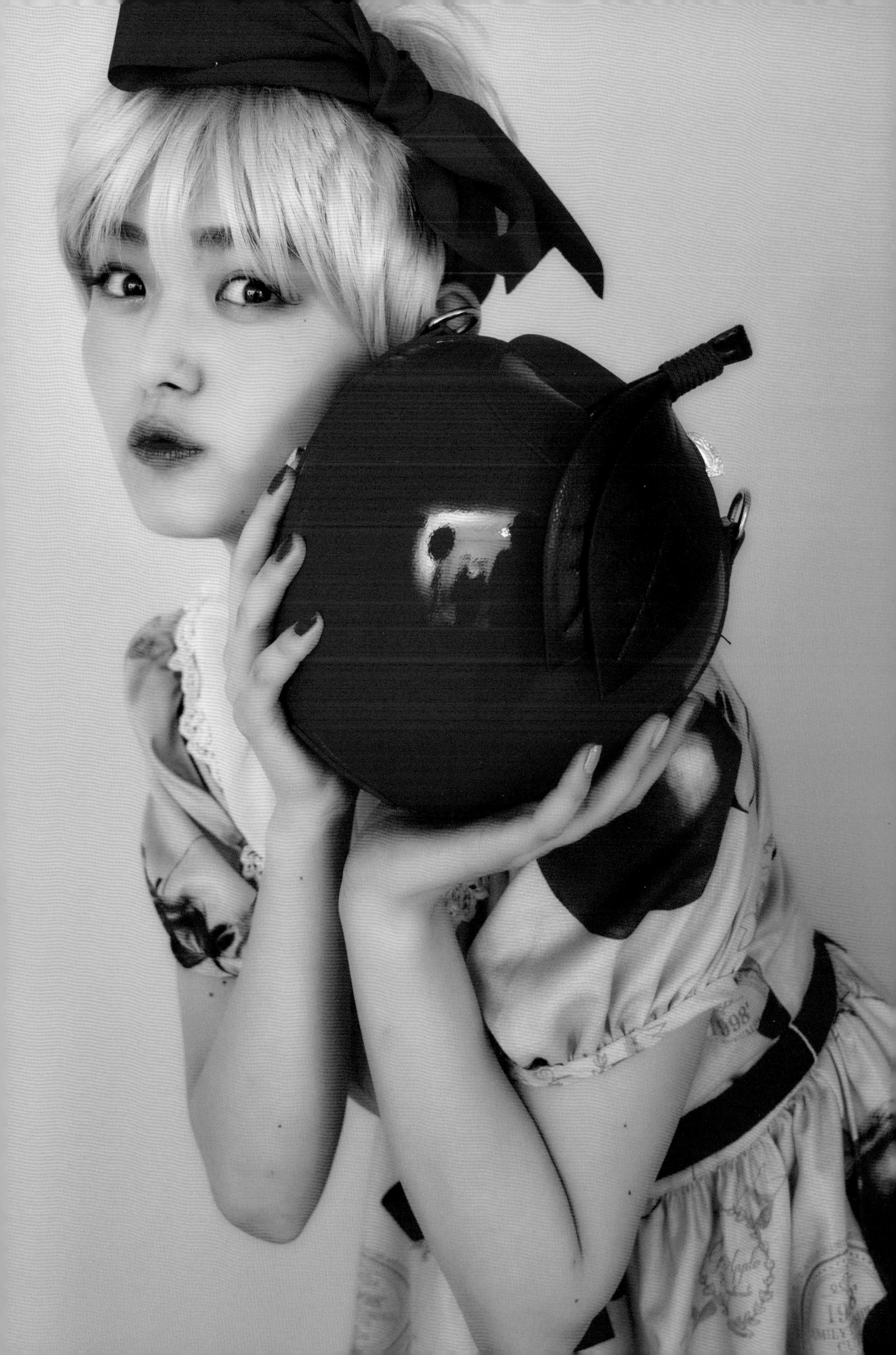

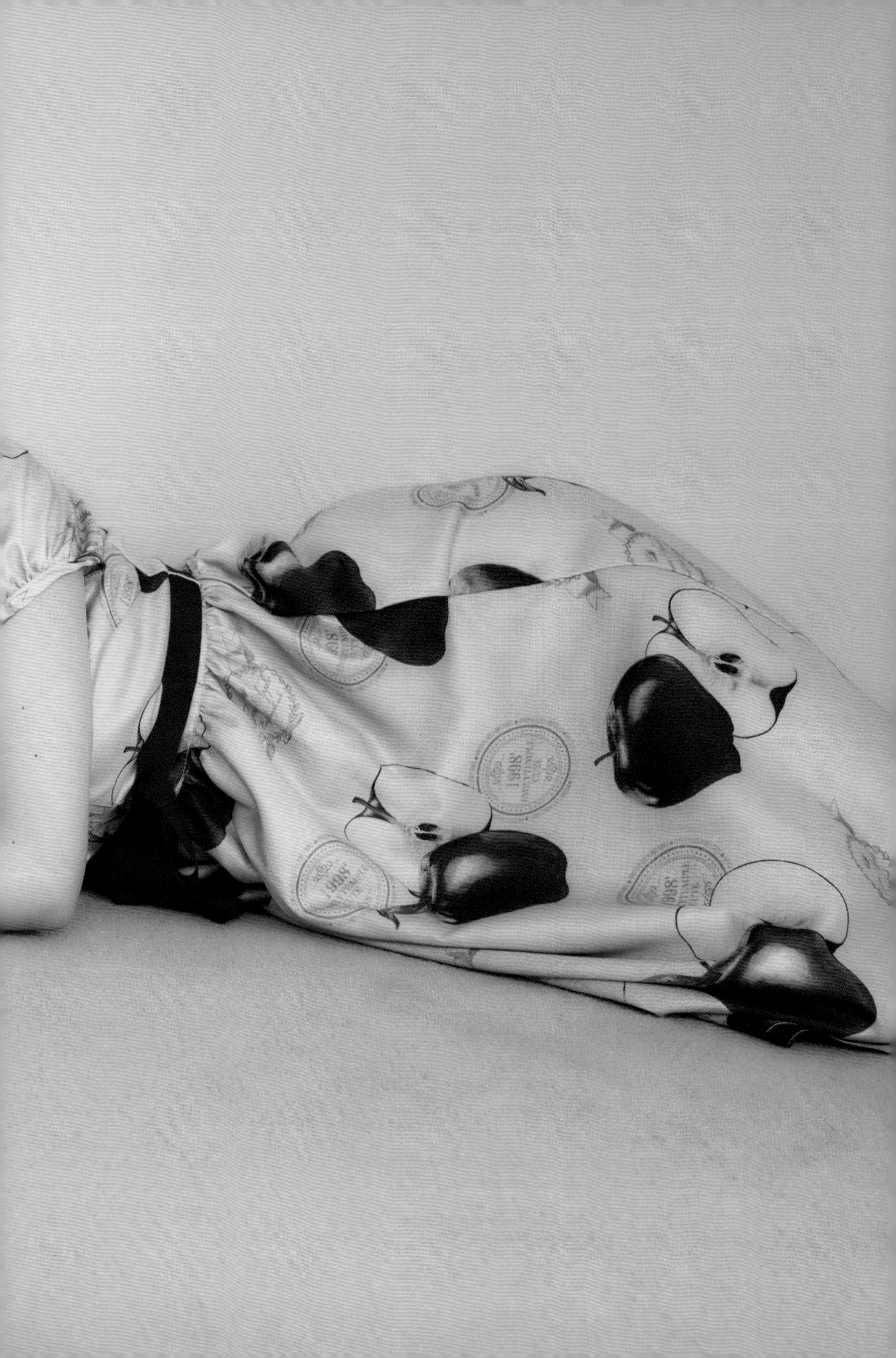

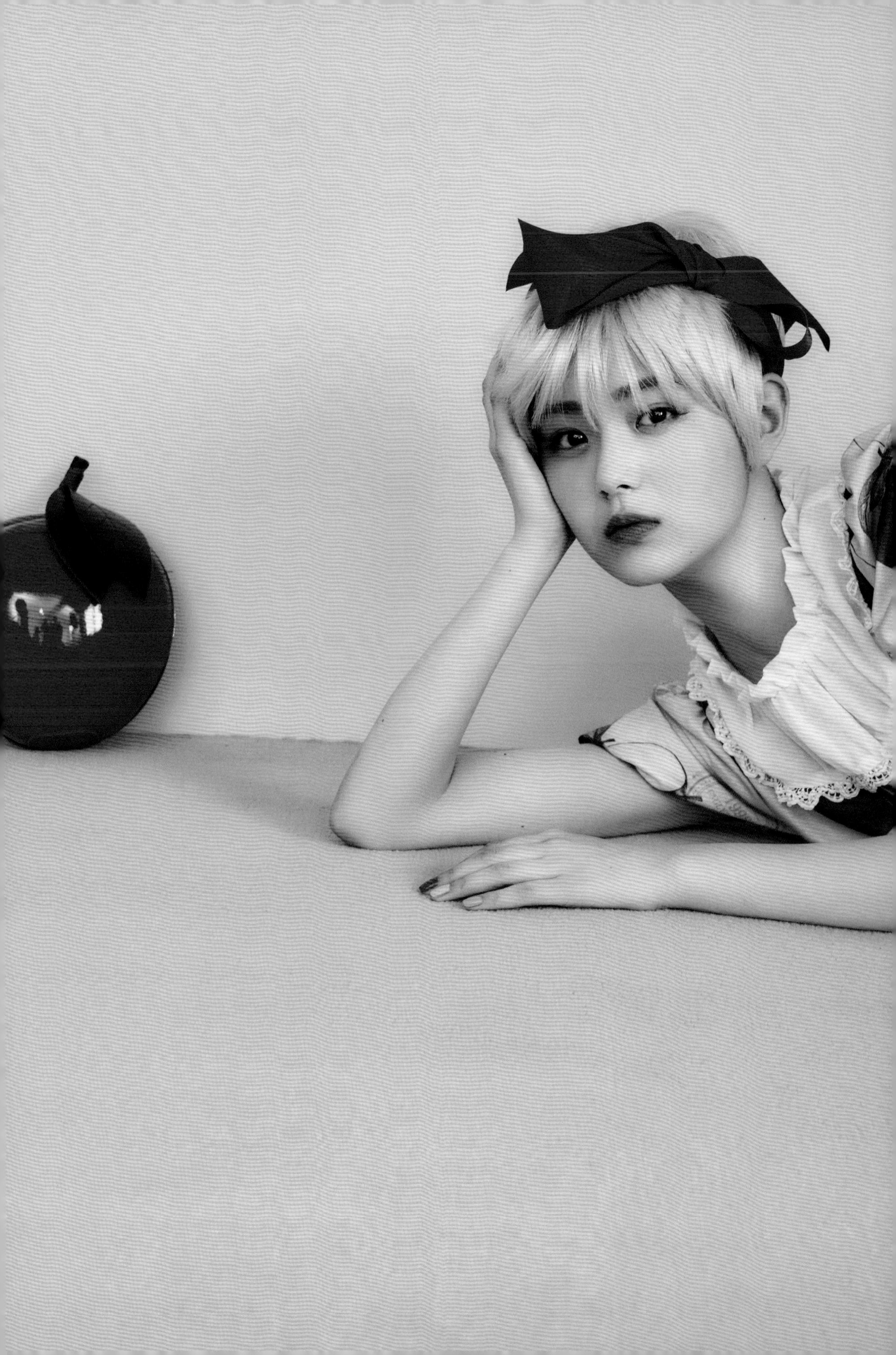

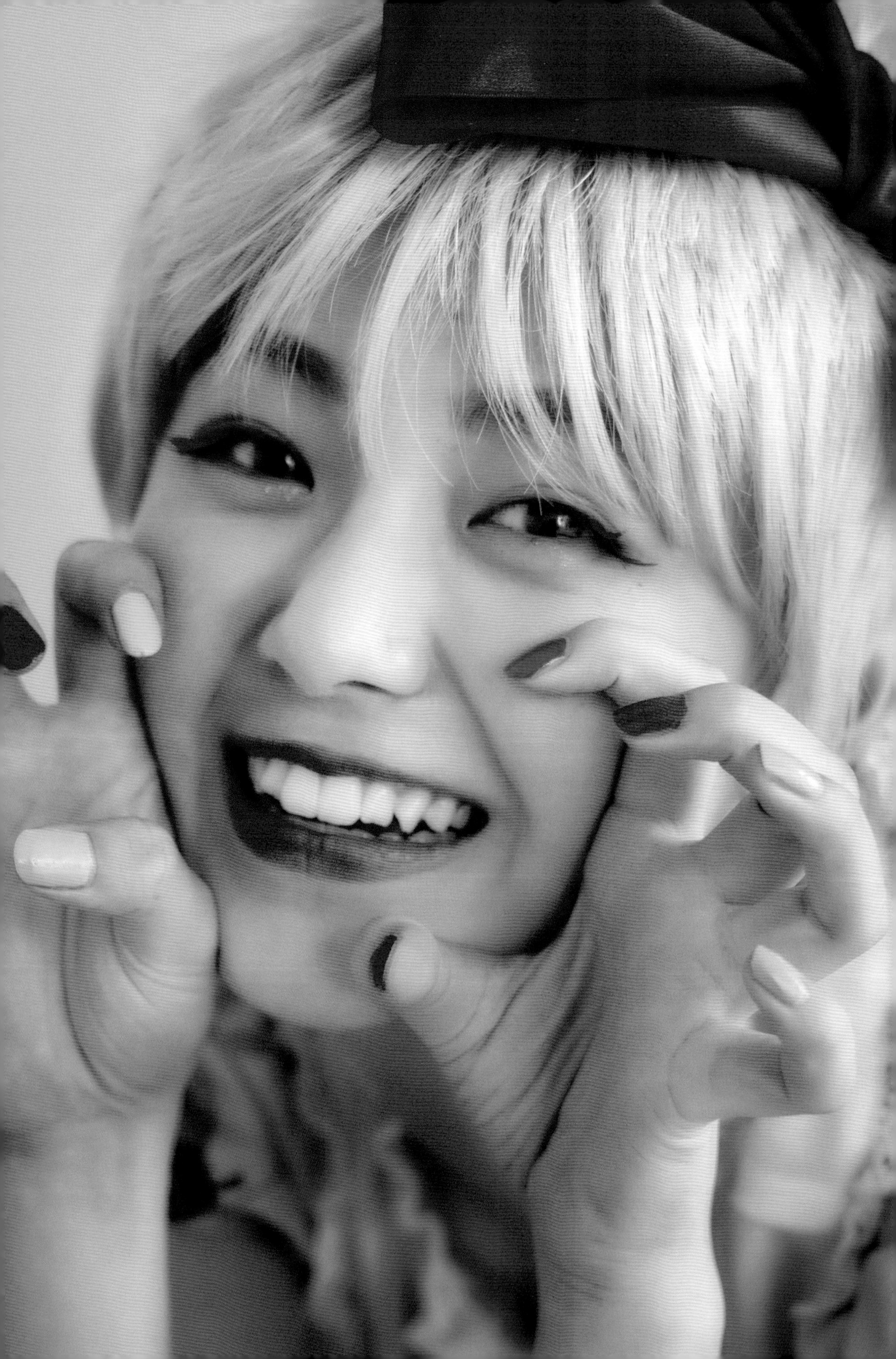

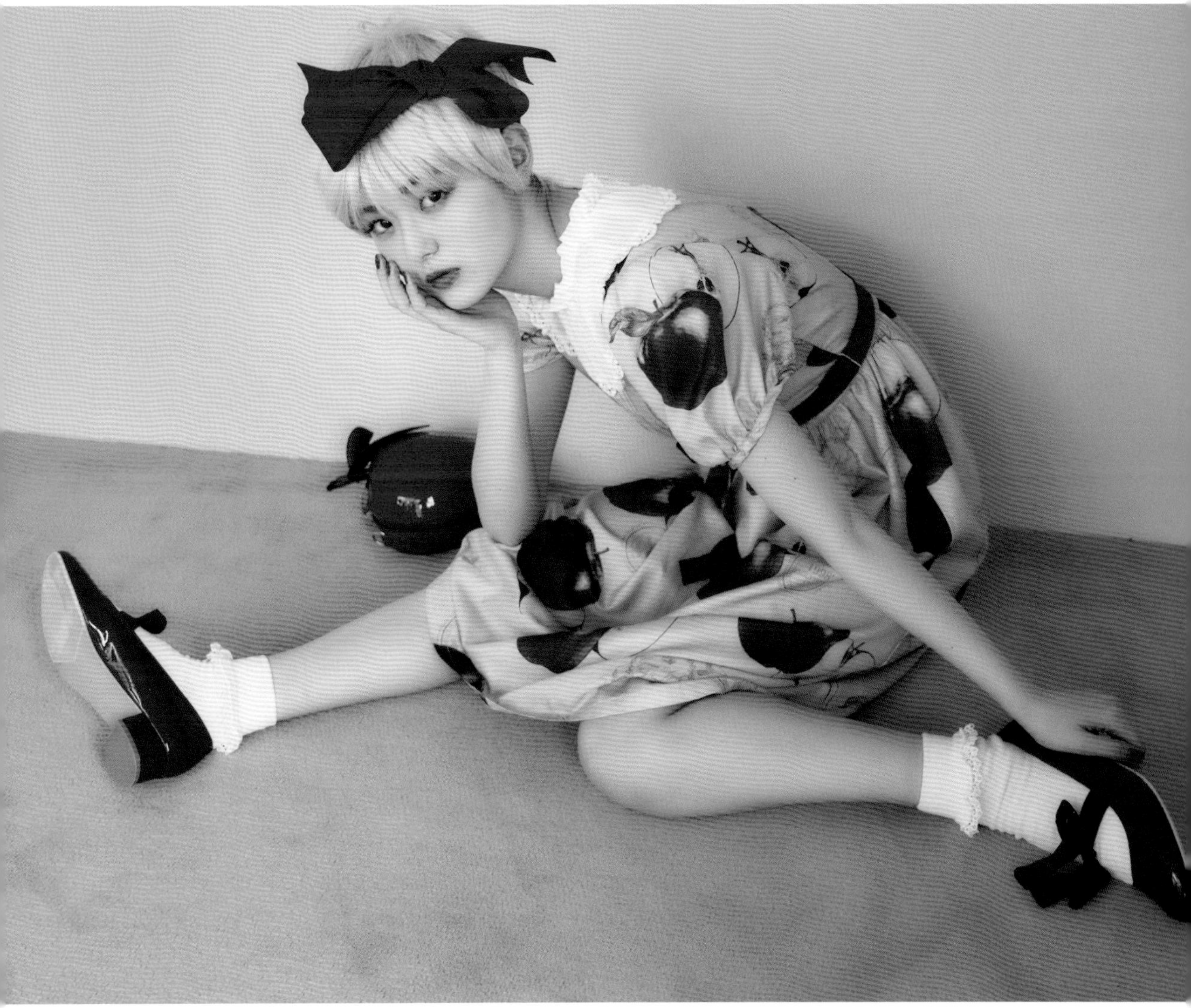

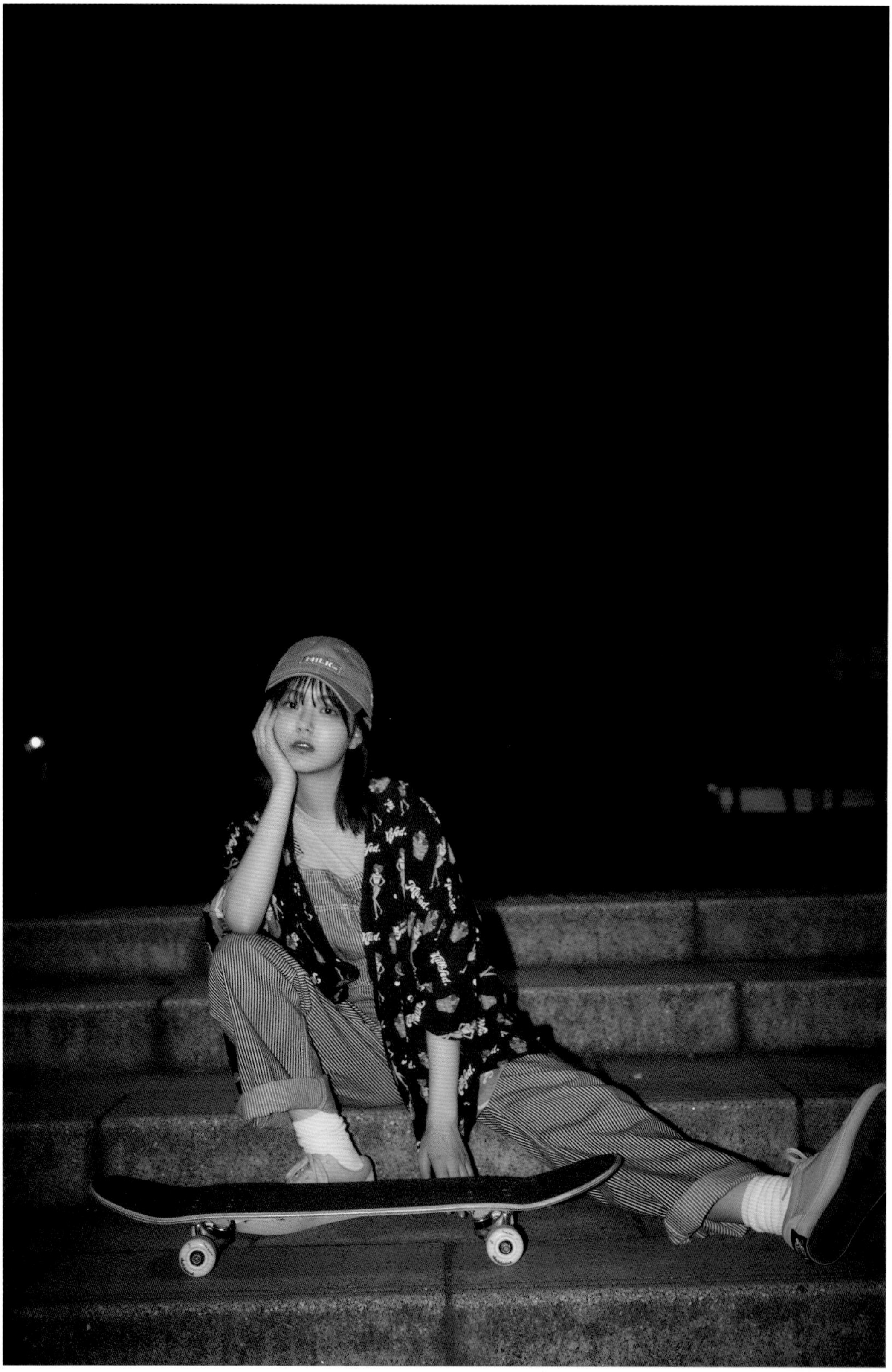

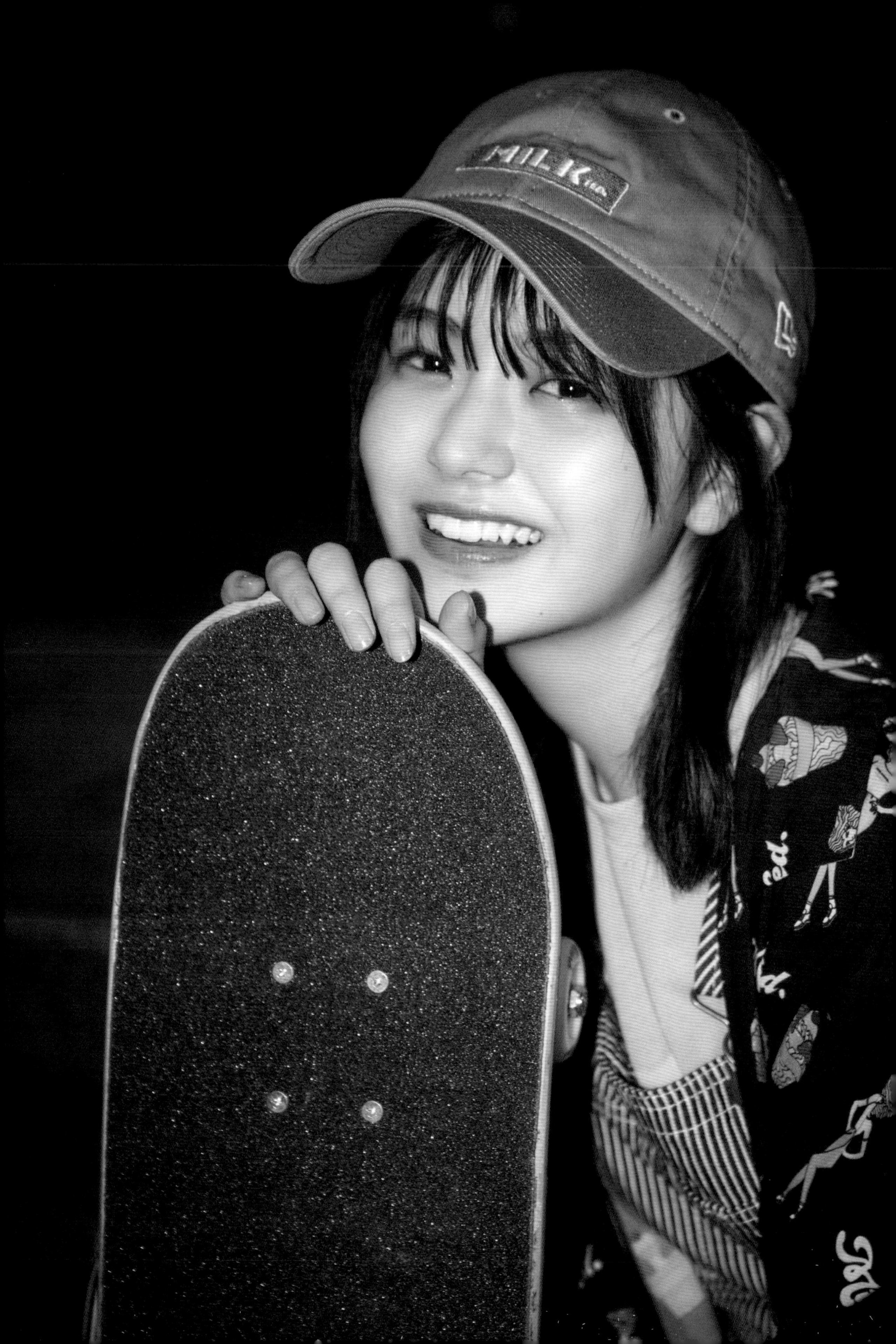
MILK

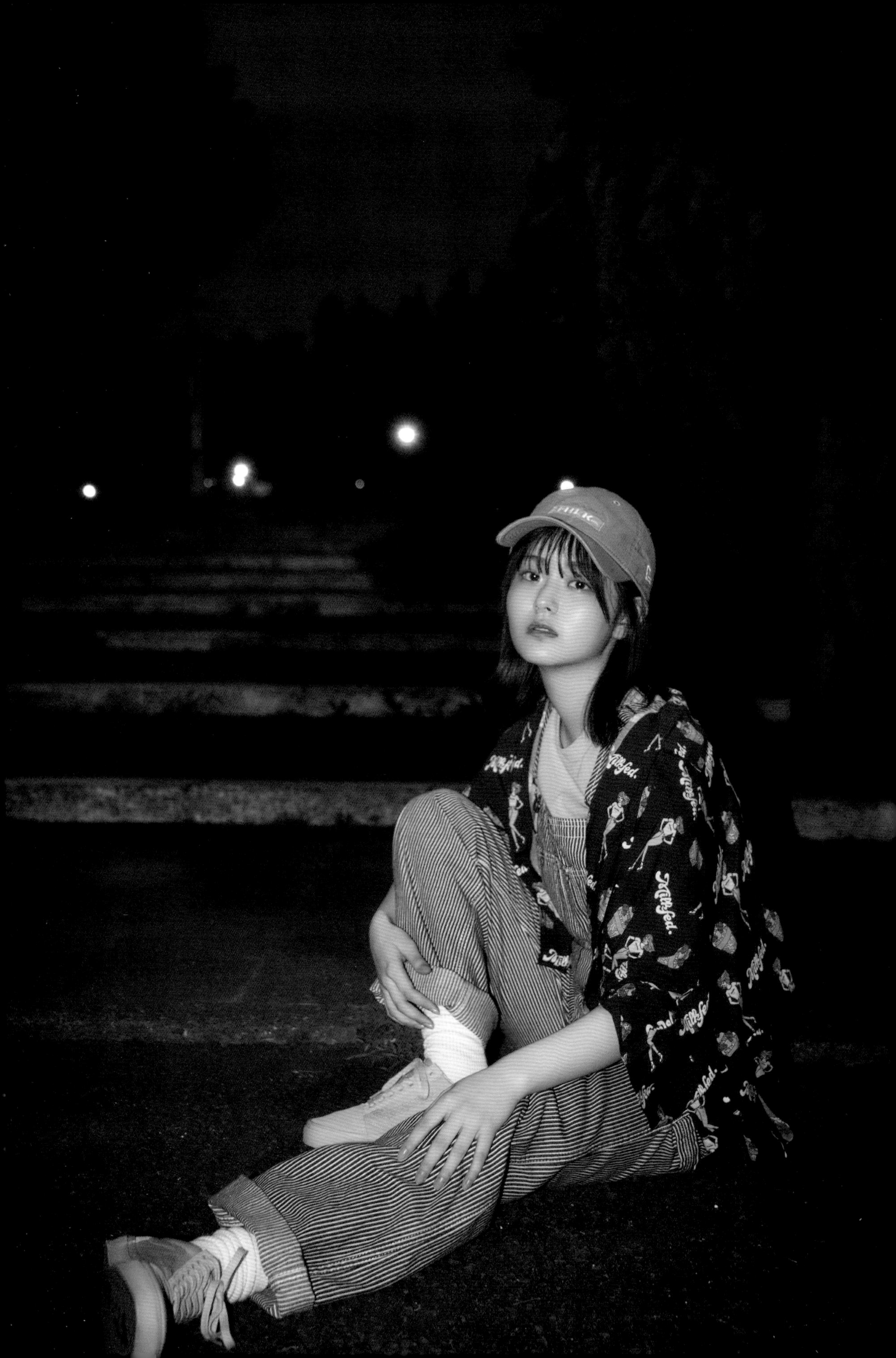
Milkfed.

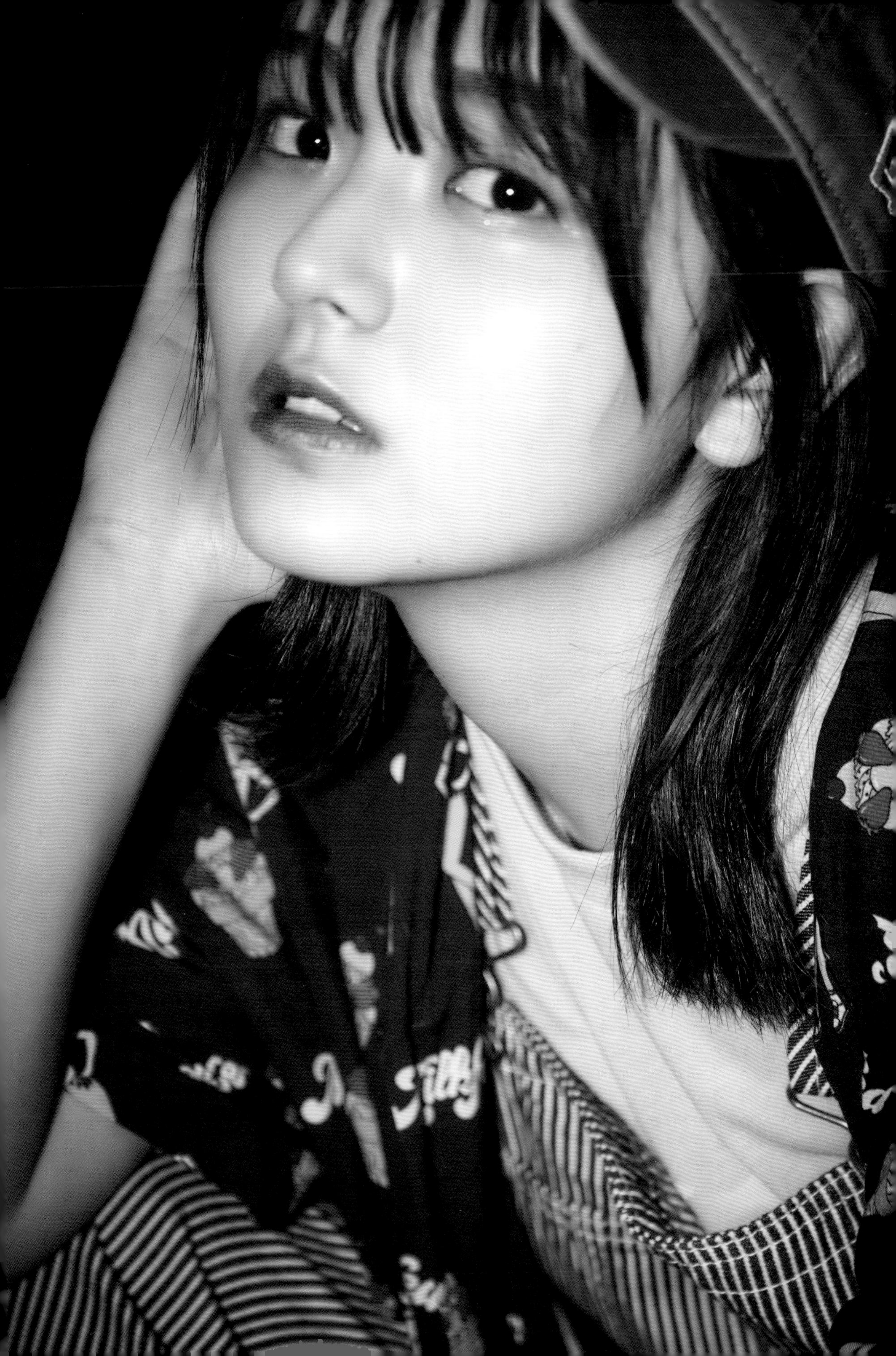

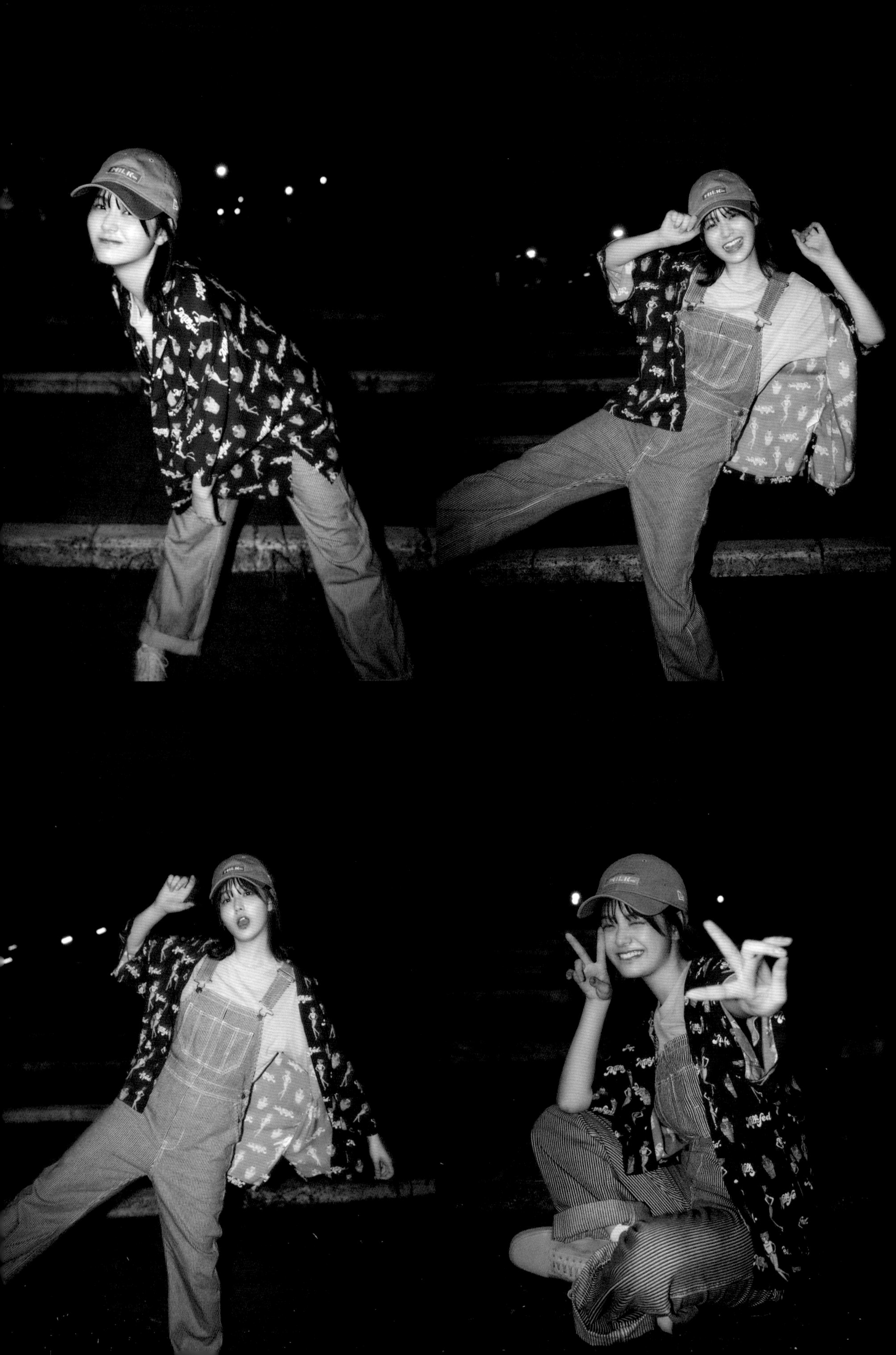

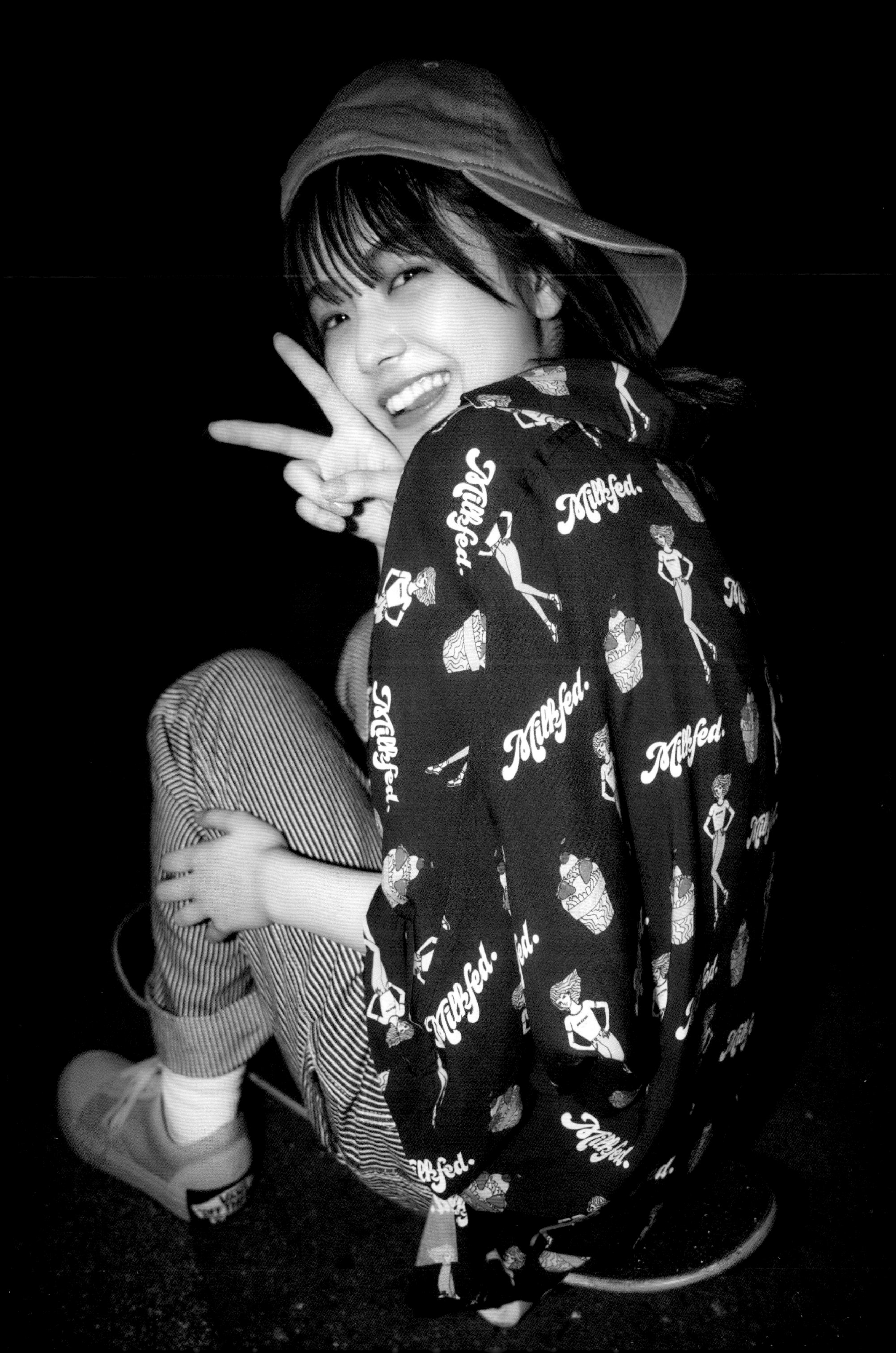
Milkfed.

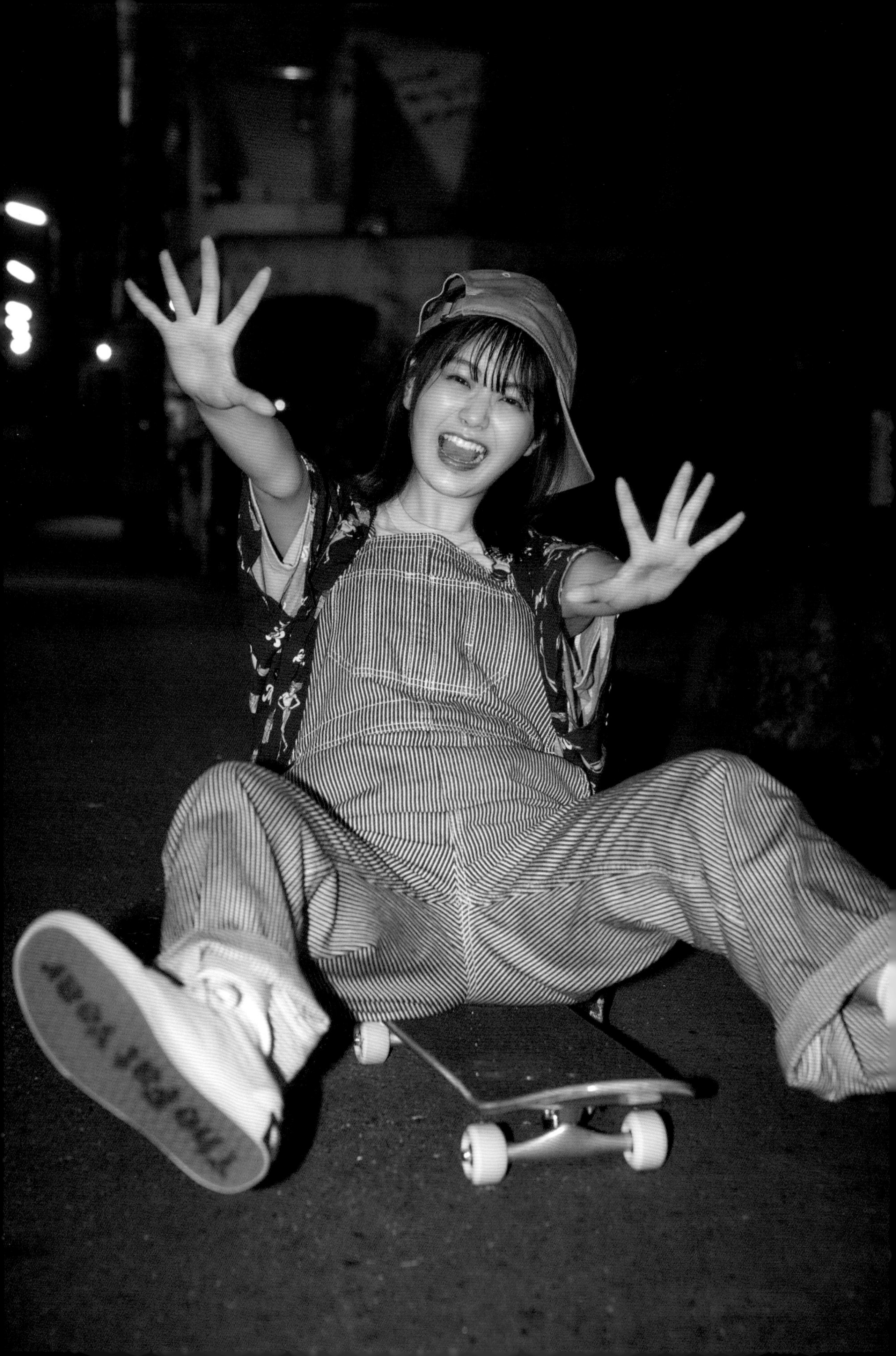

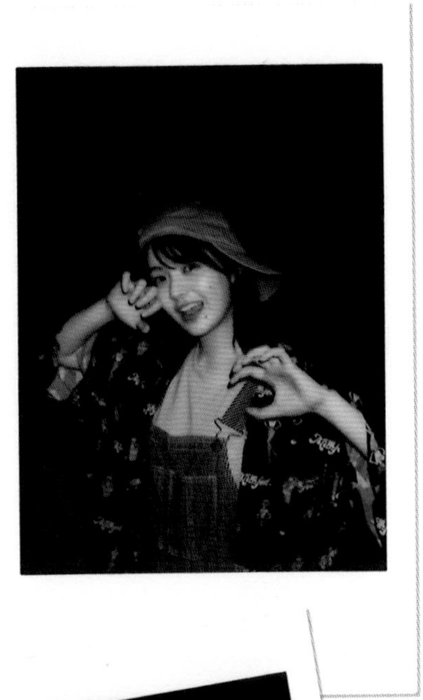
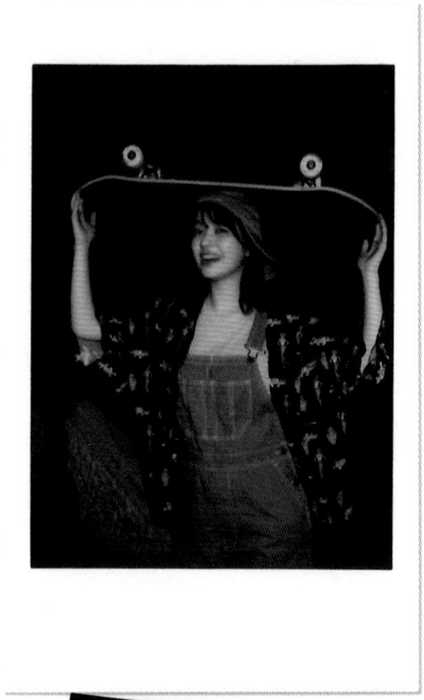
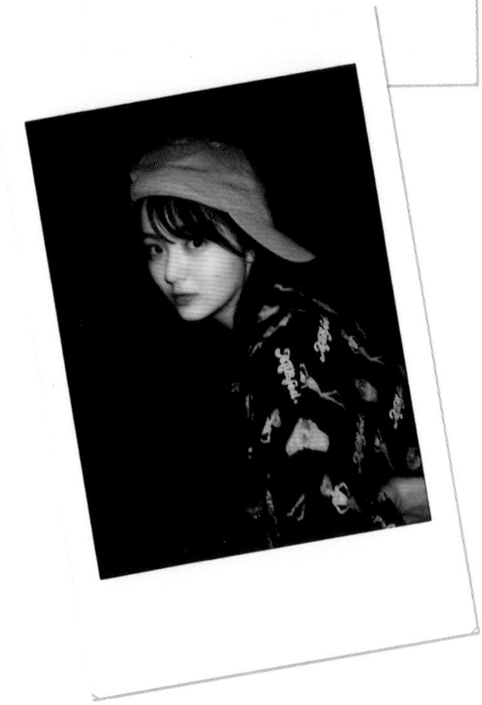
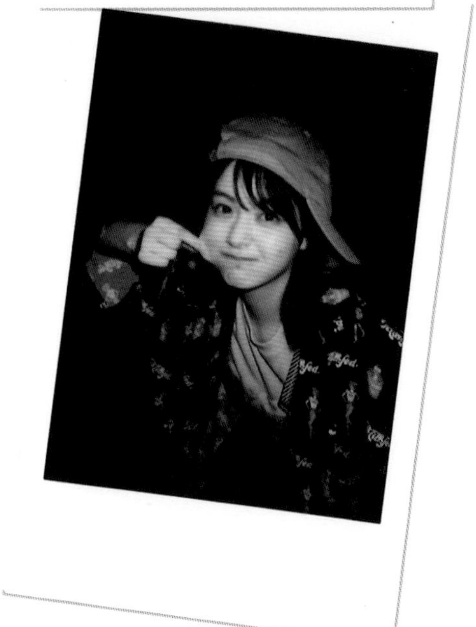

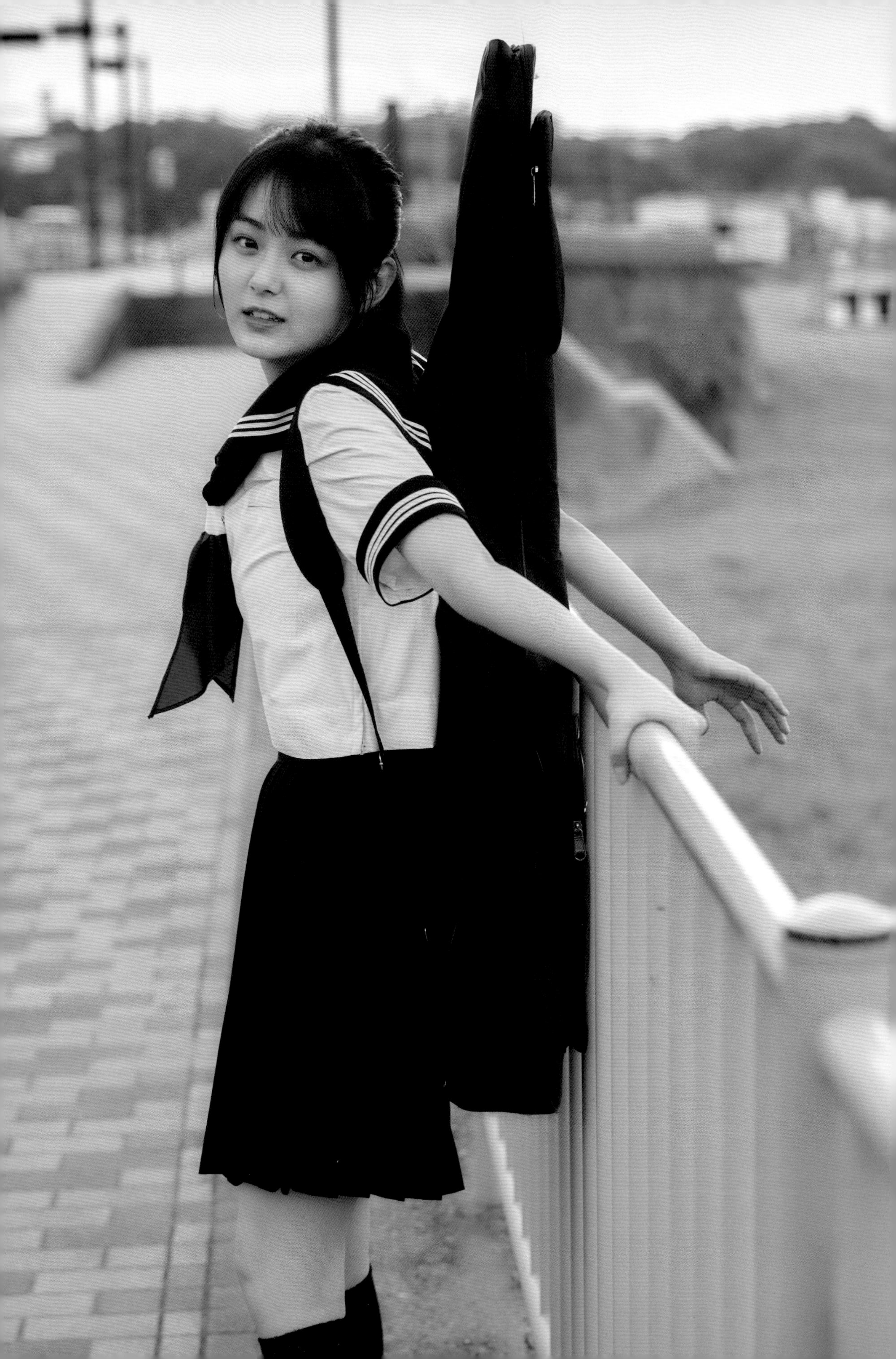

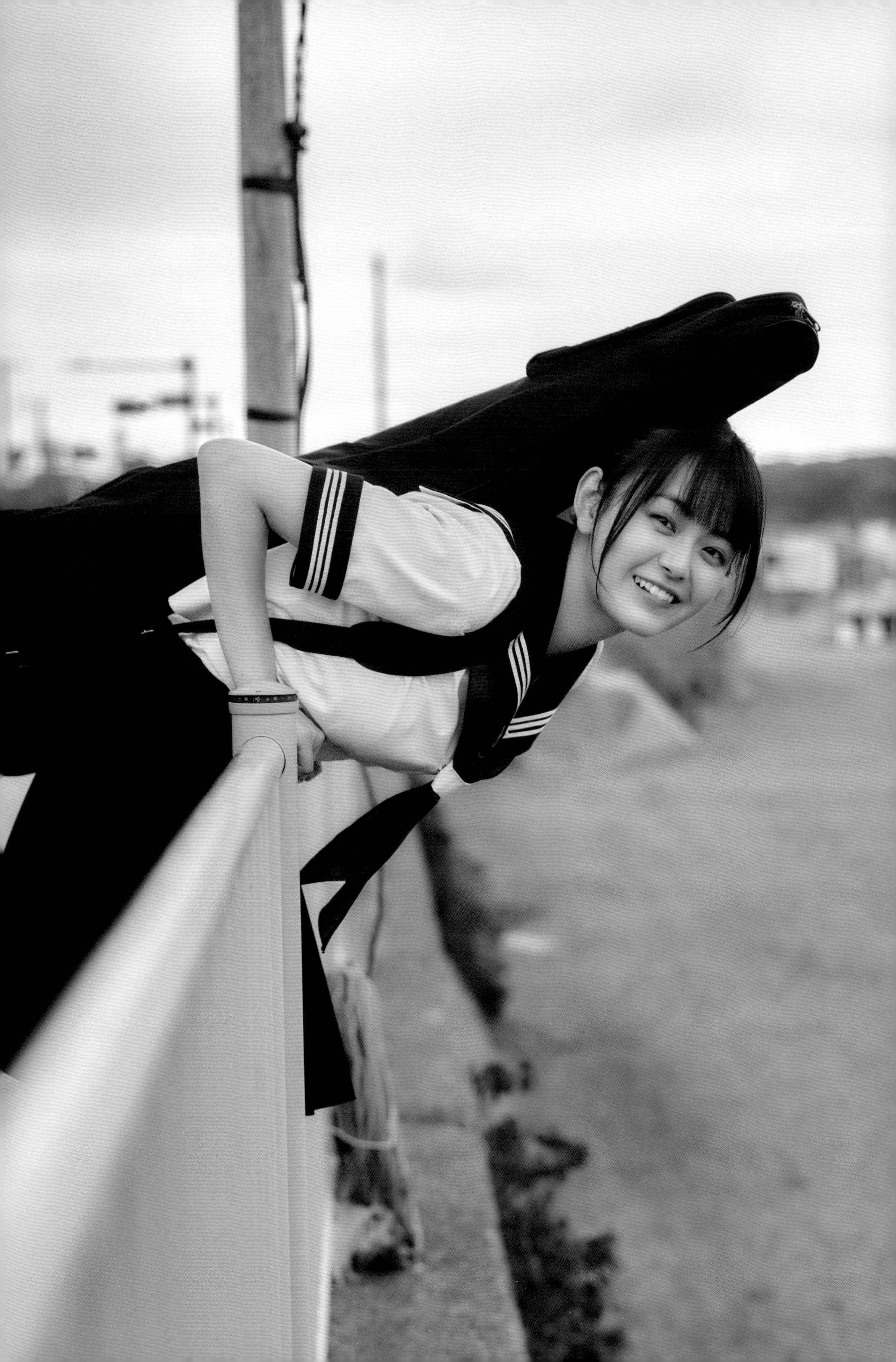

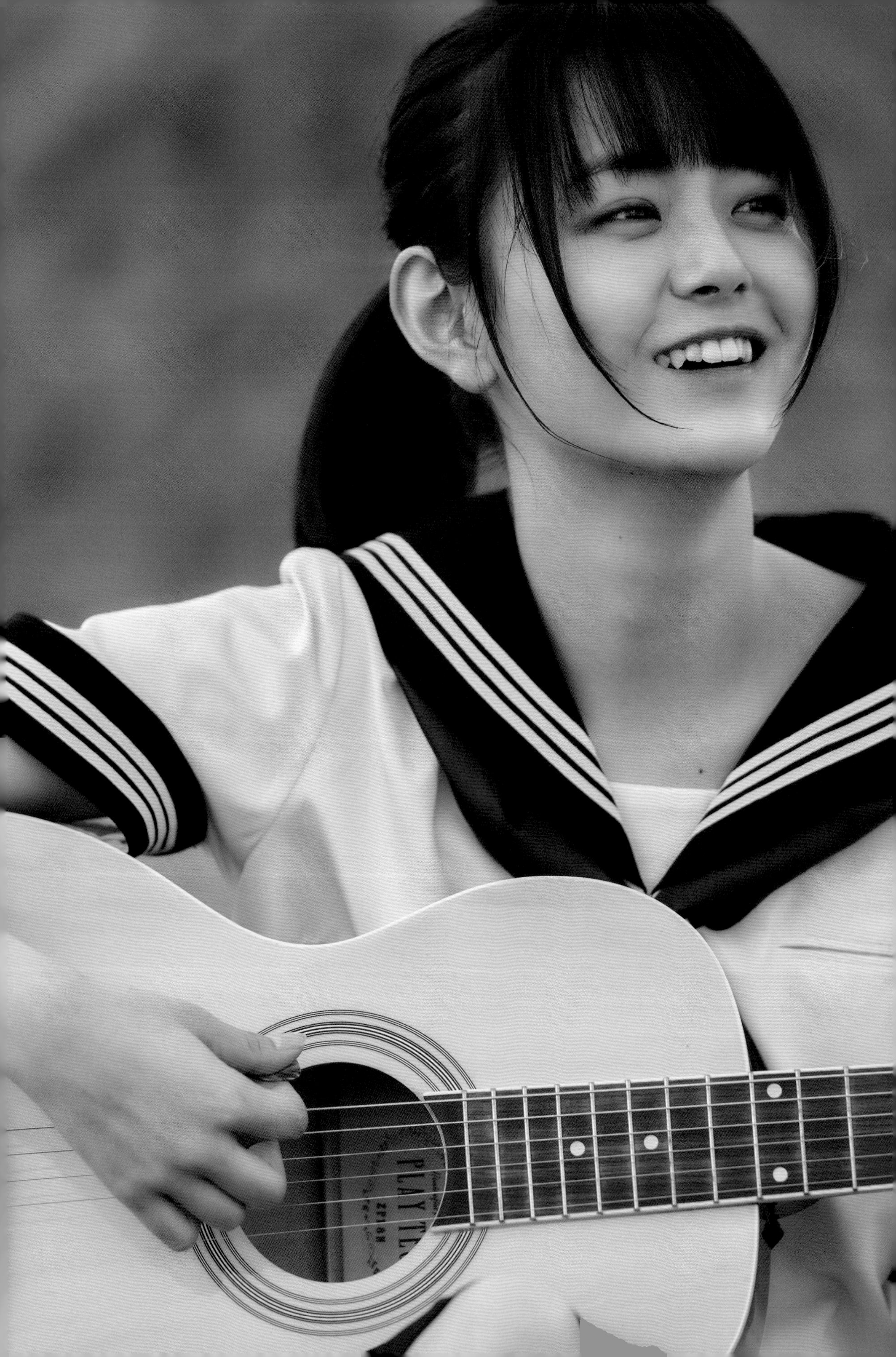

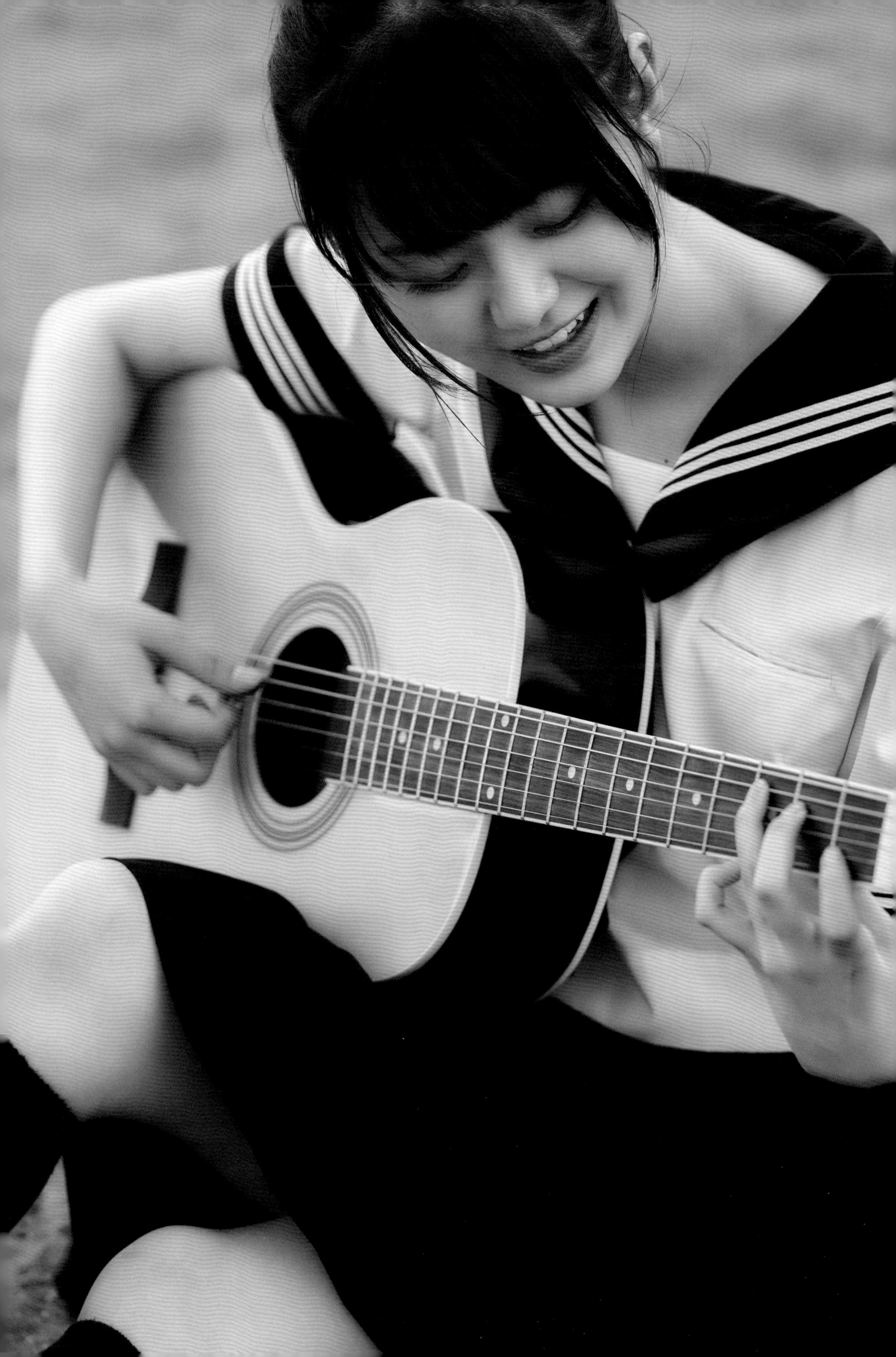

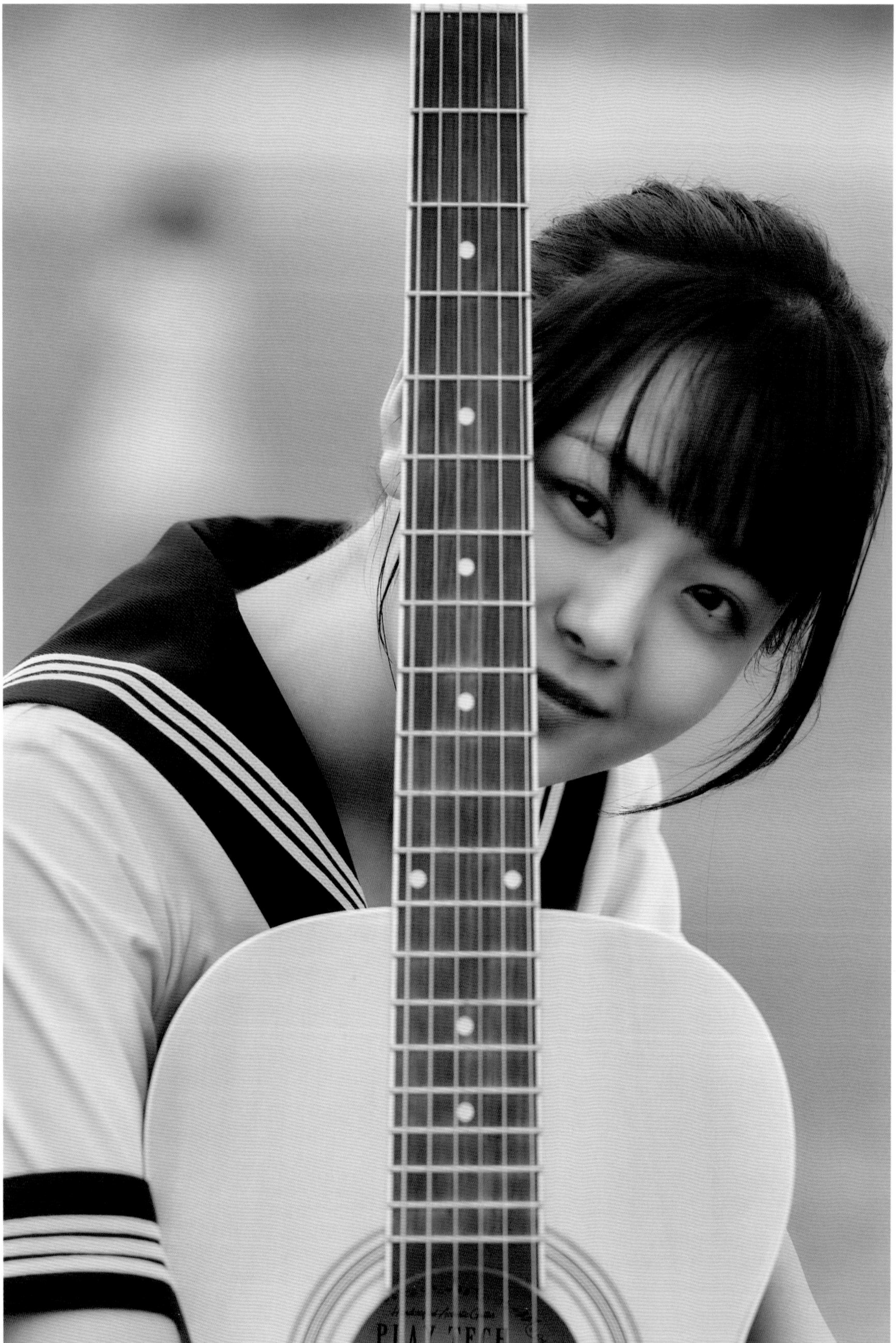

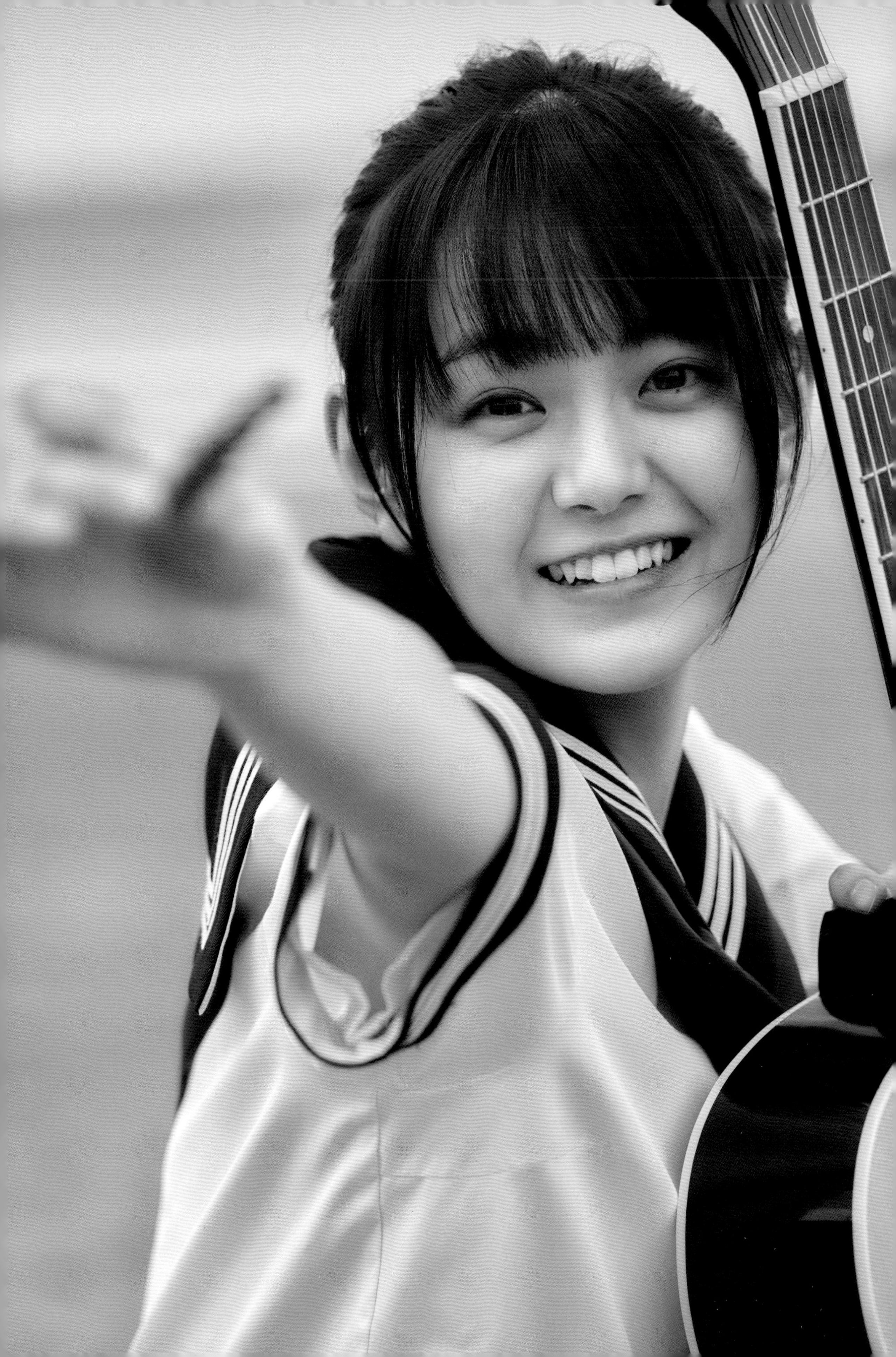

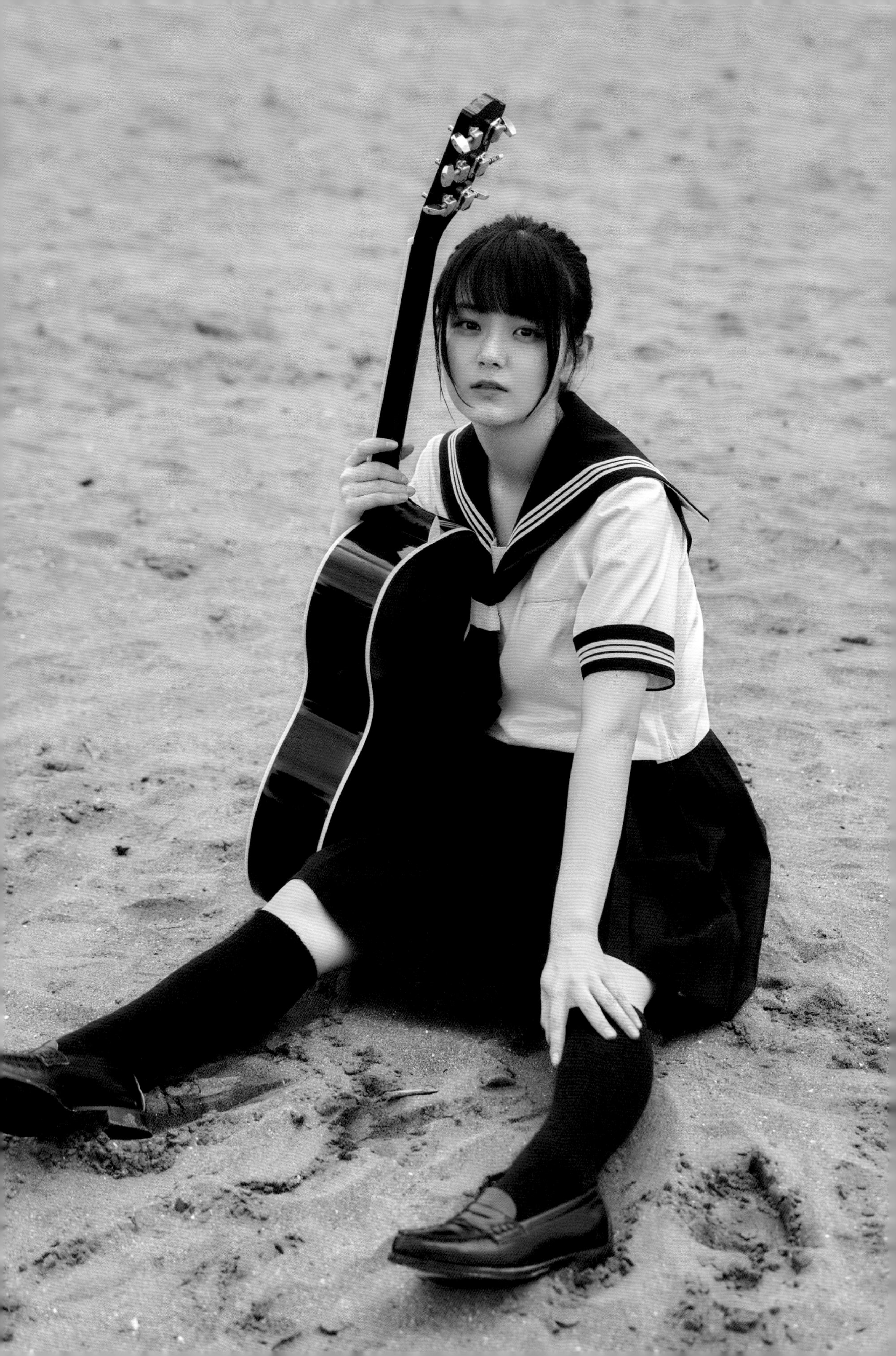

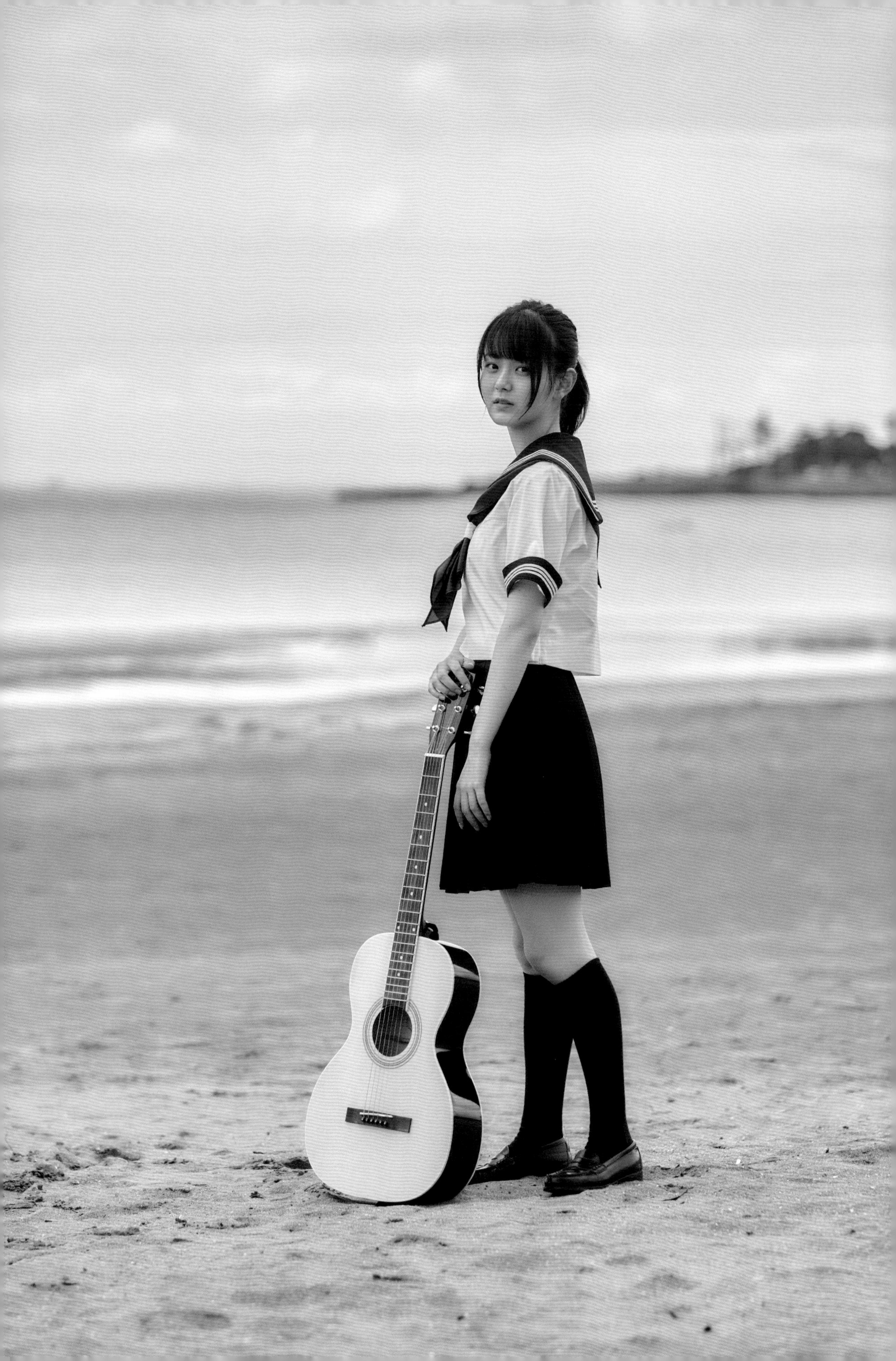

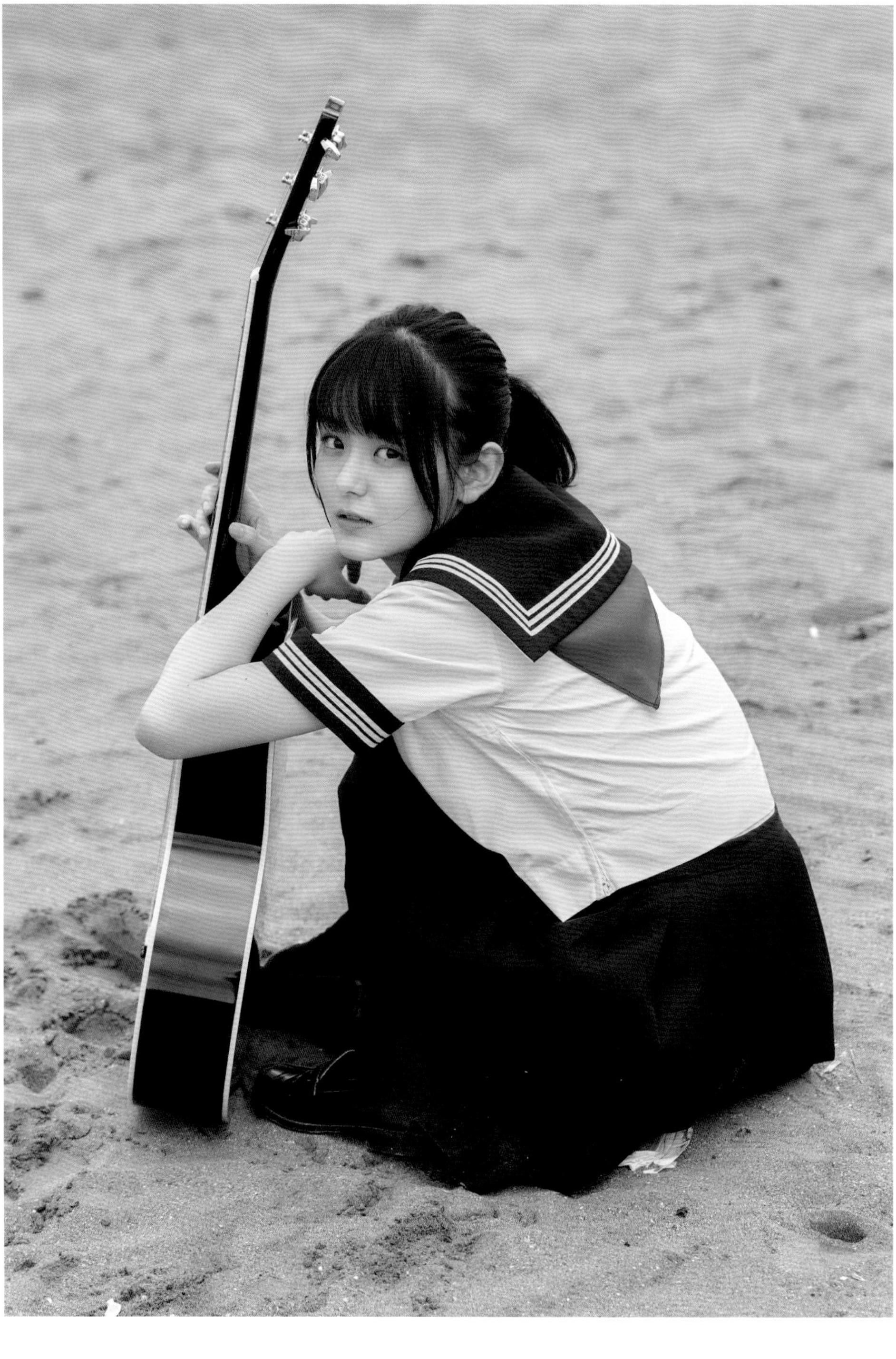

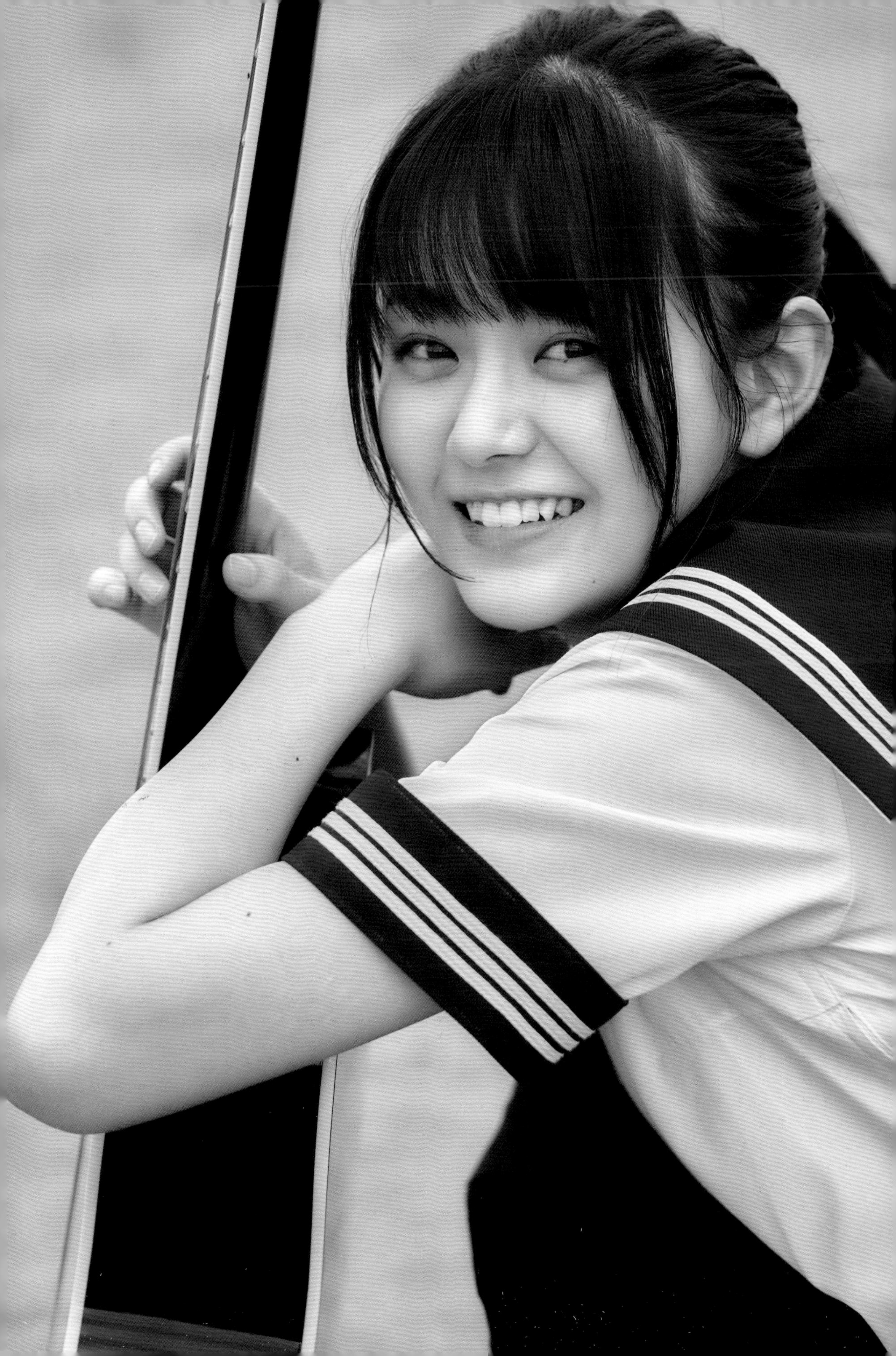

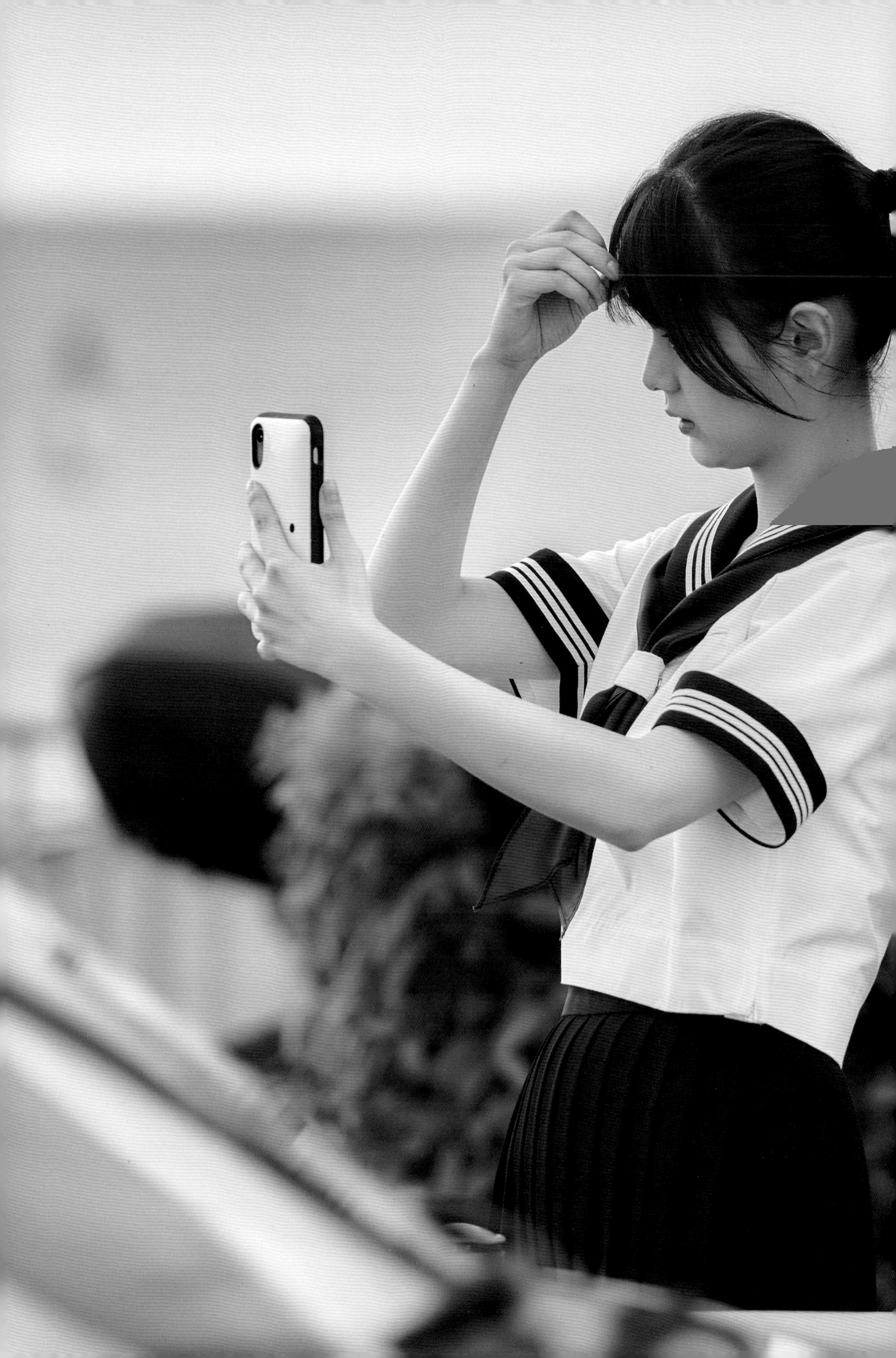

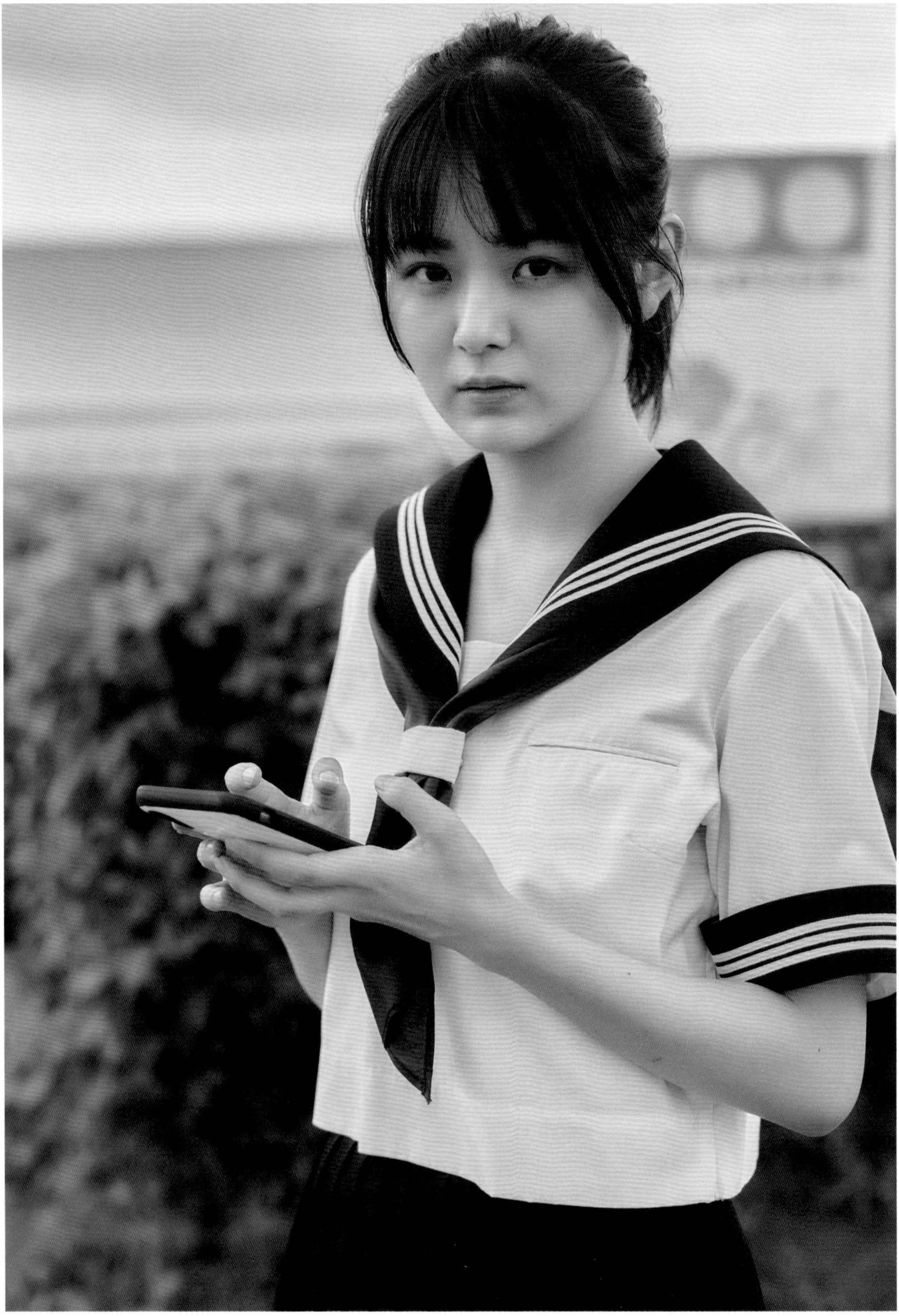

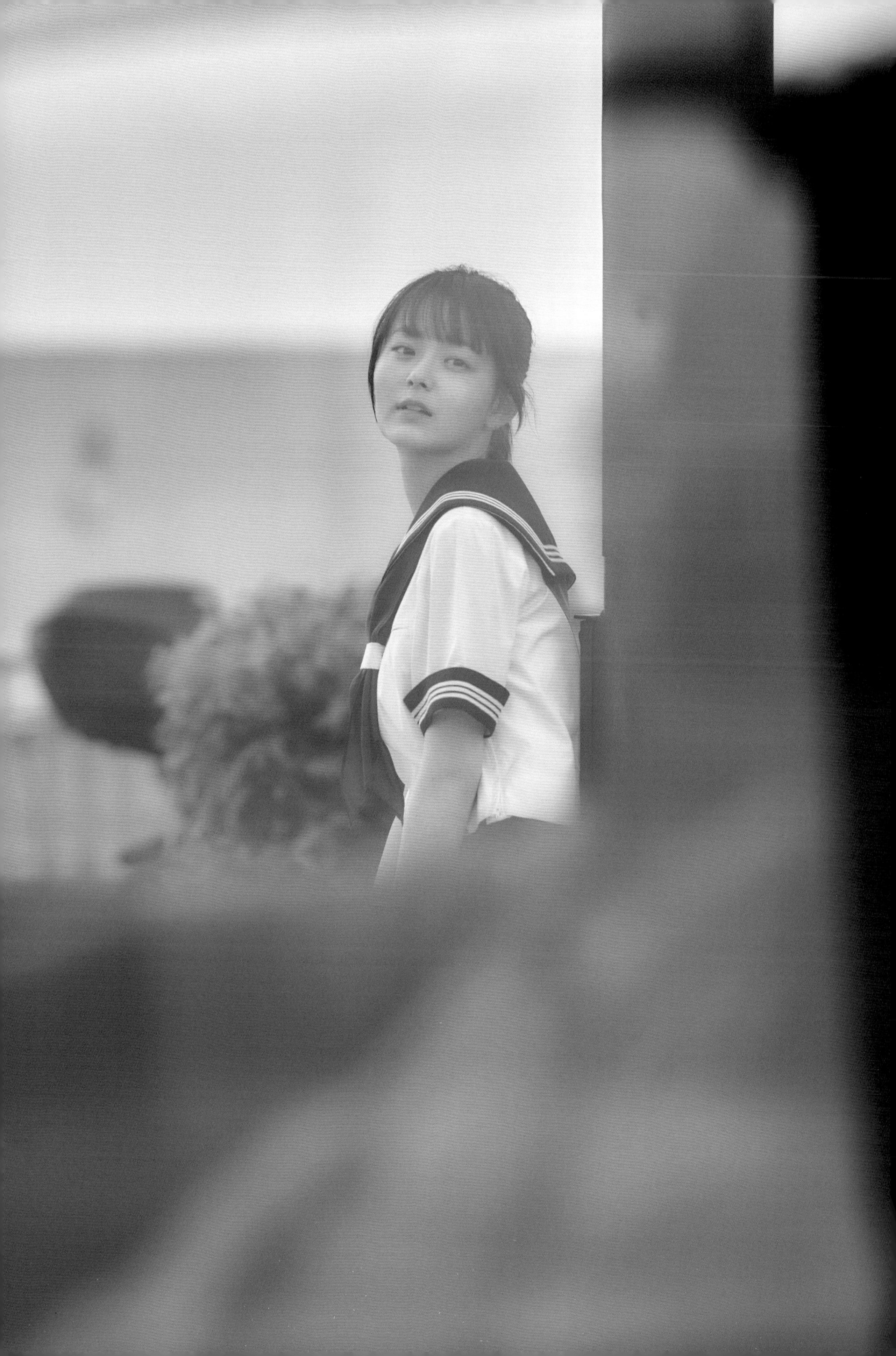

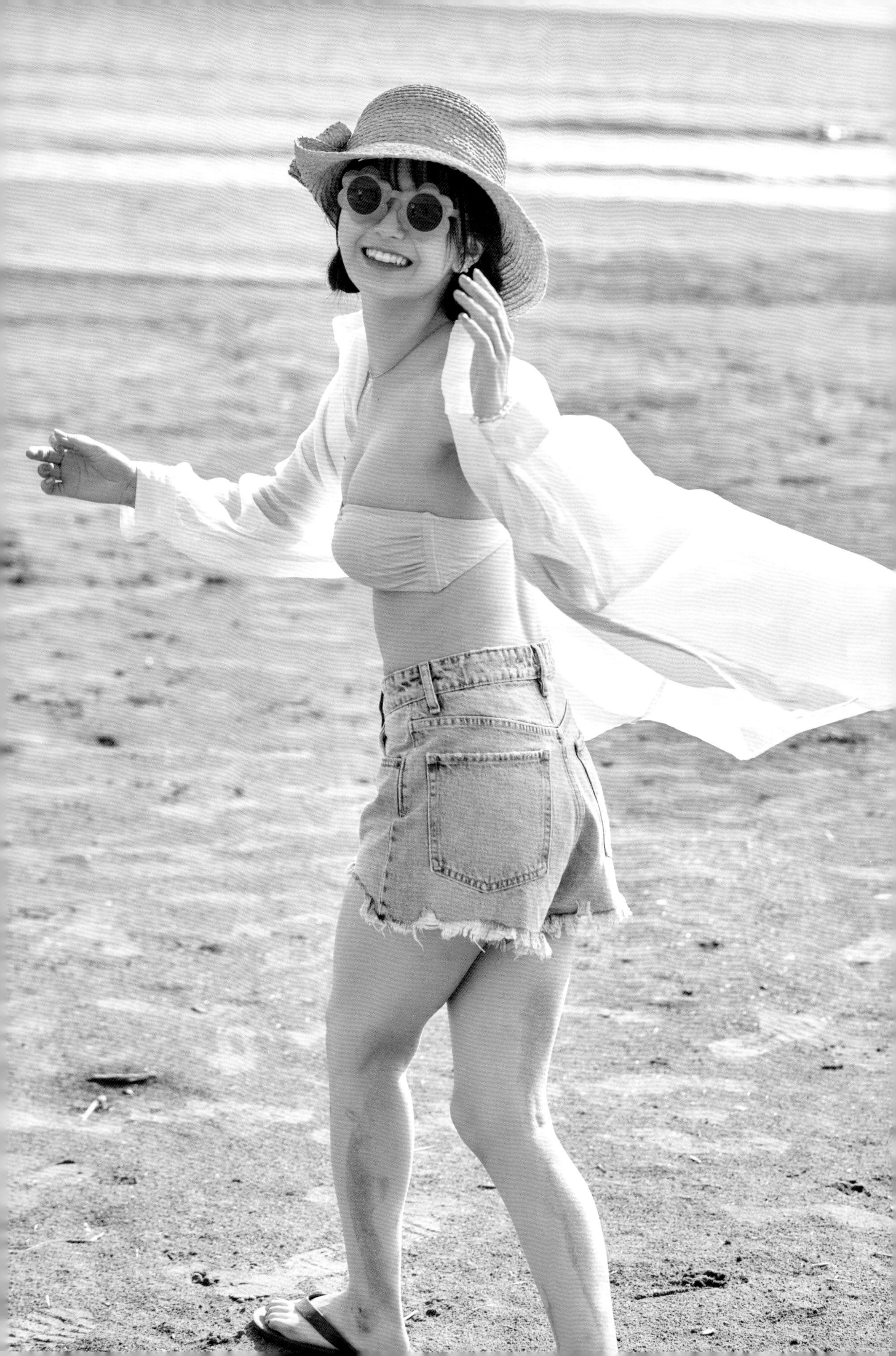

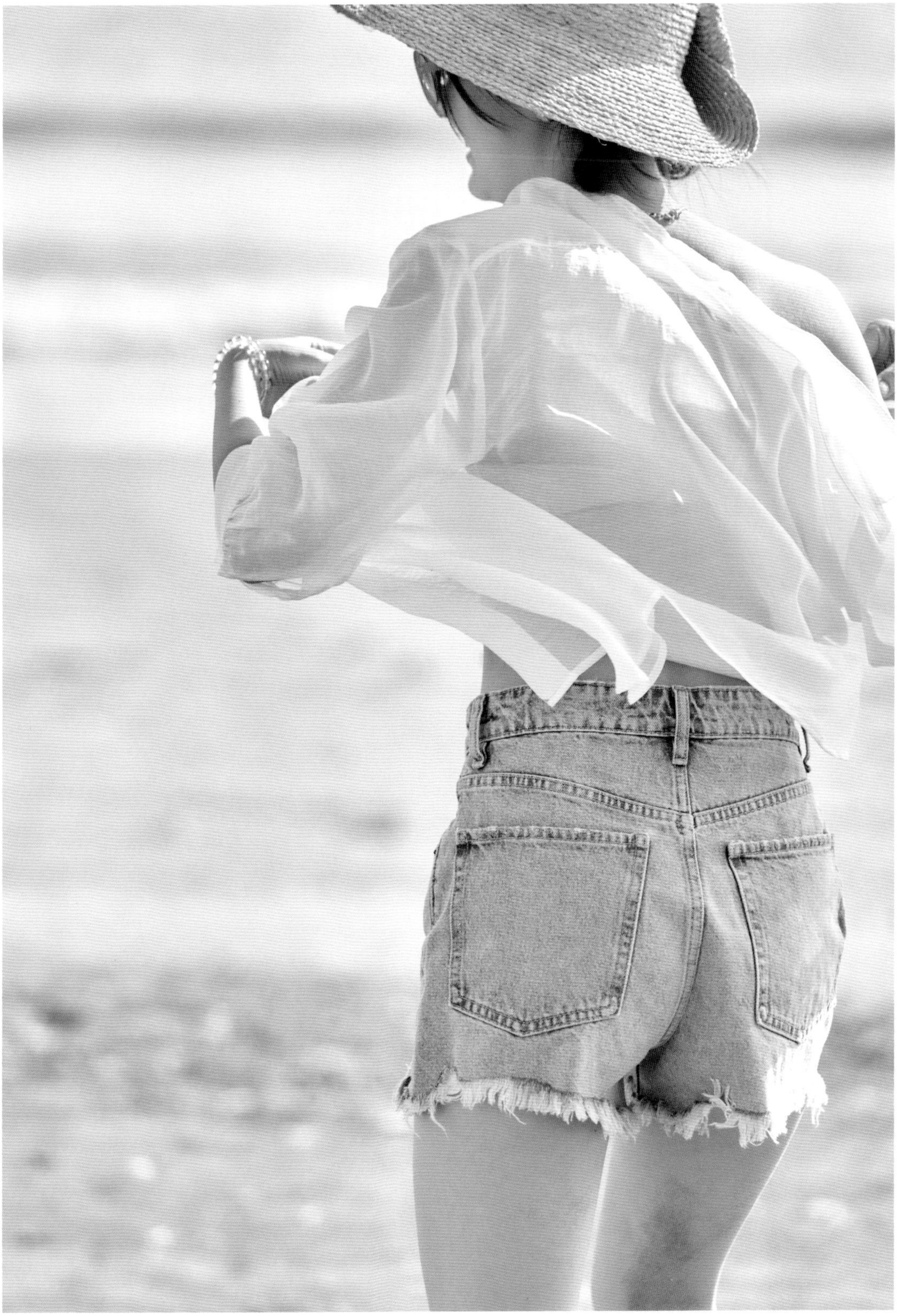

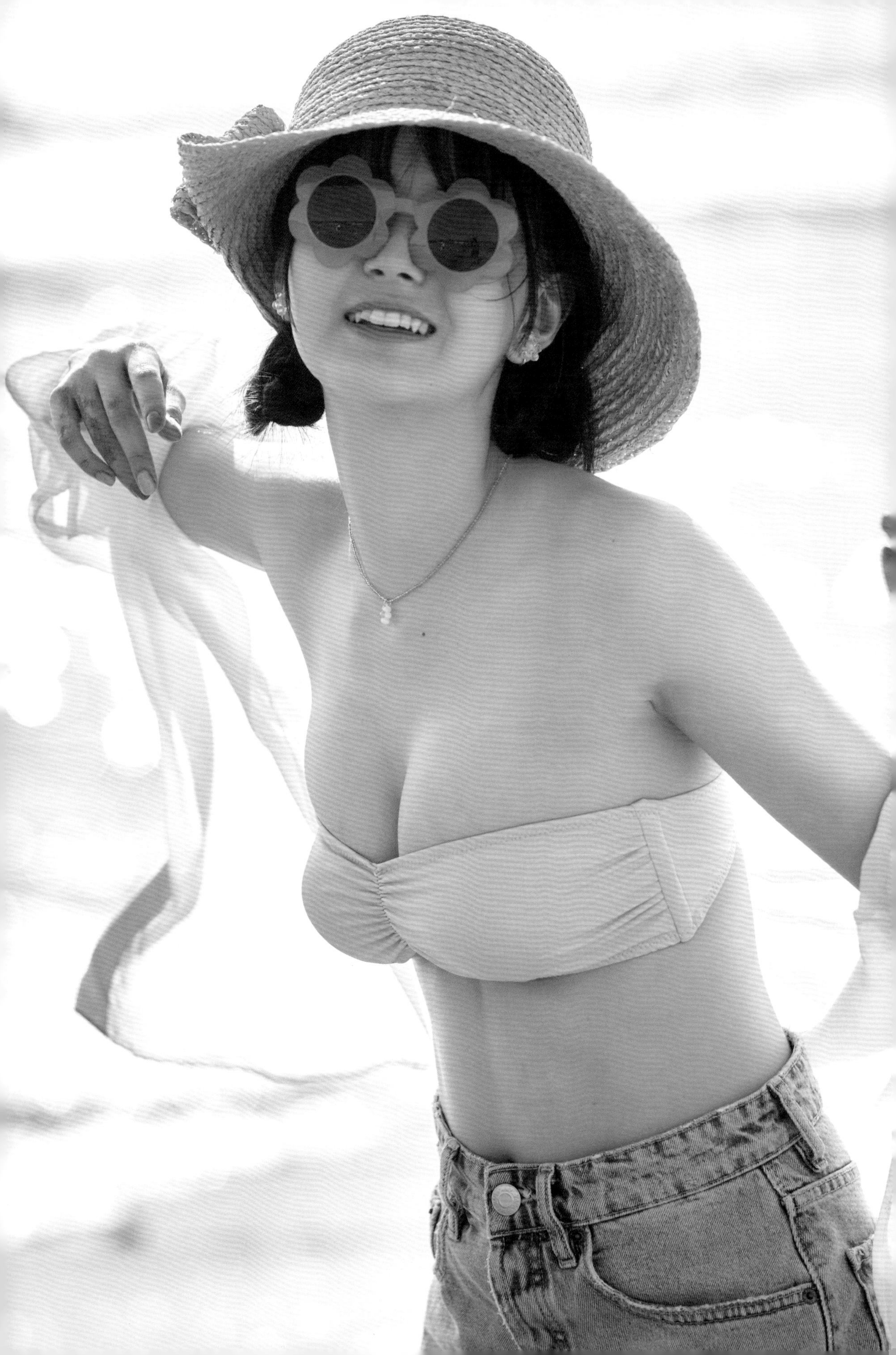

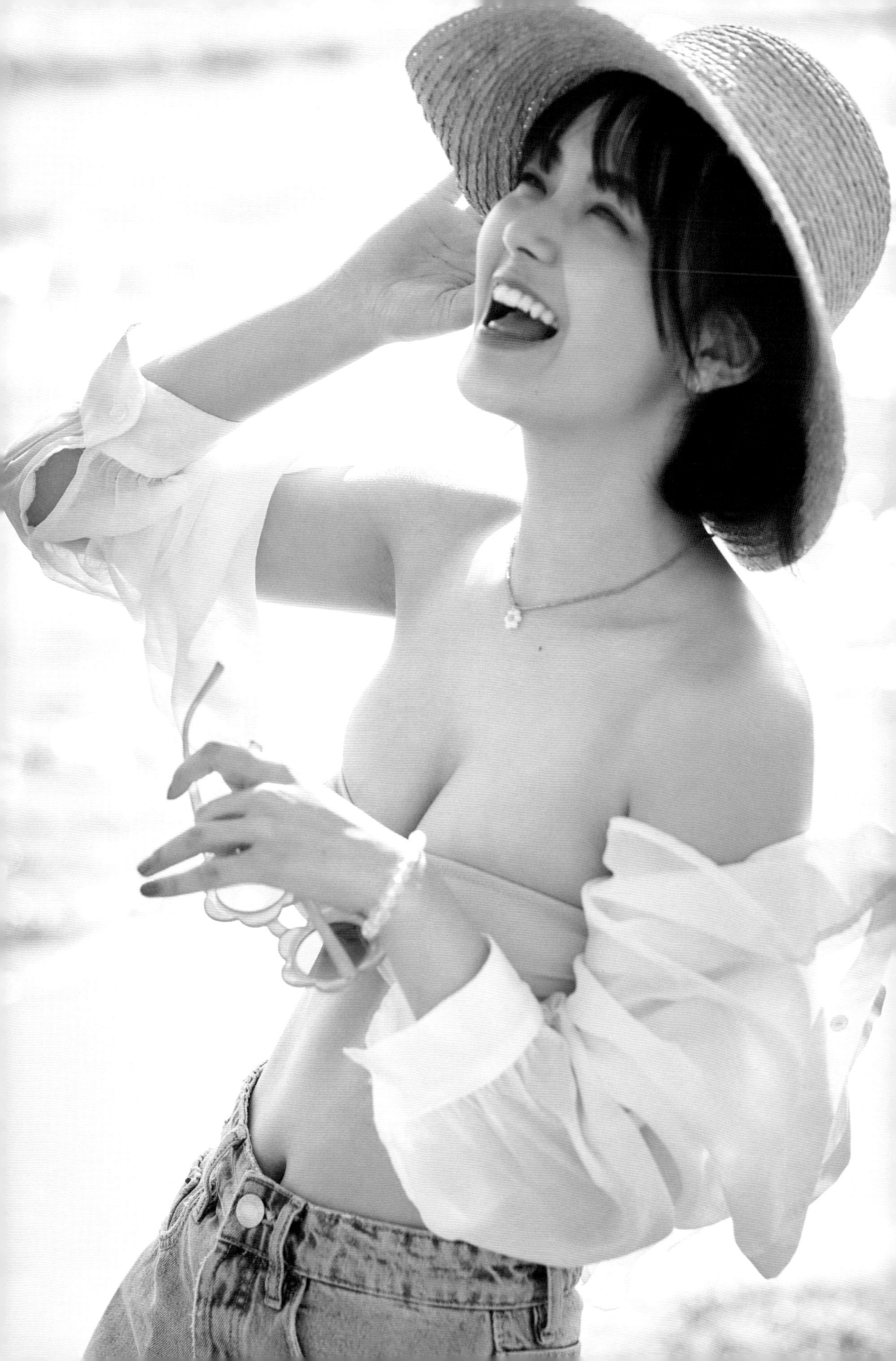

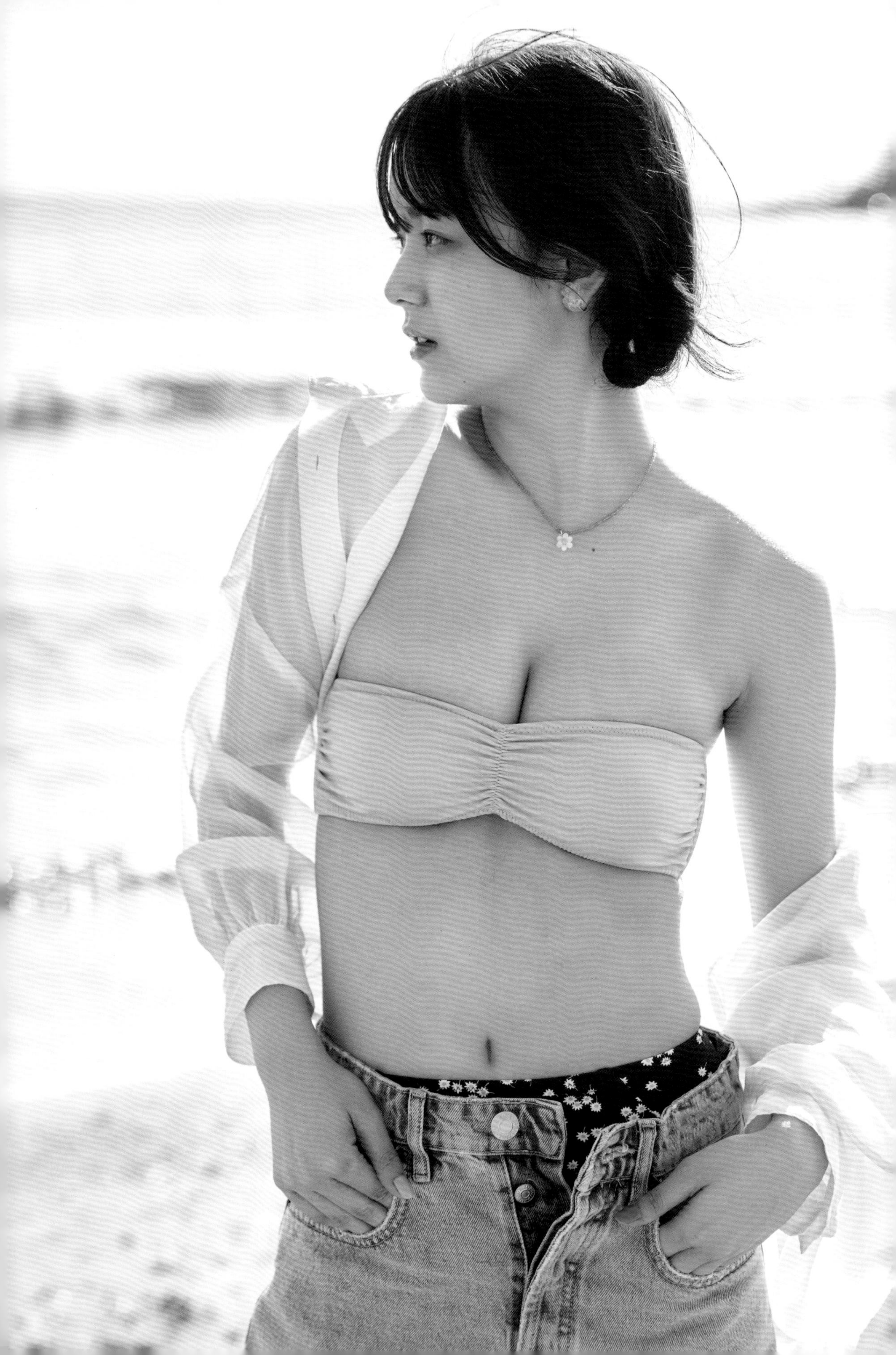

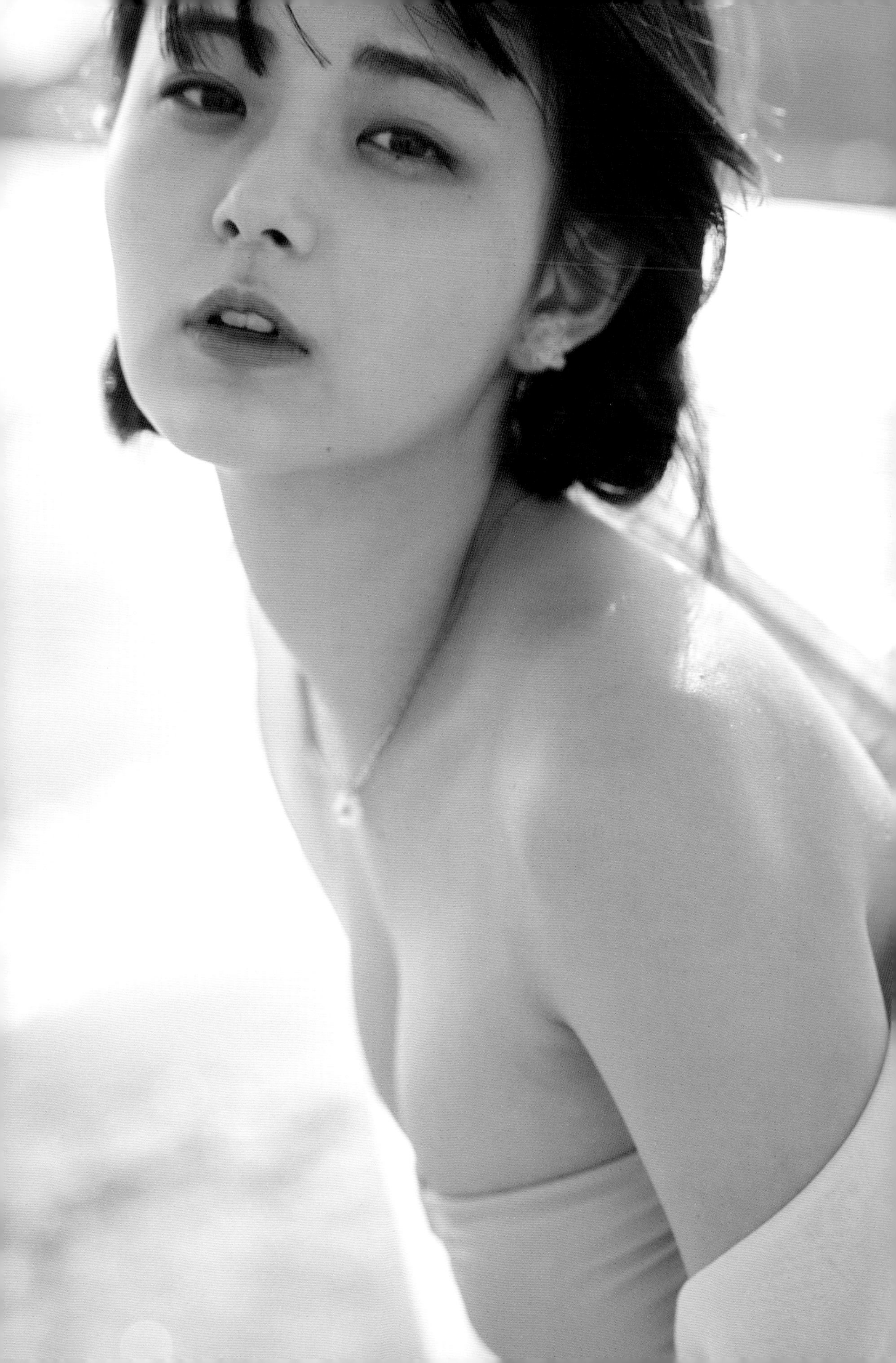

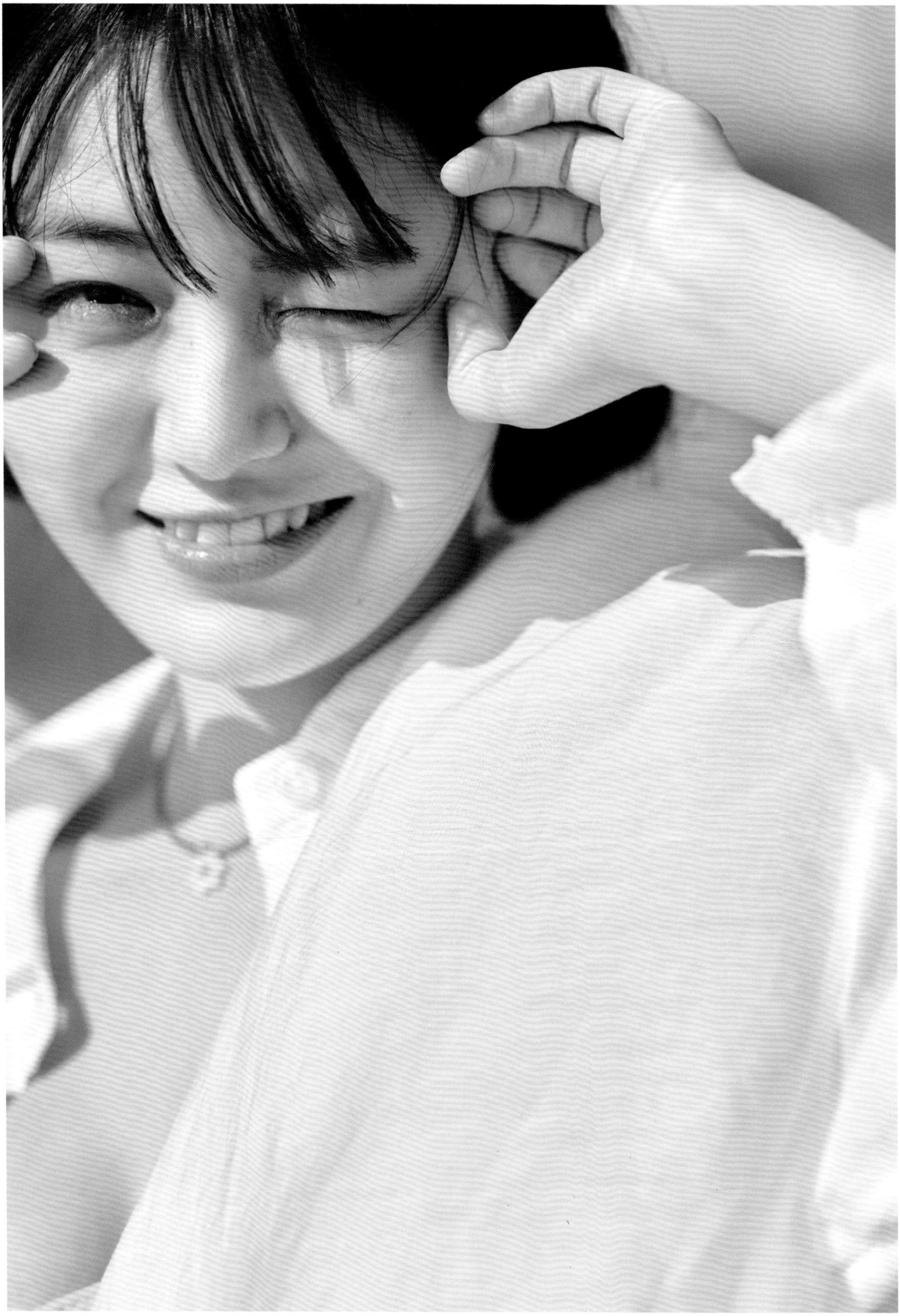

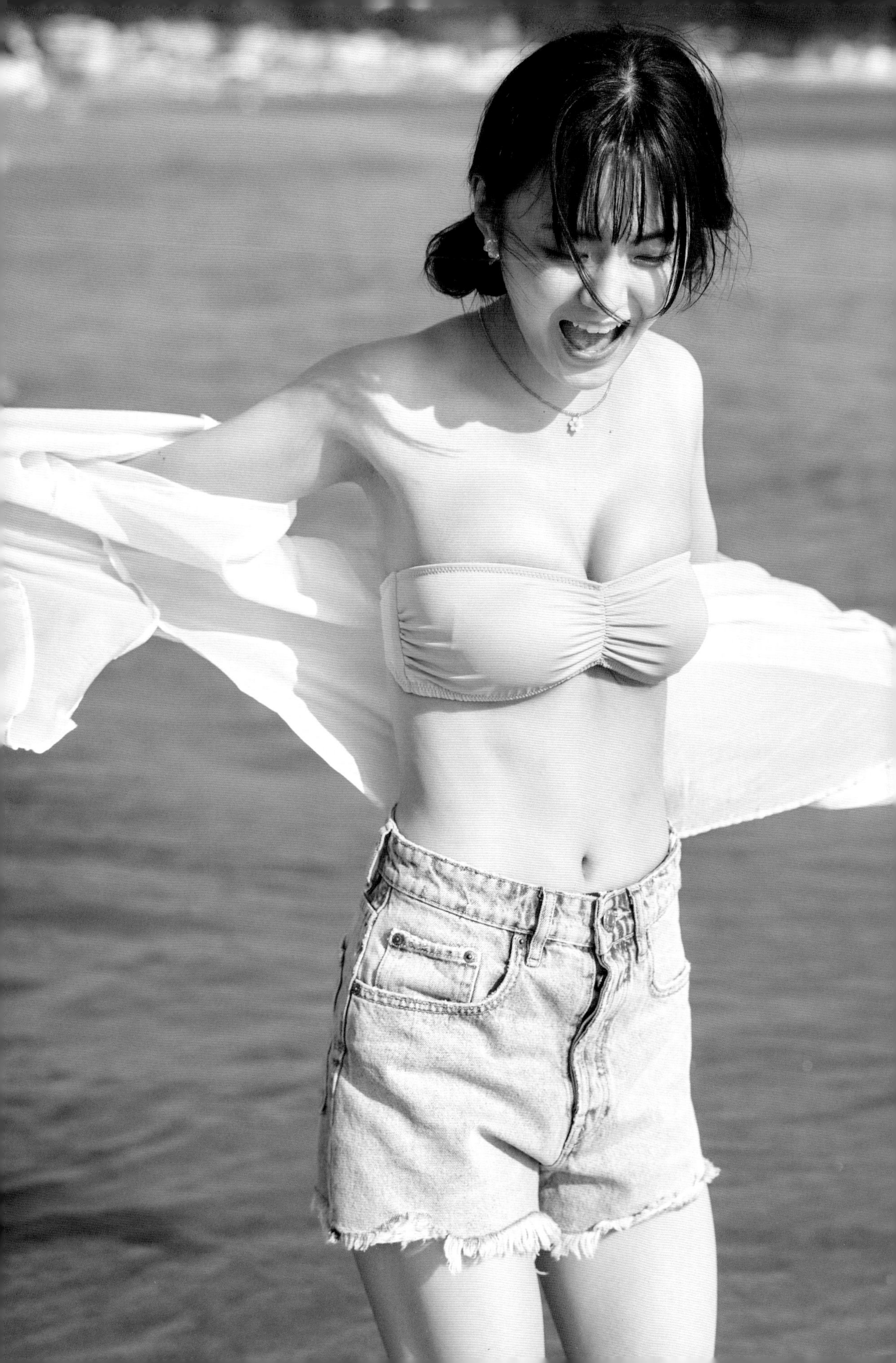

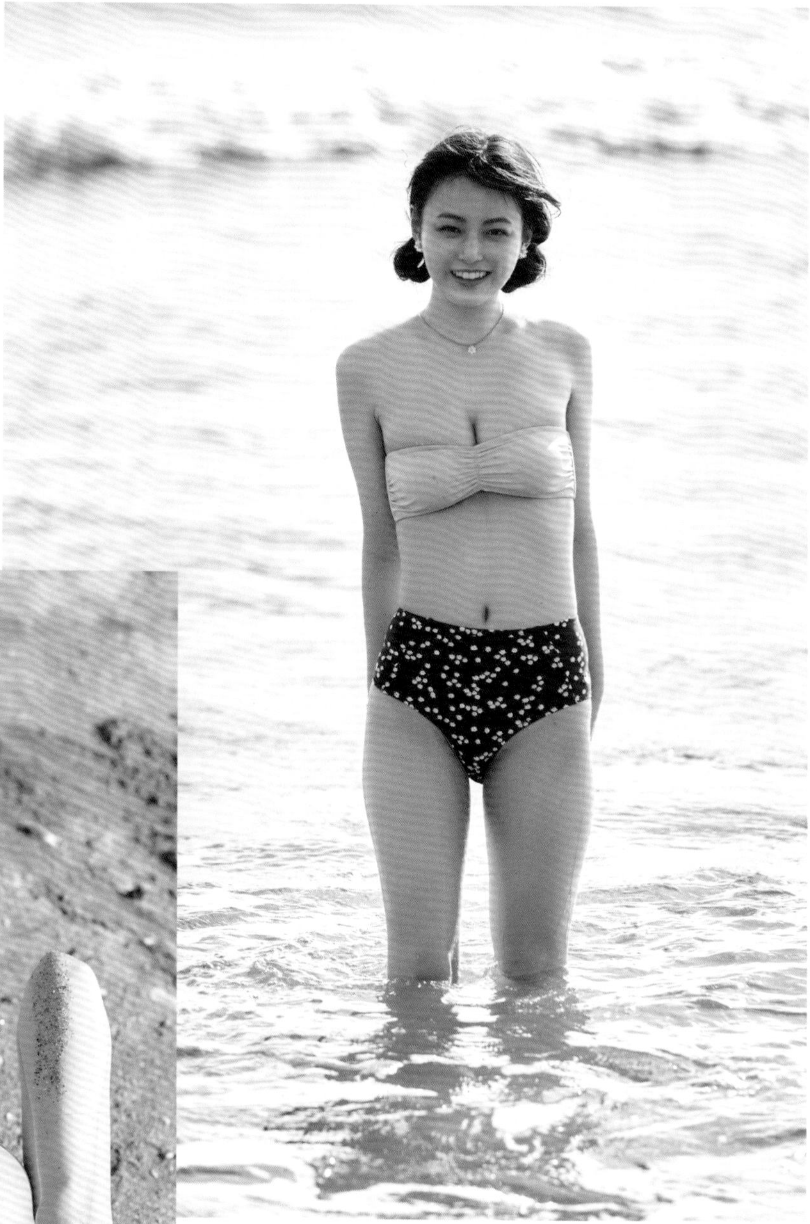

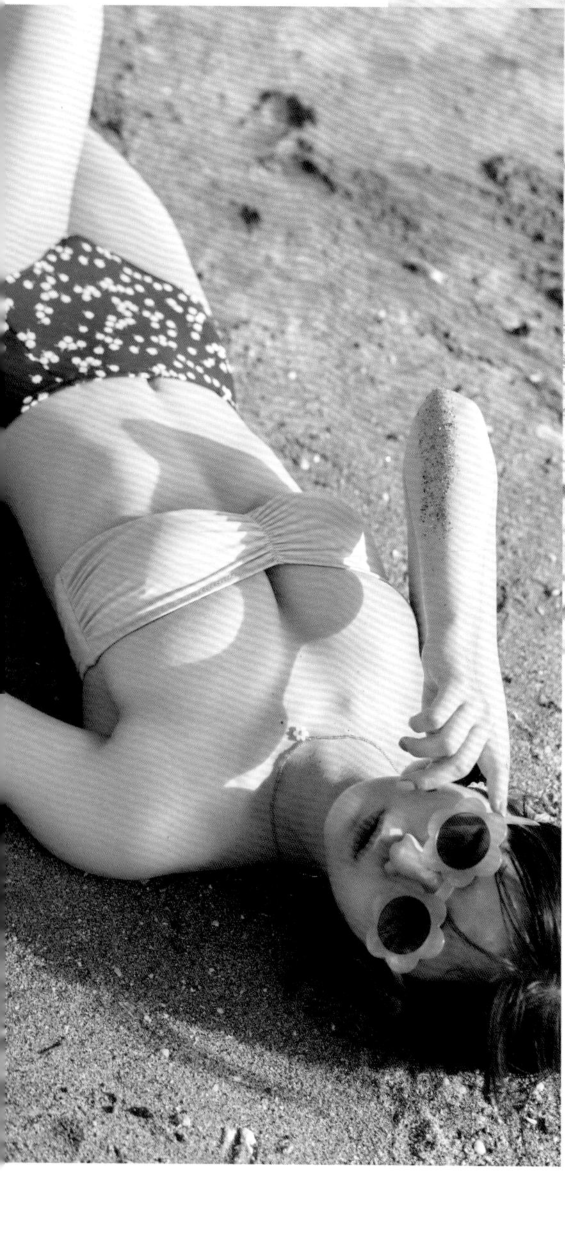

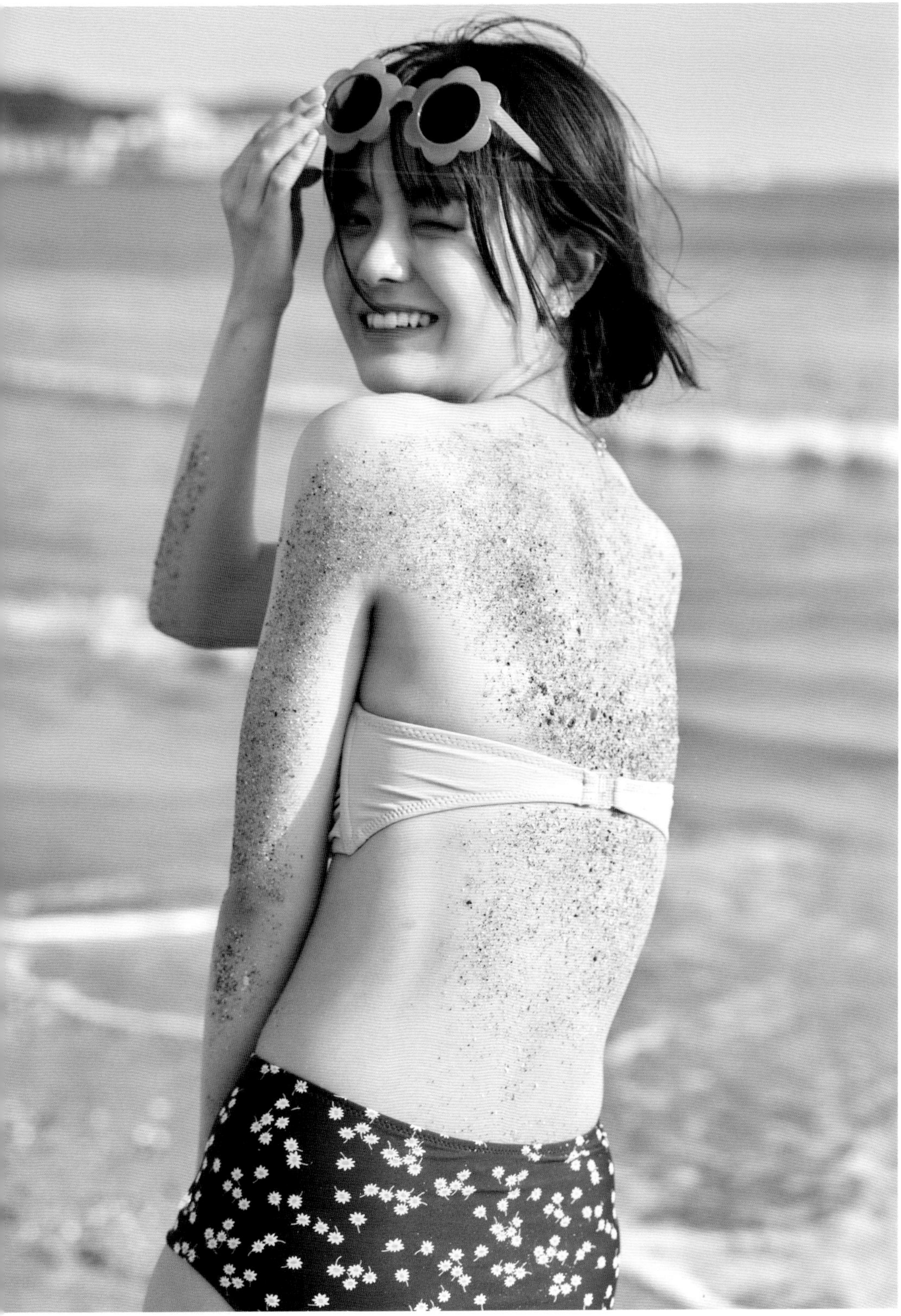

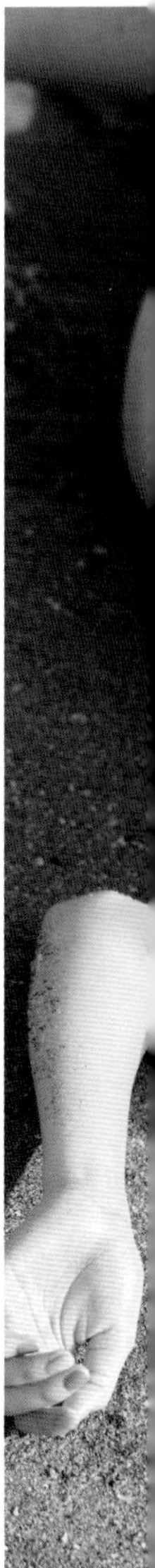

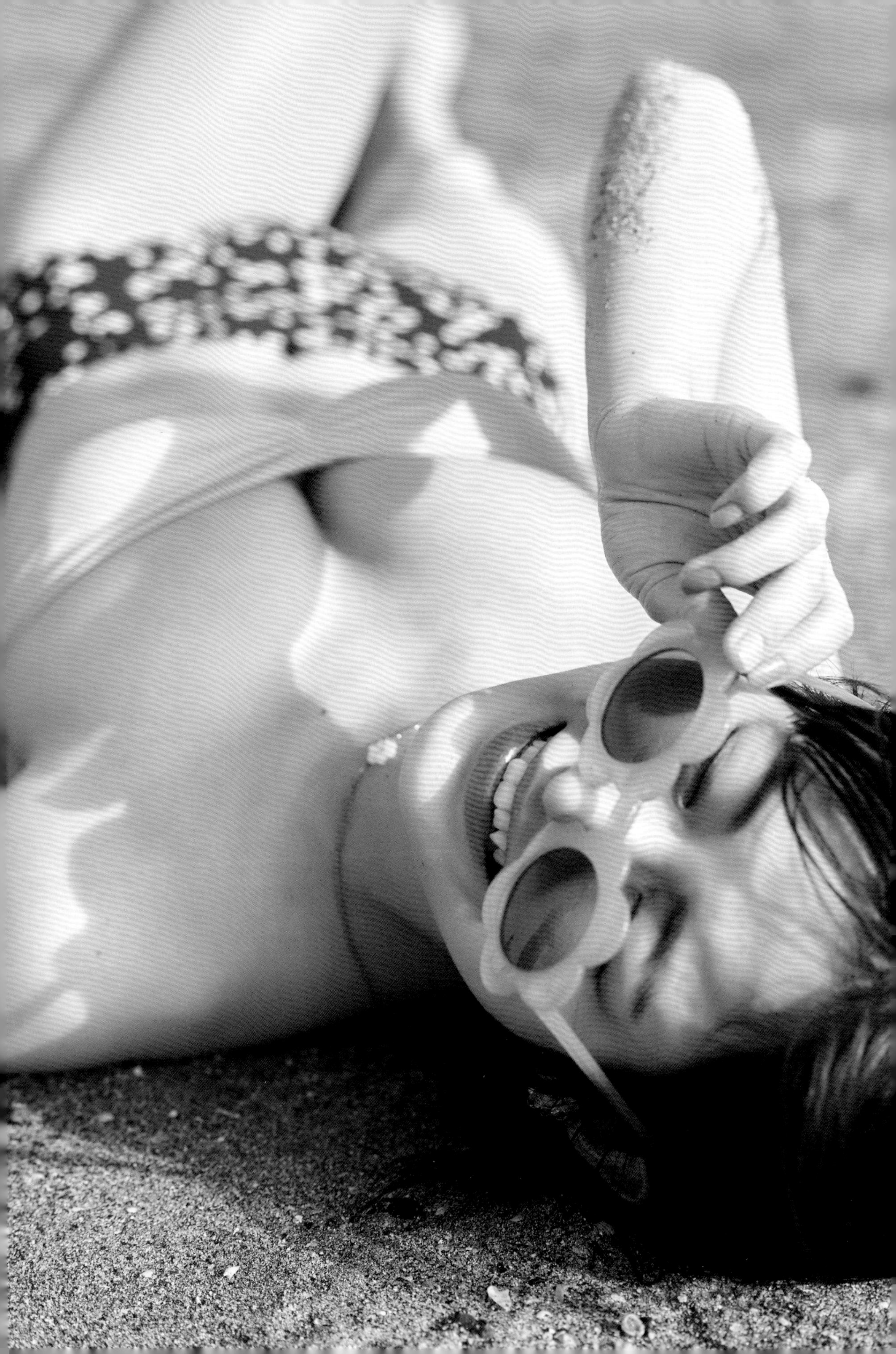

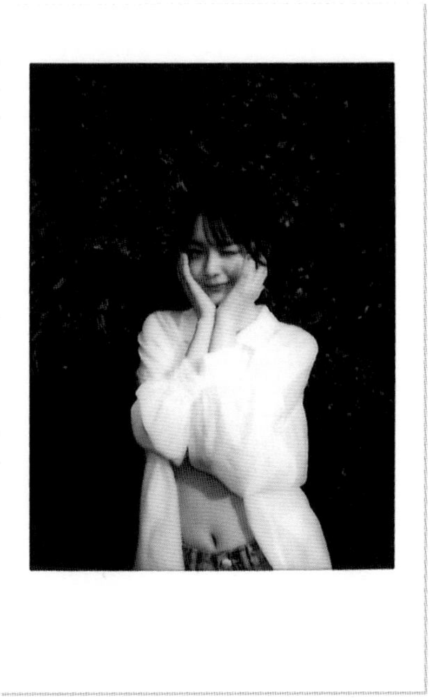
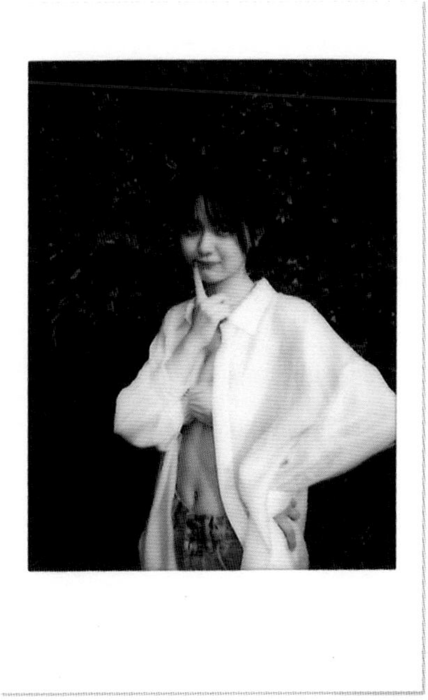
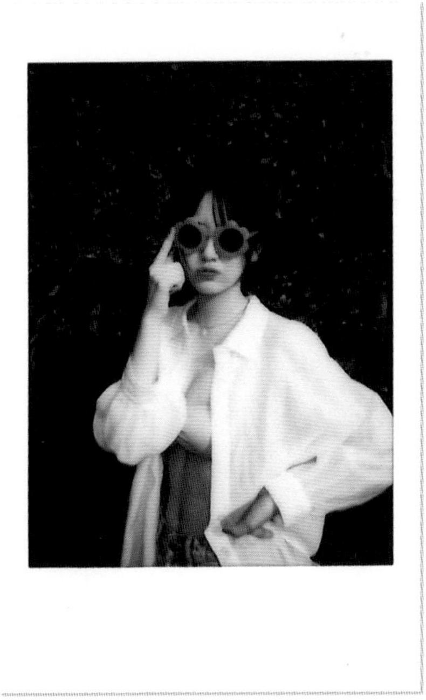
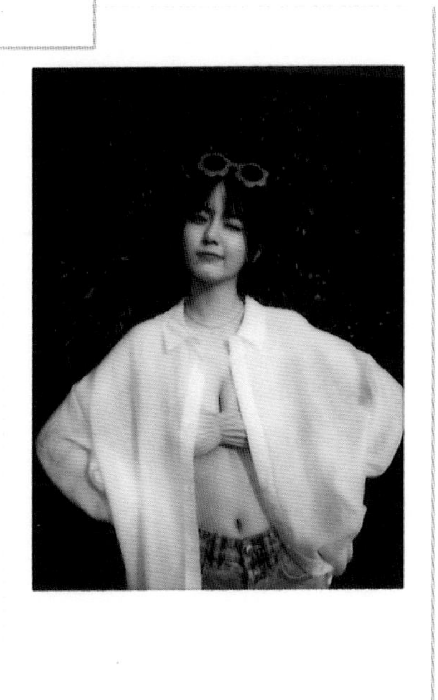

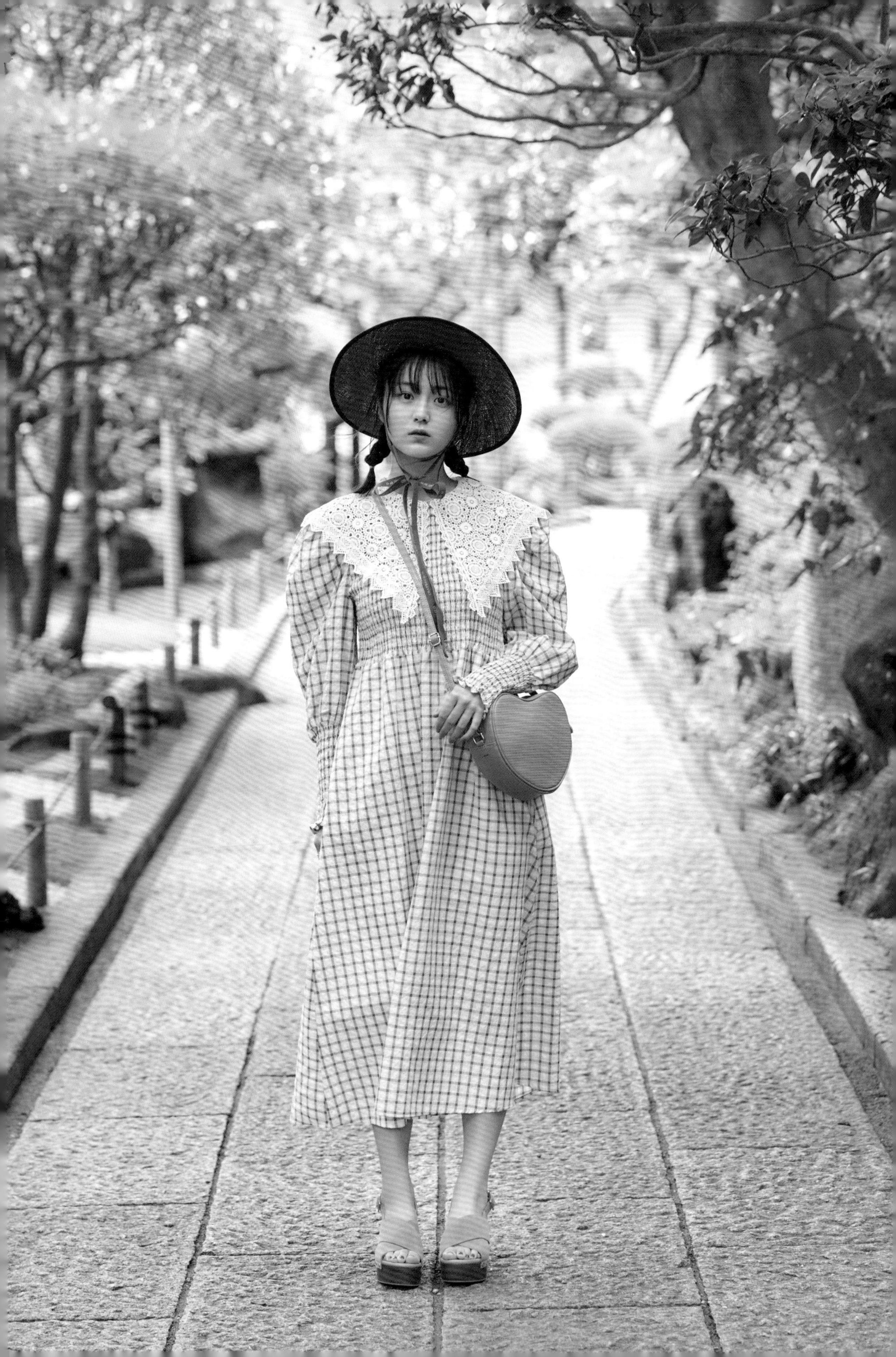

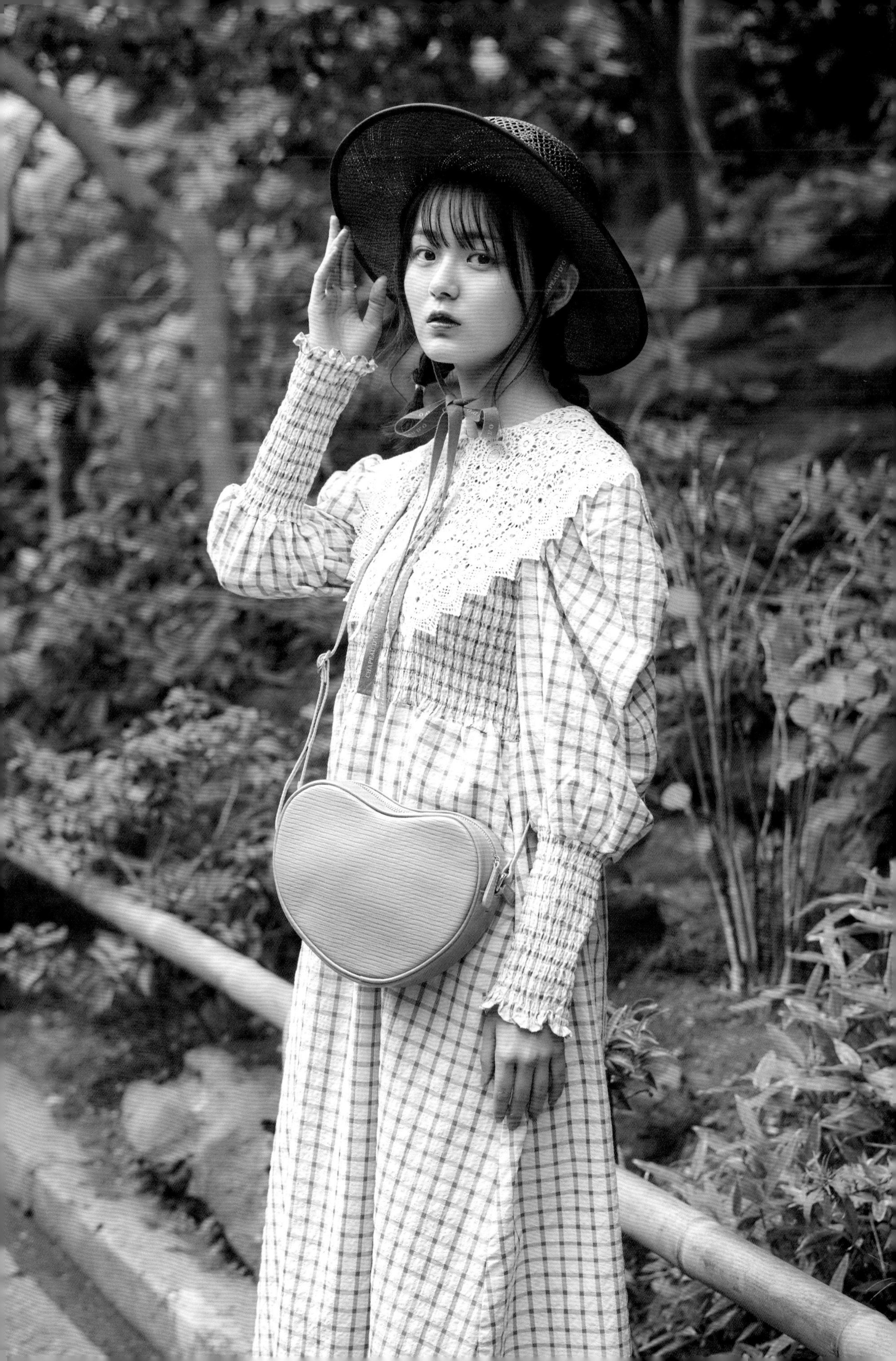

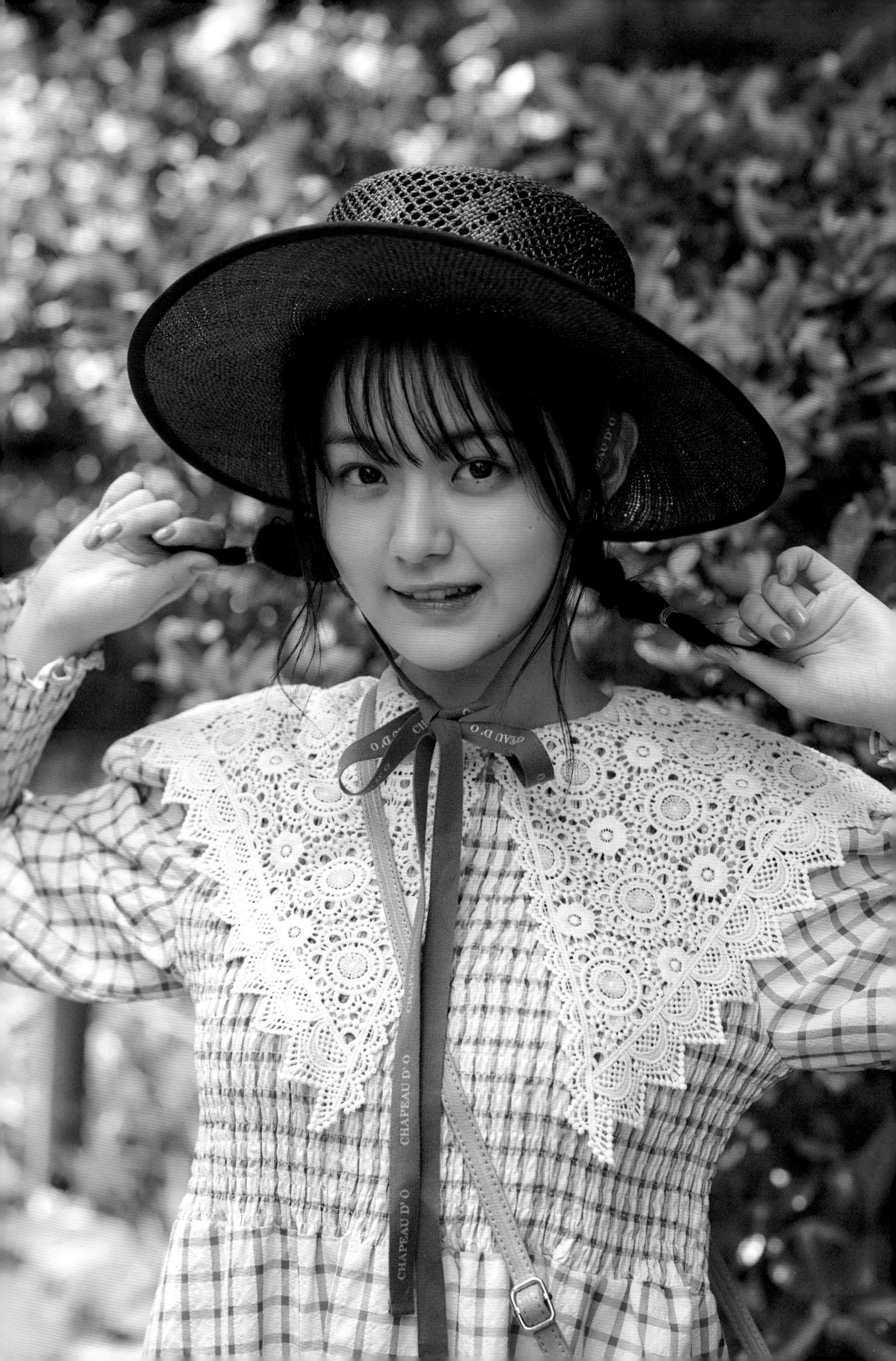
CHAPEAU D'O

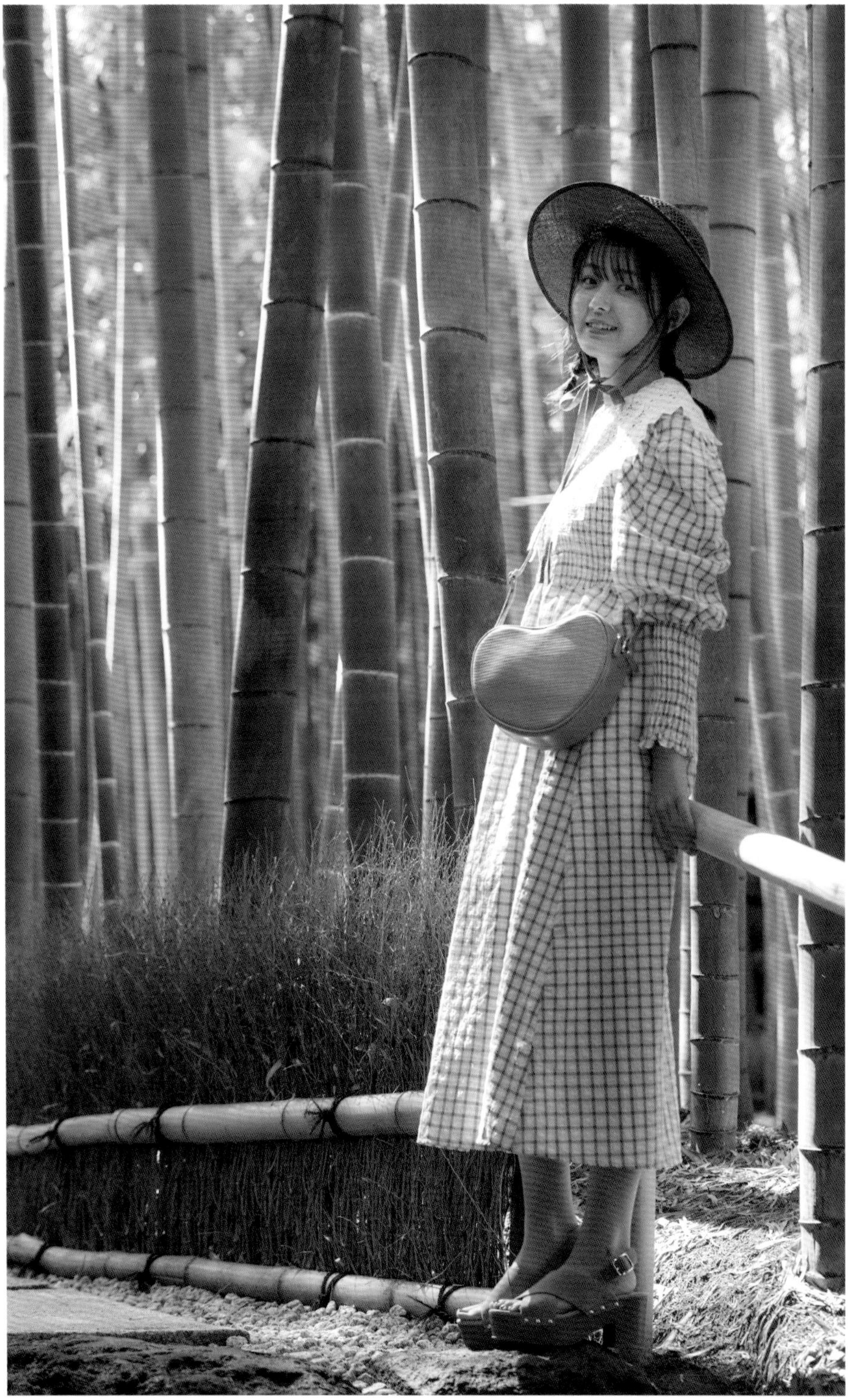

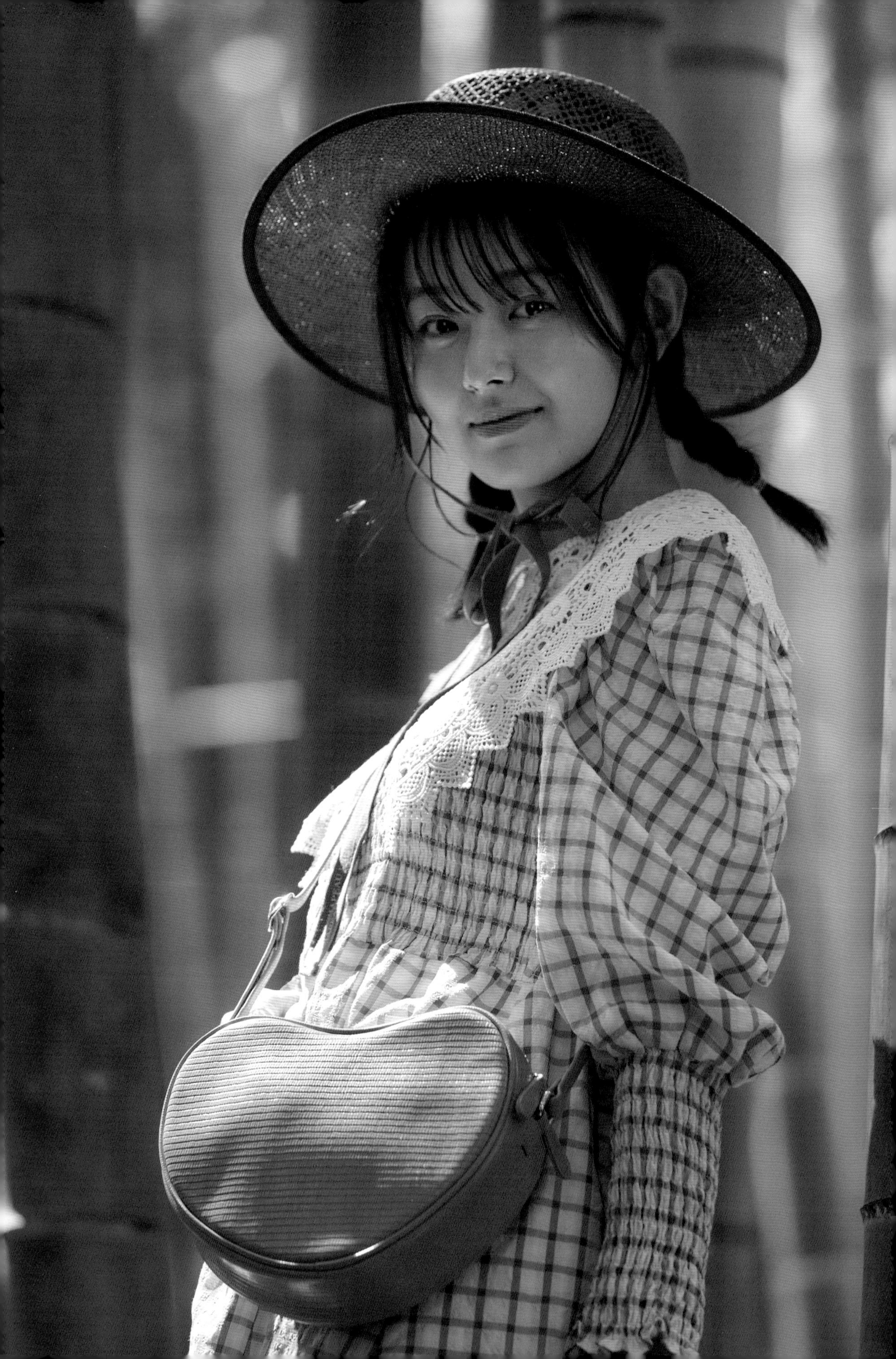

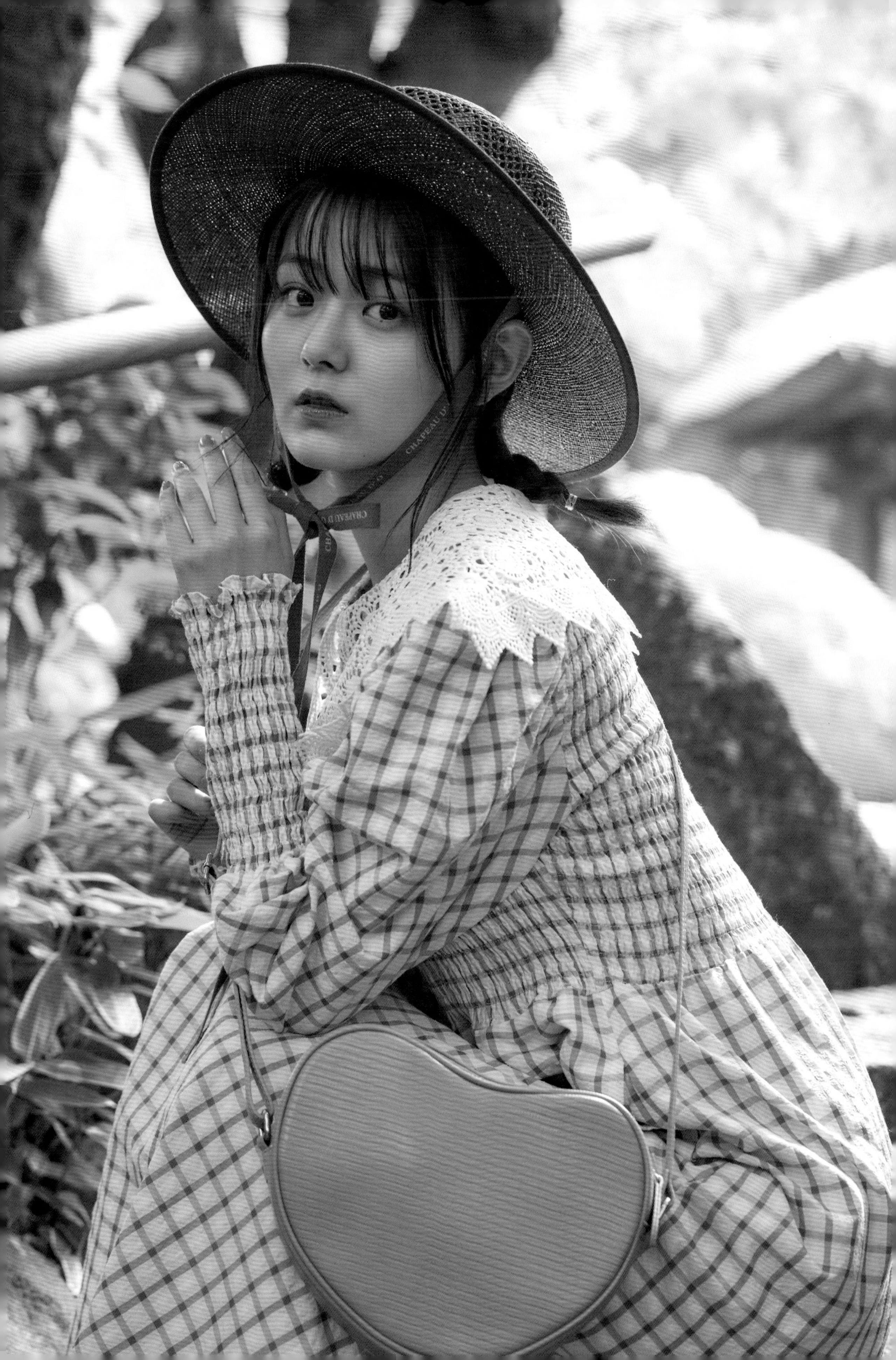

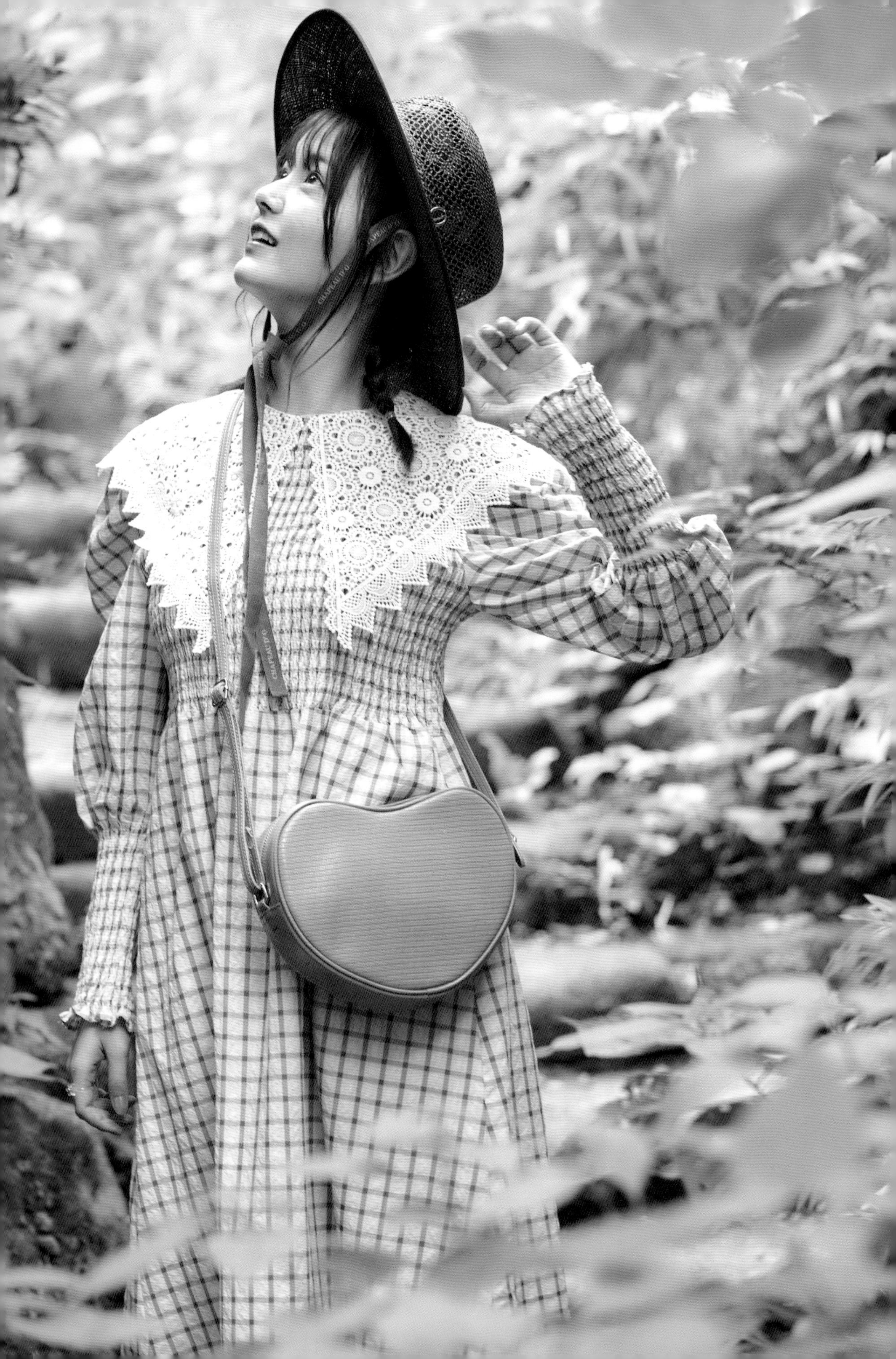

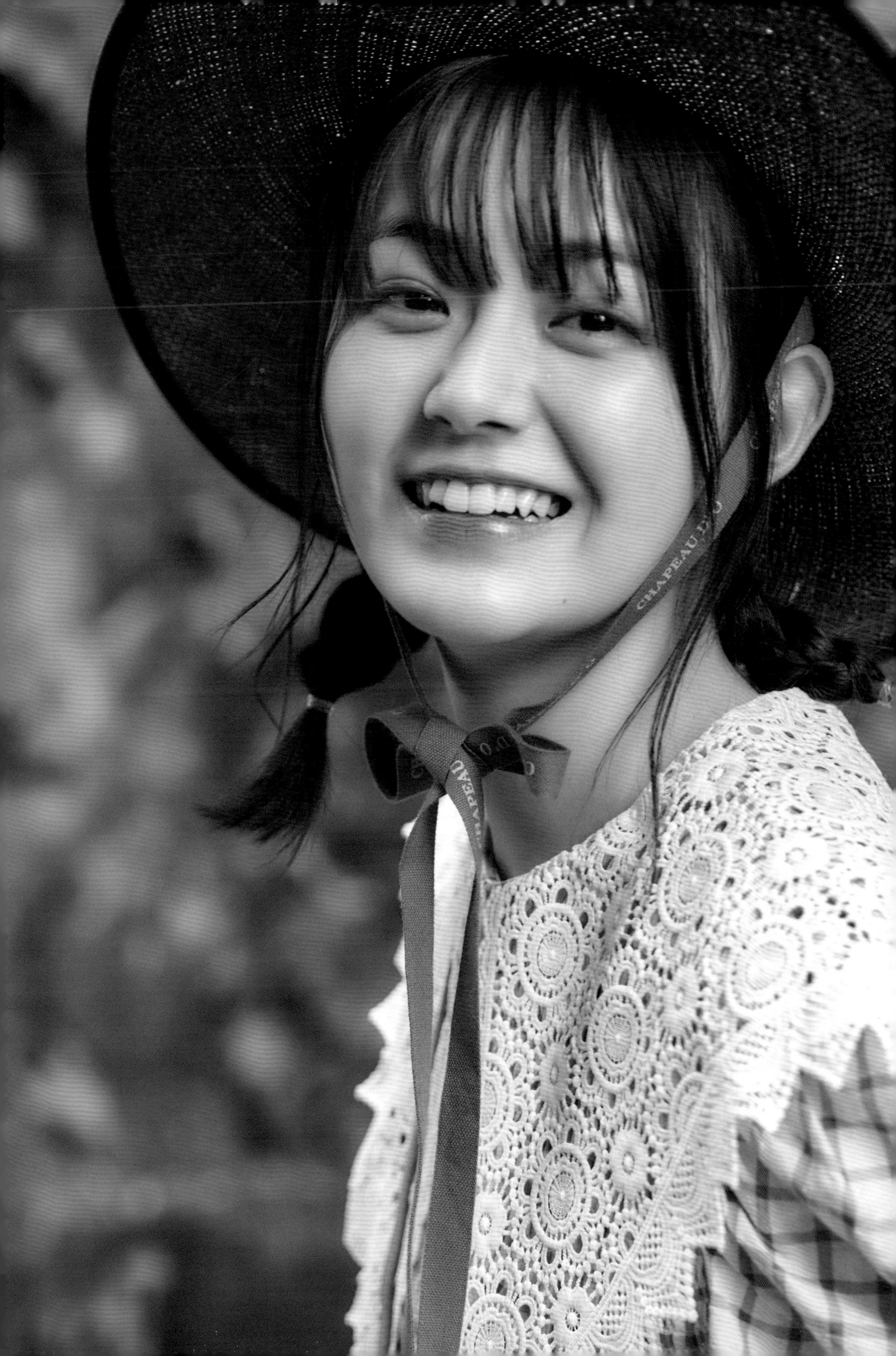
CHAPEAU

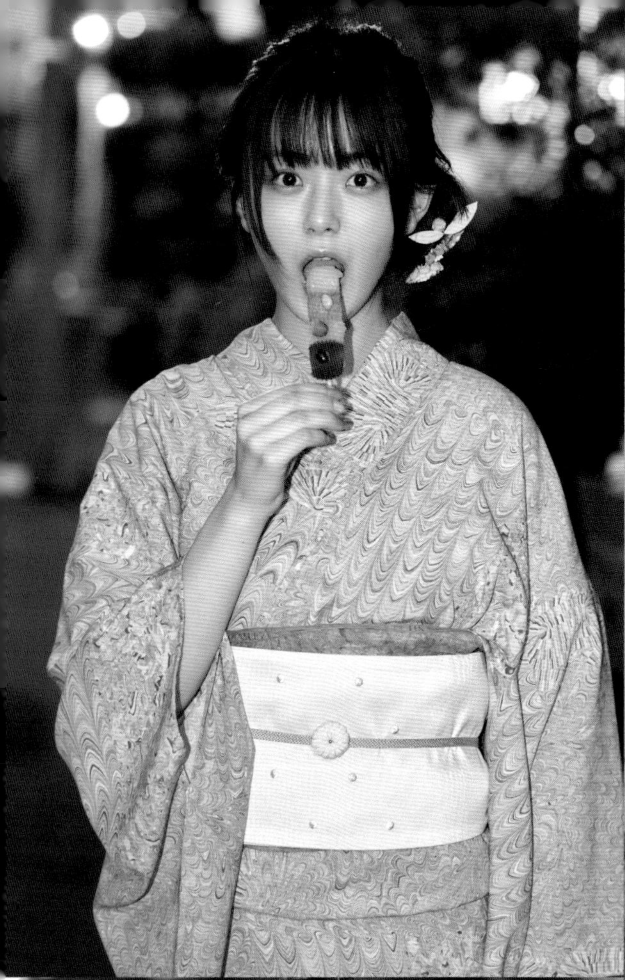
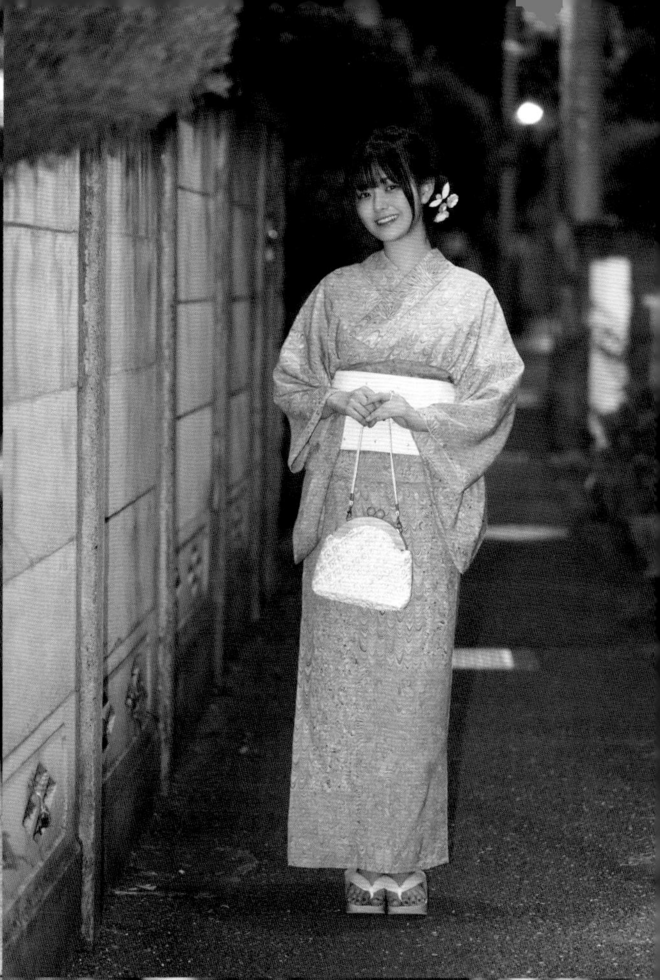
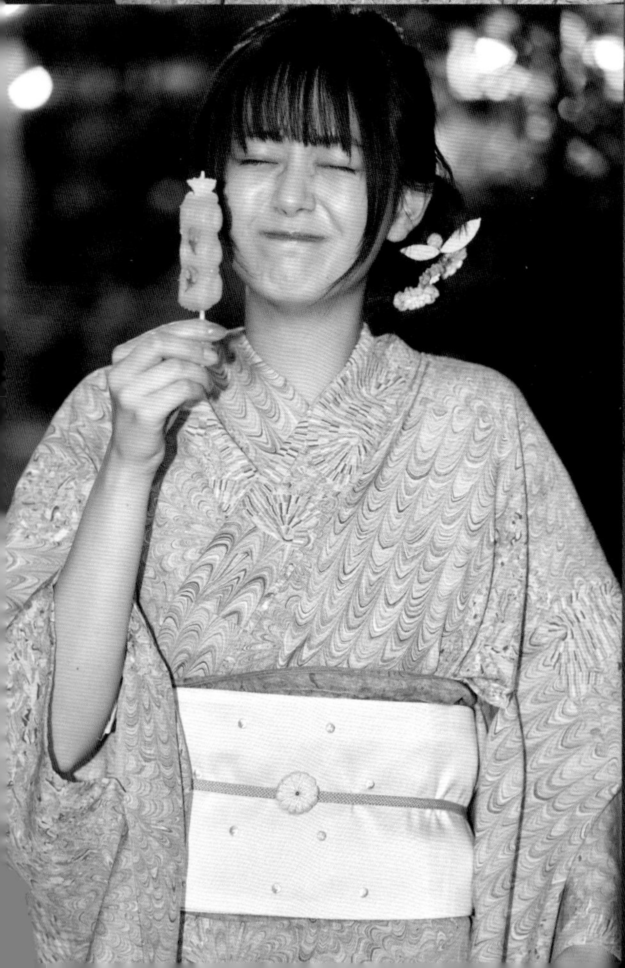
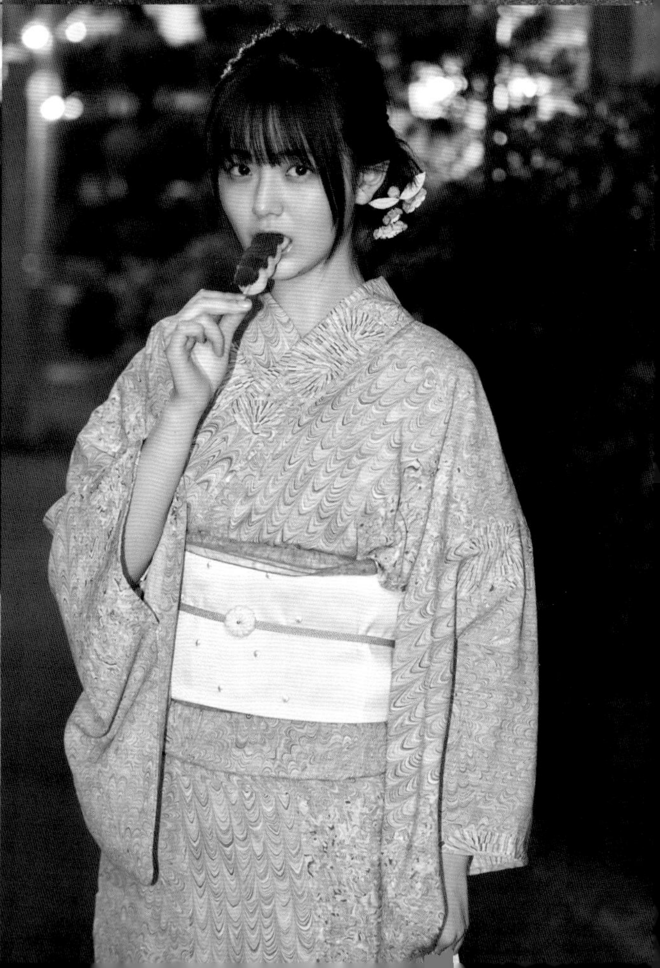

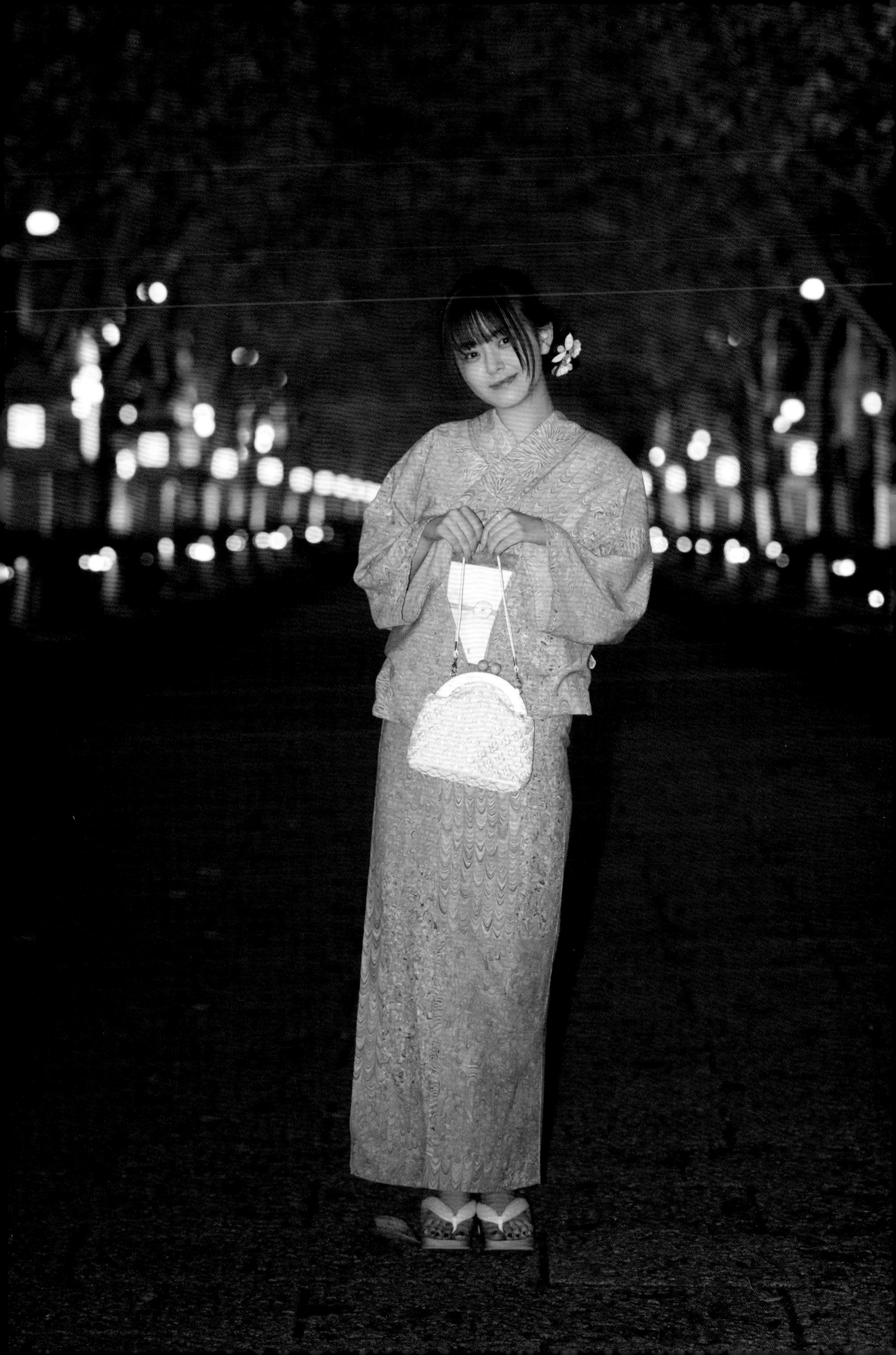

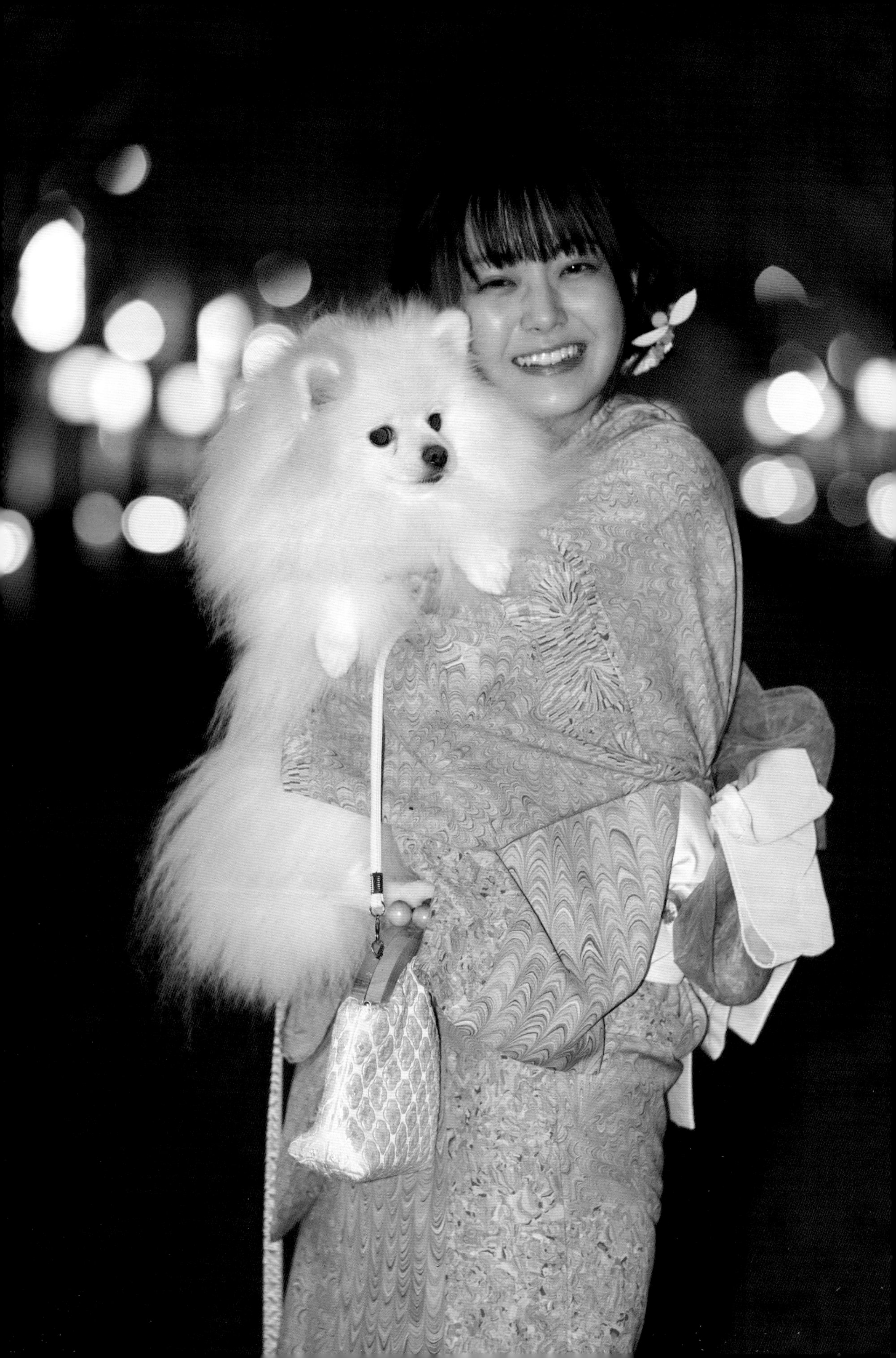

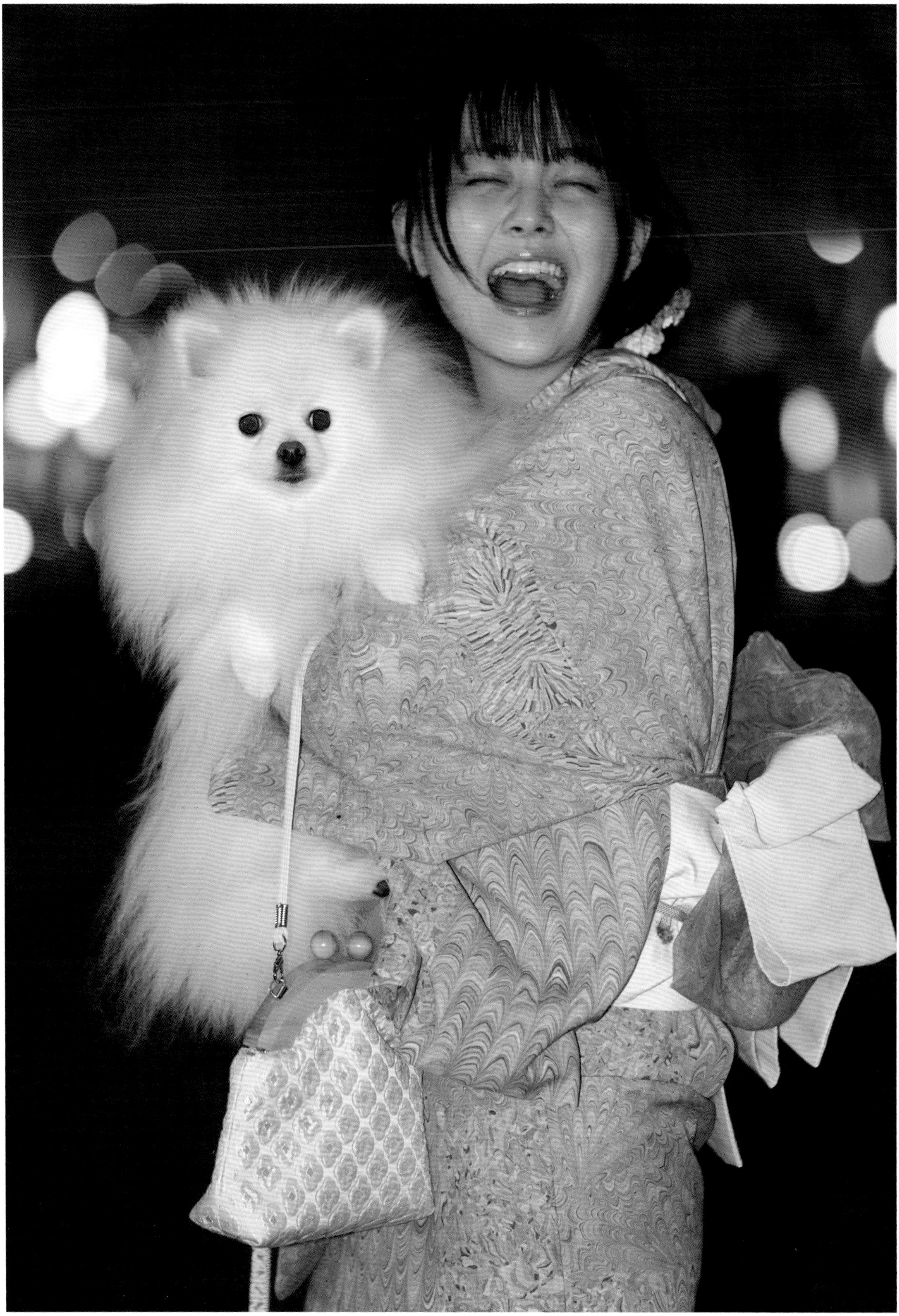

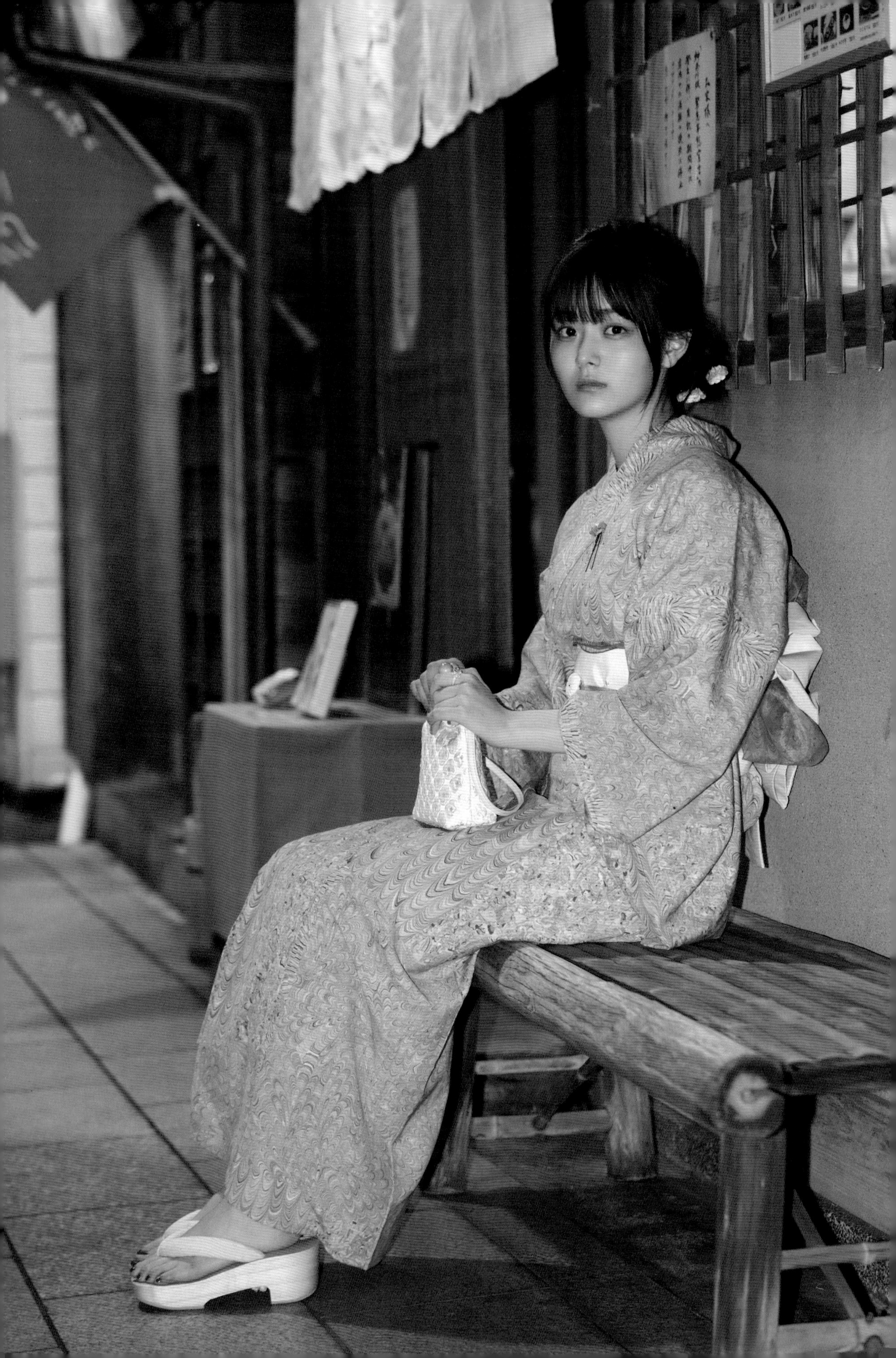

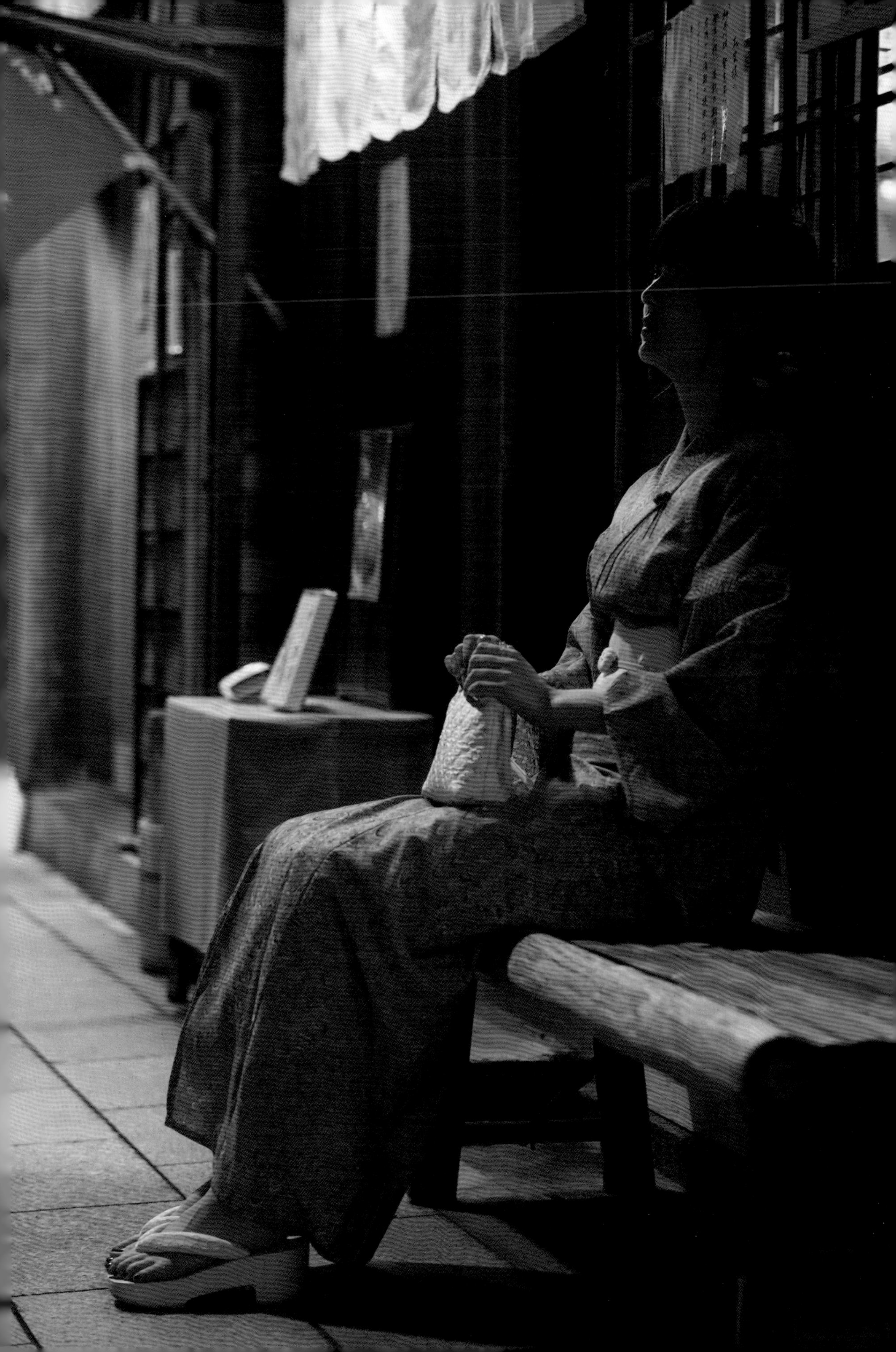

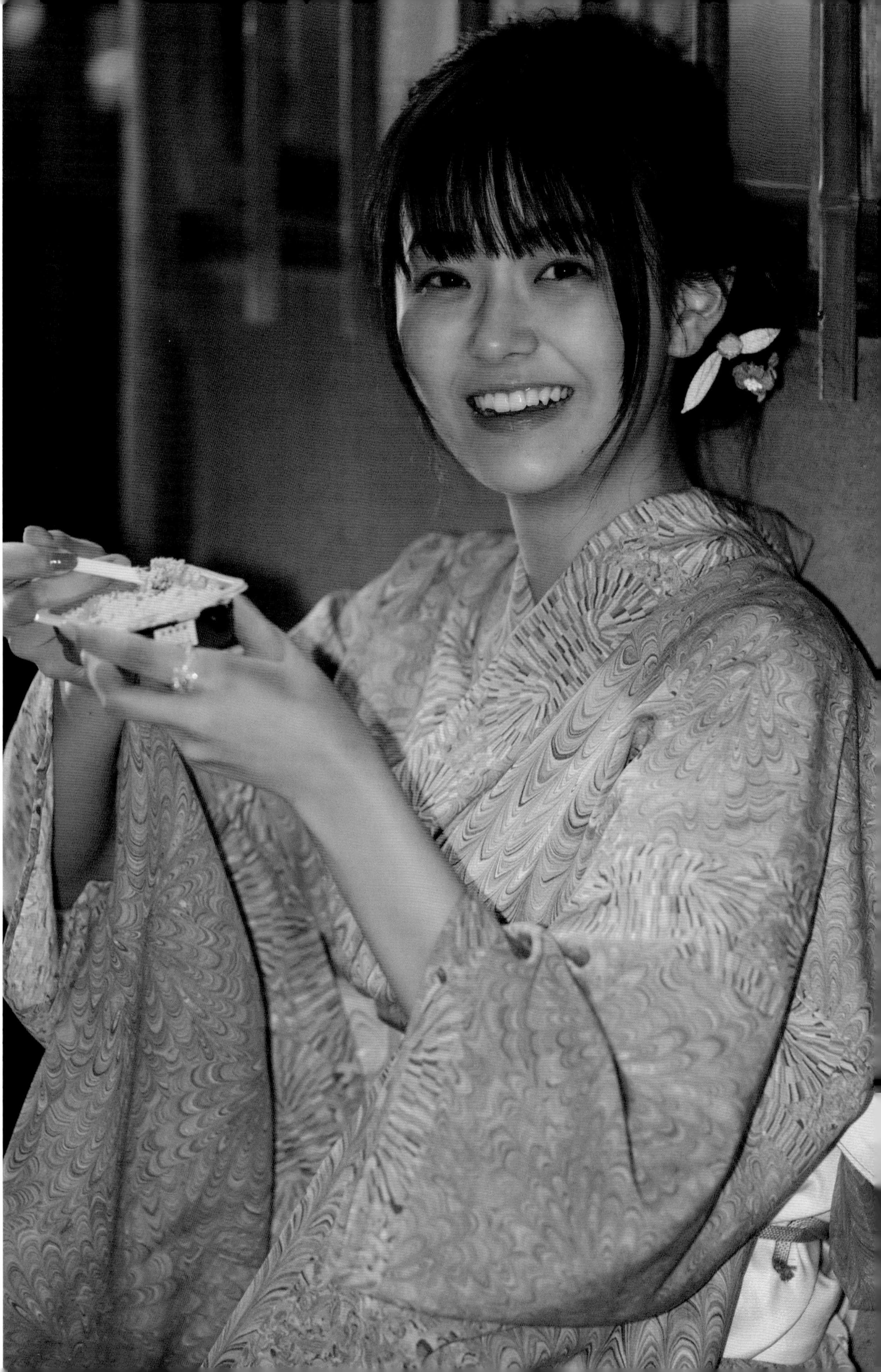

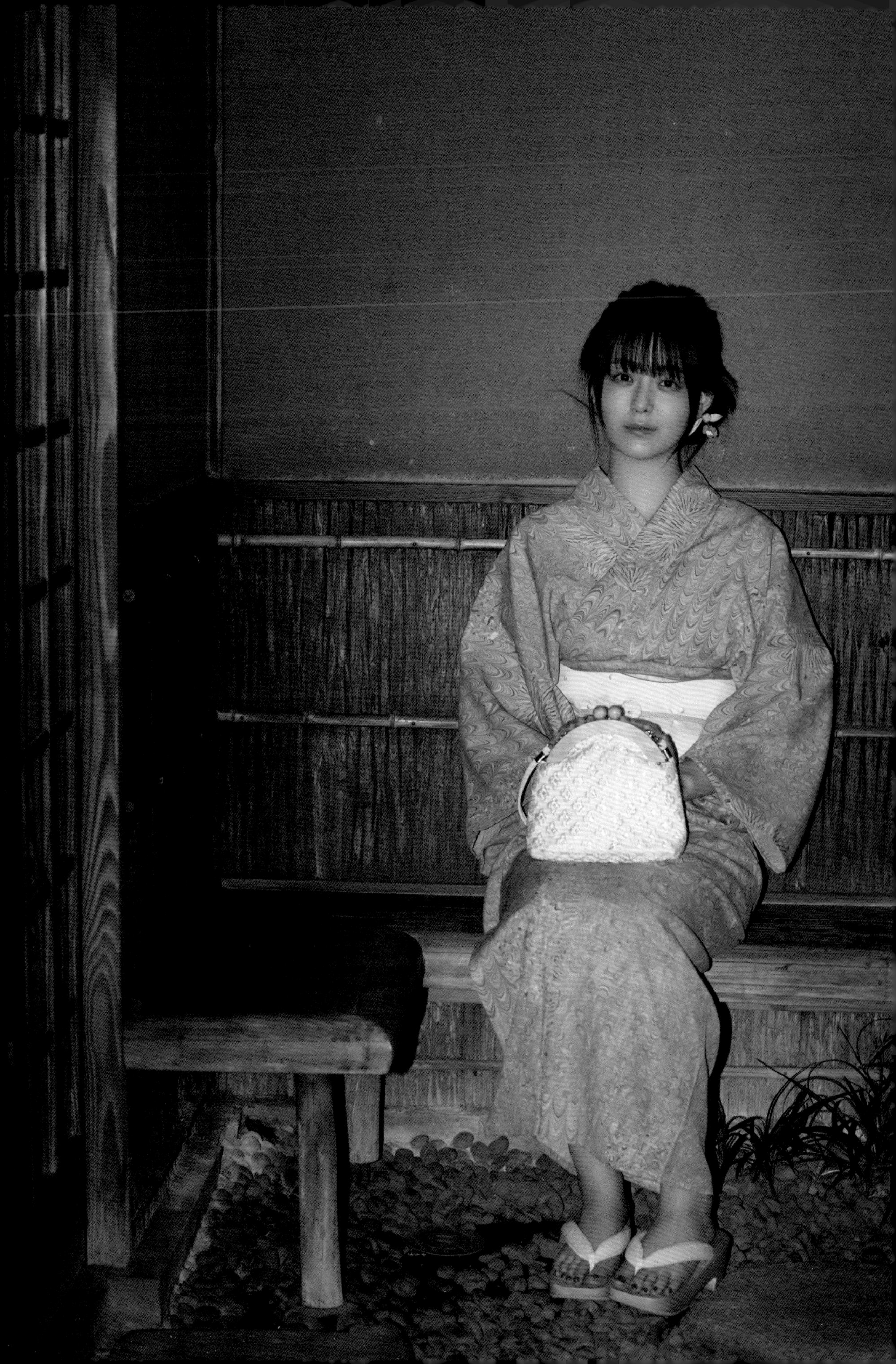

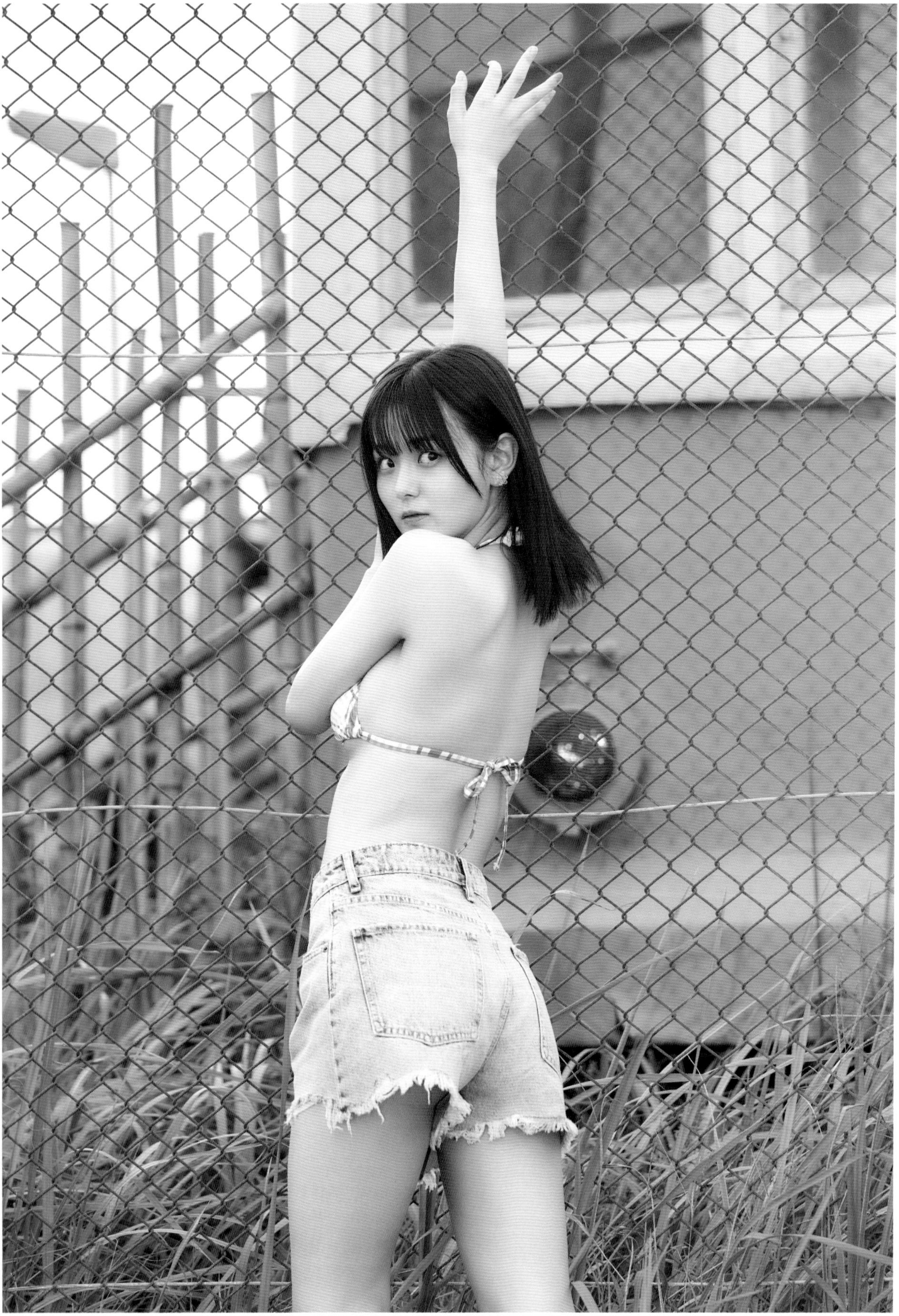

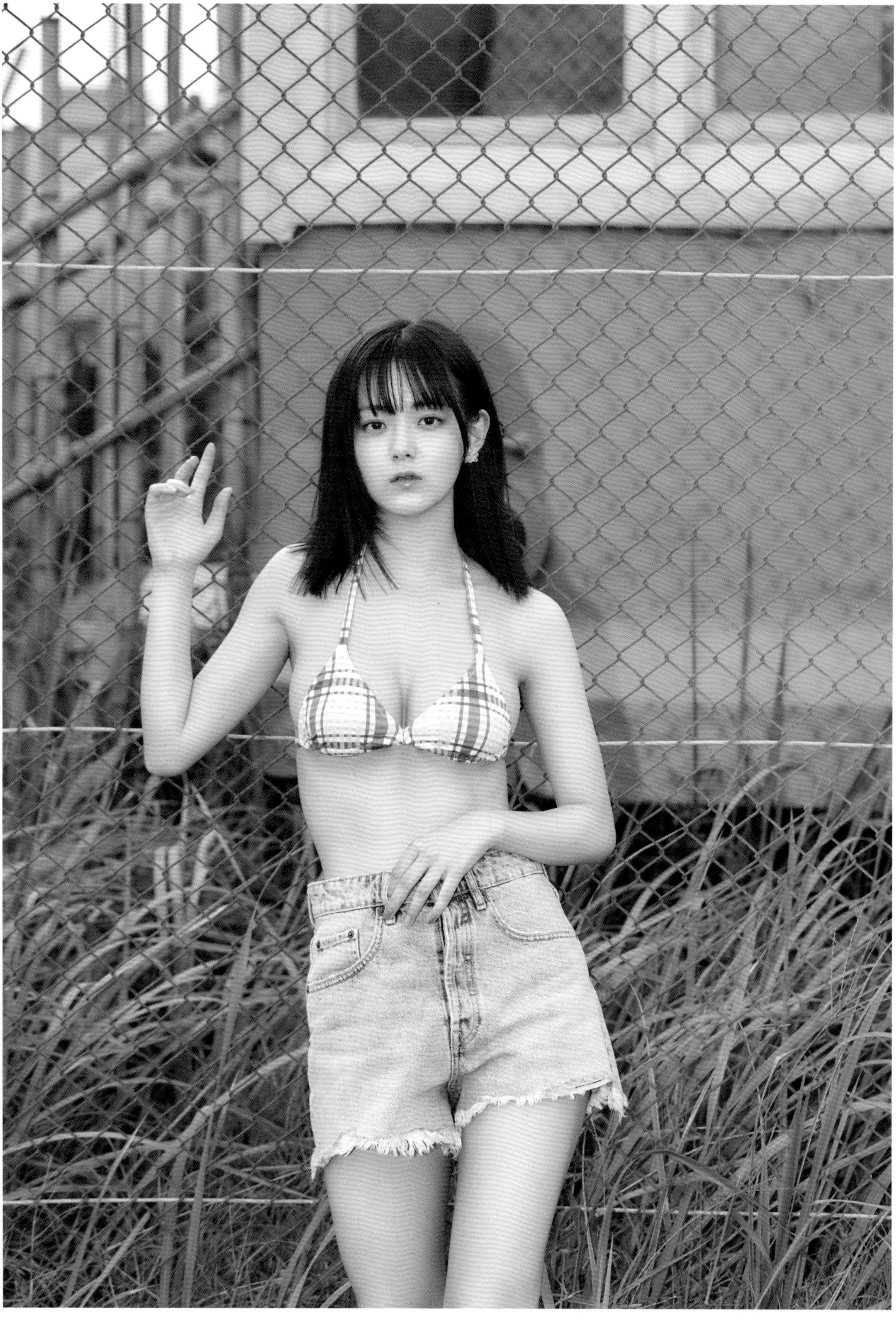

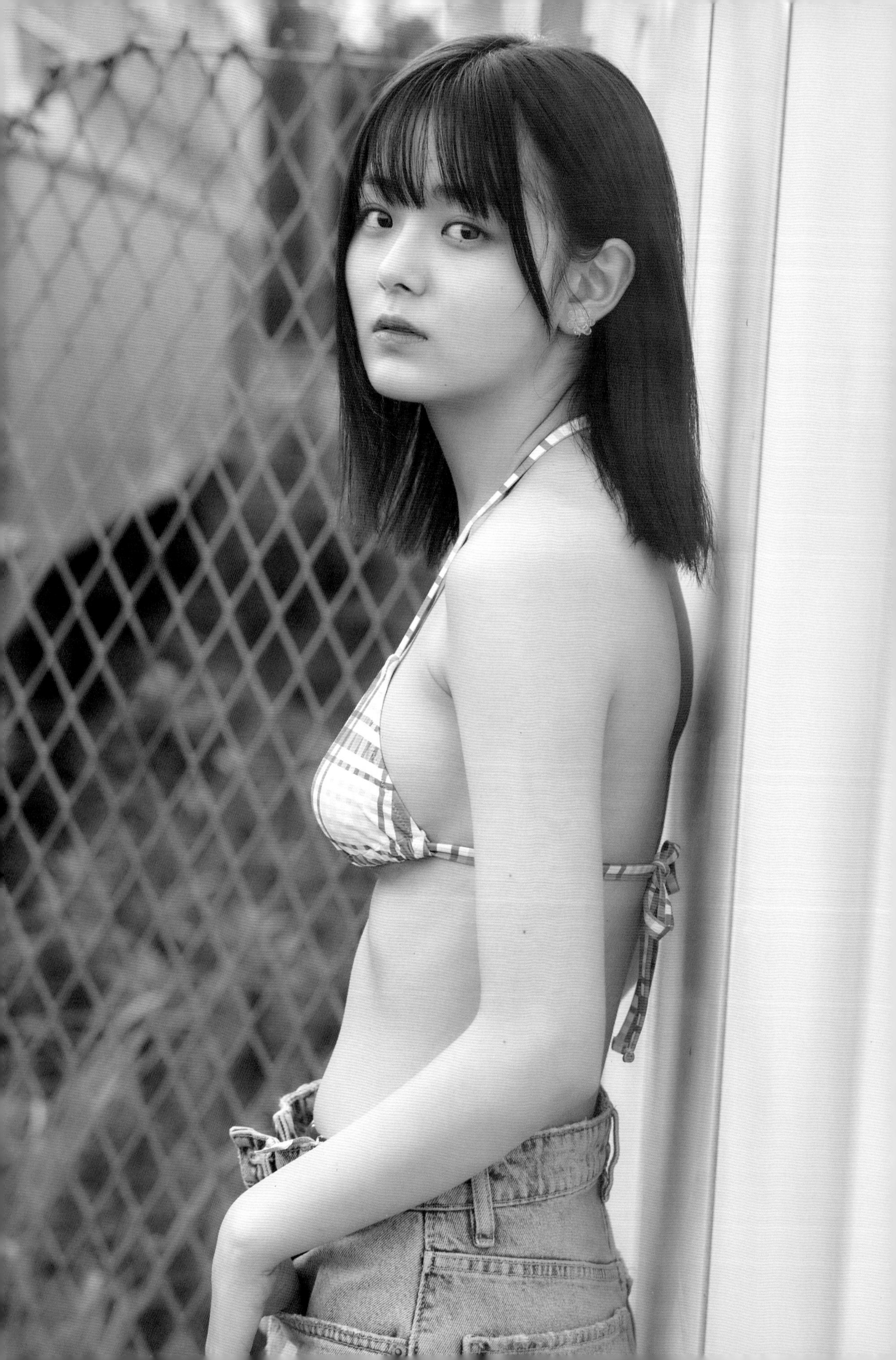

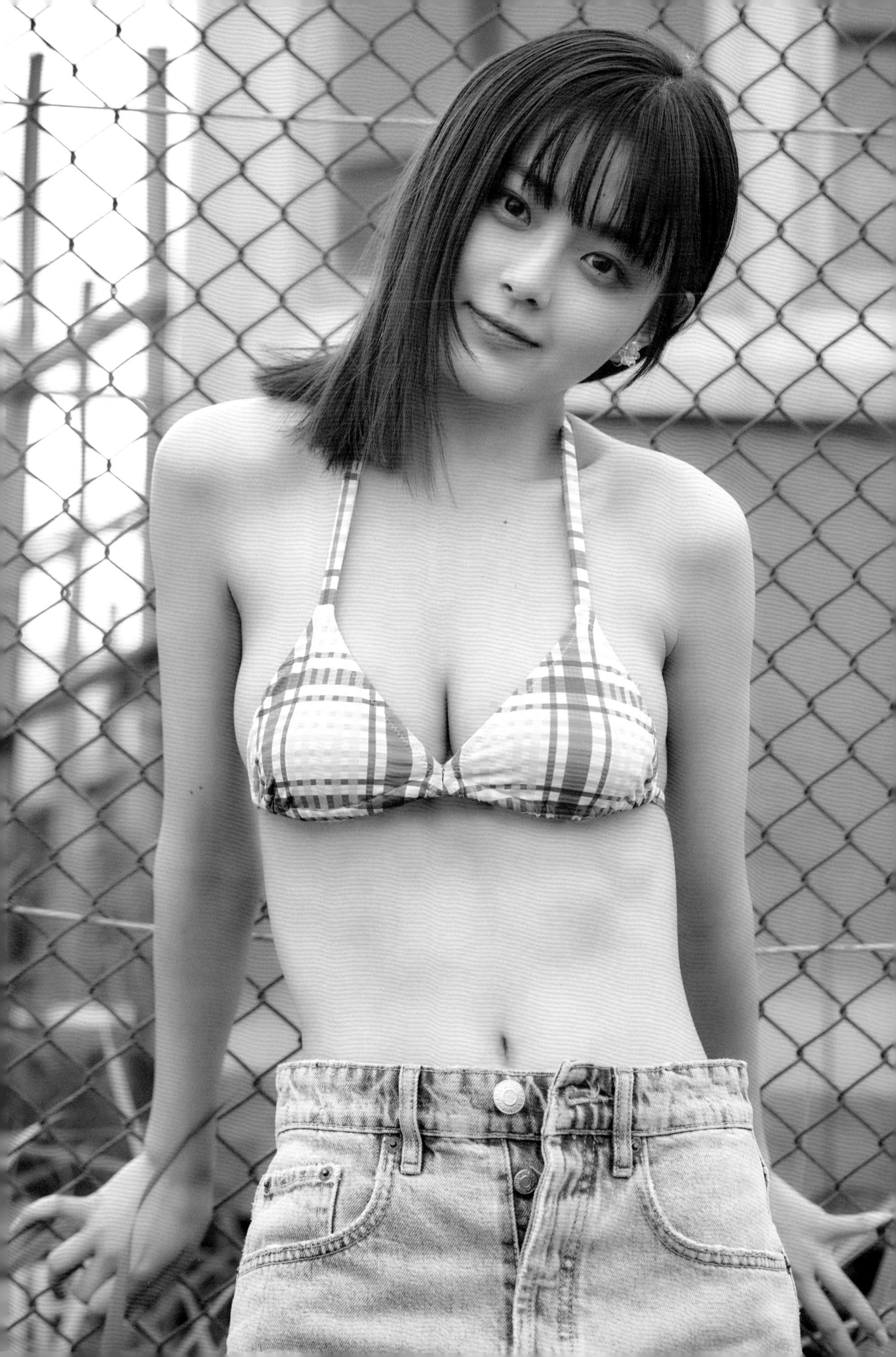

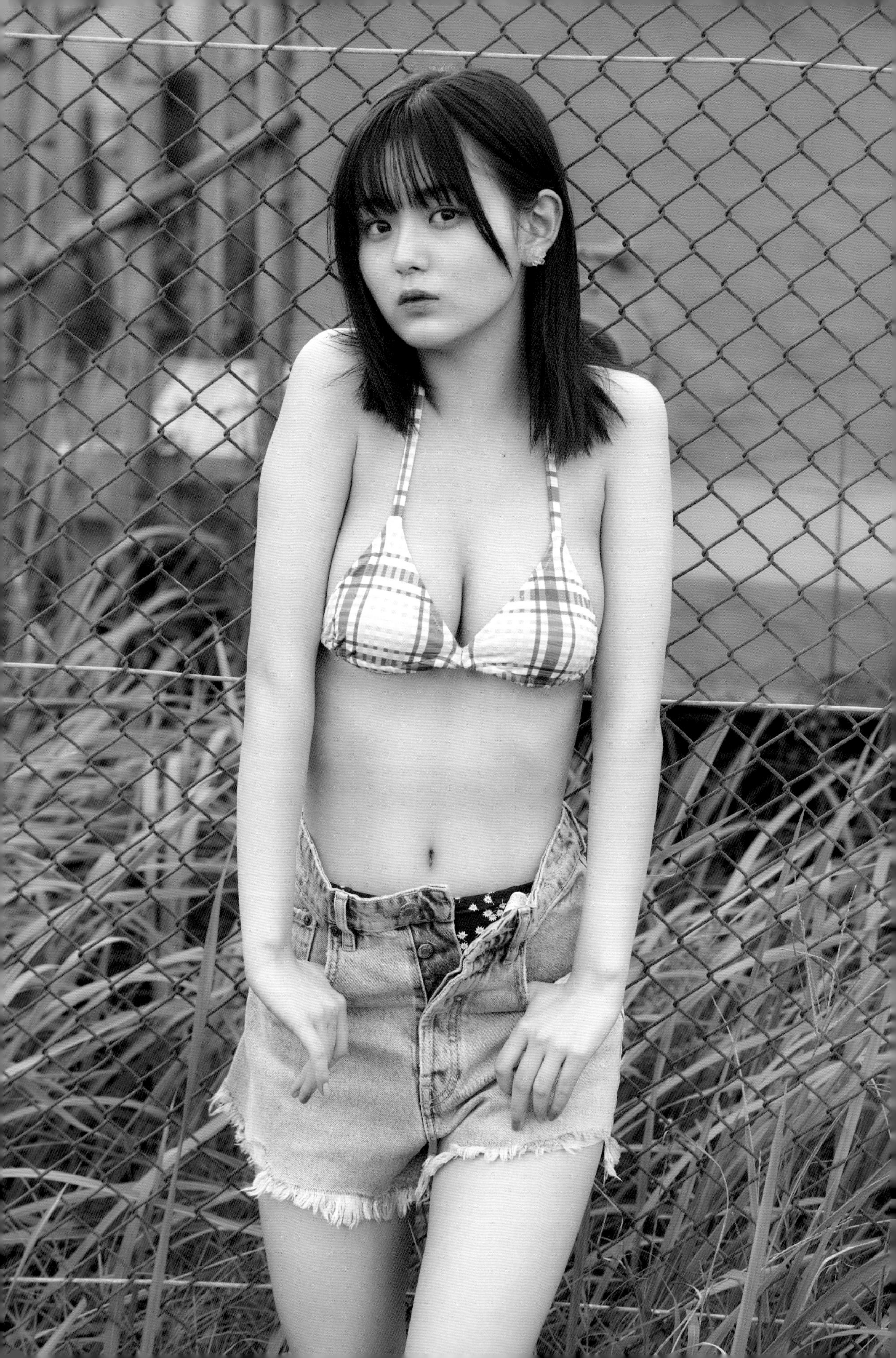

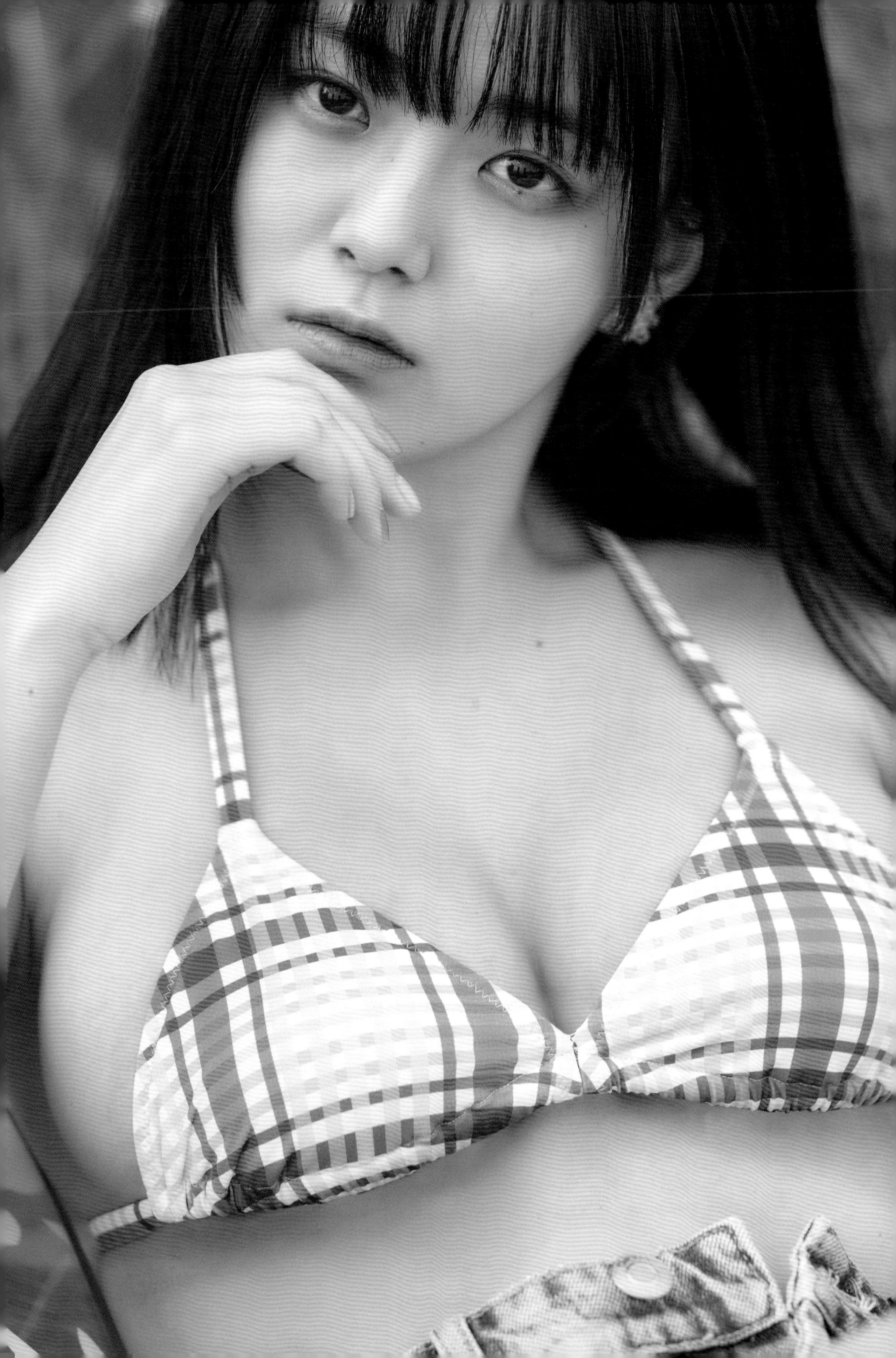

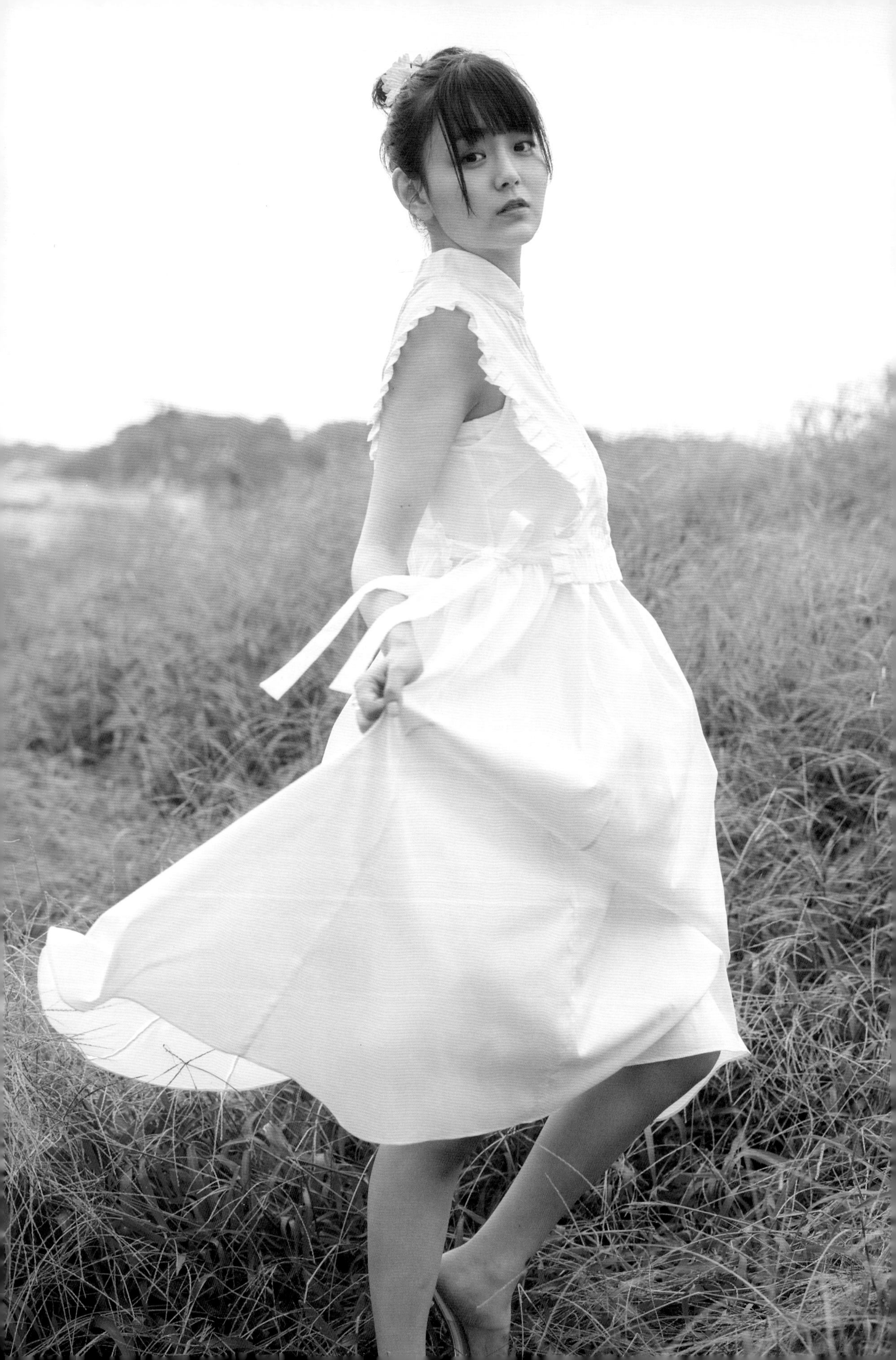

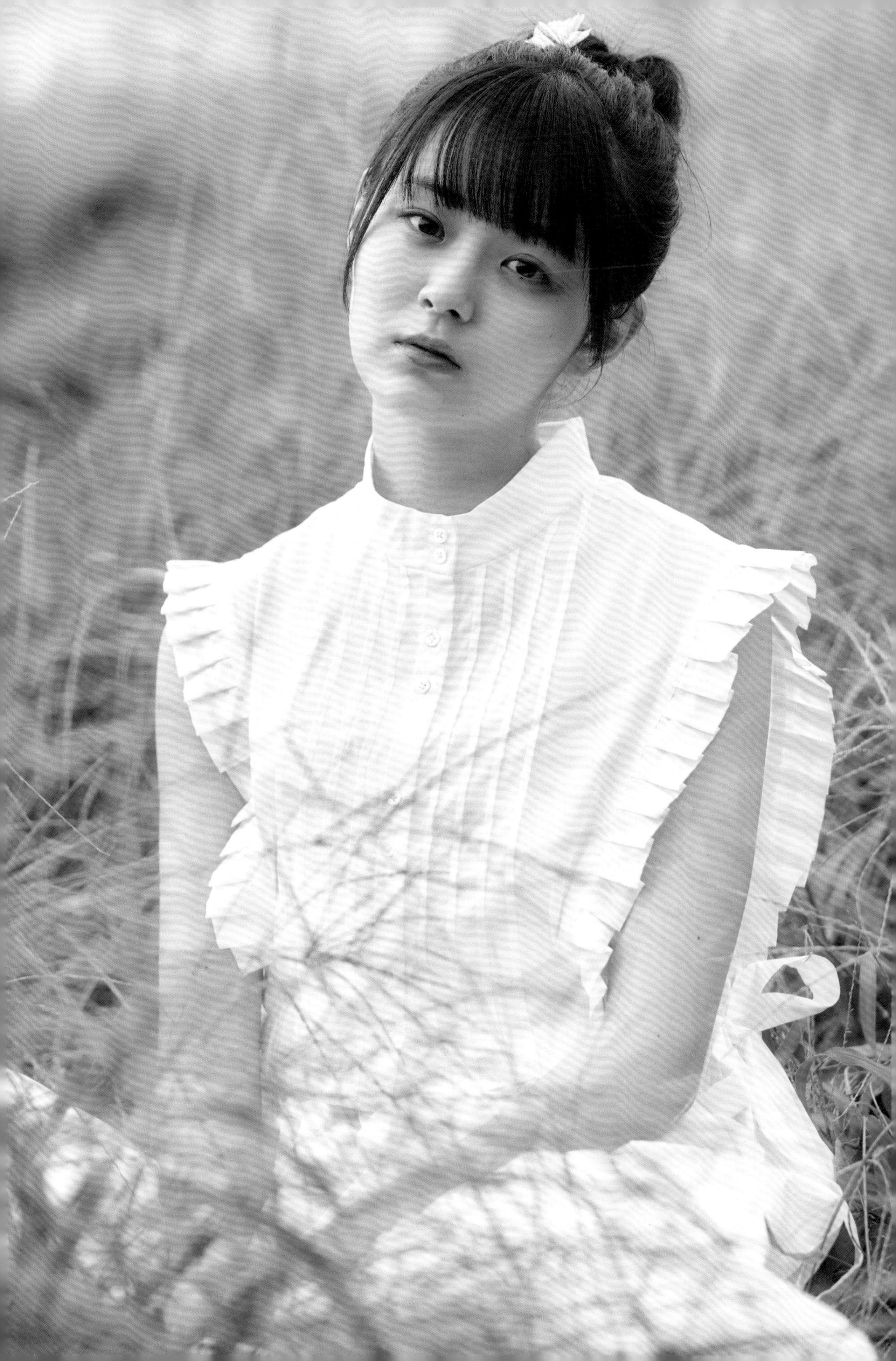

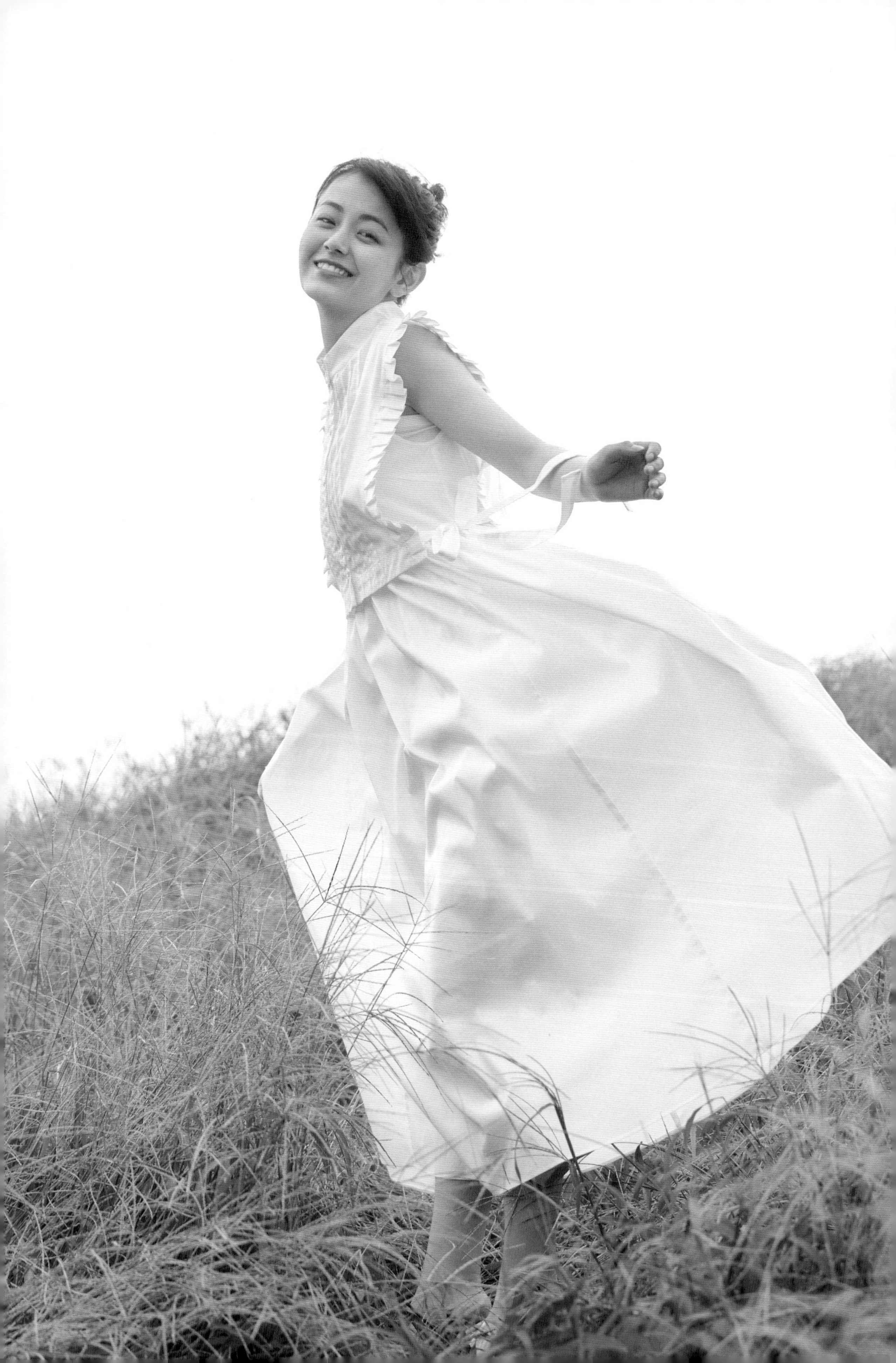

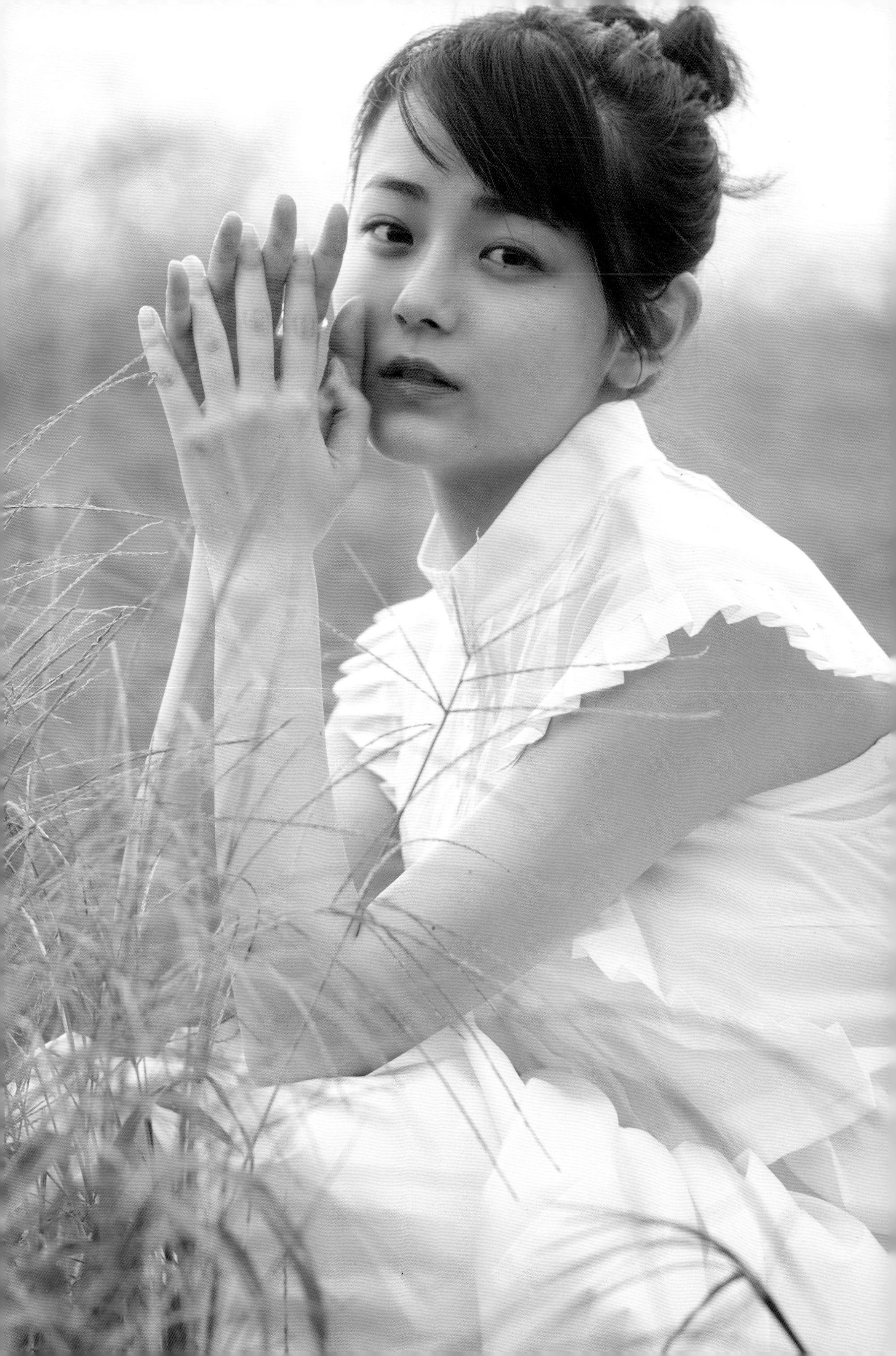

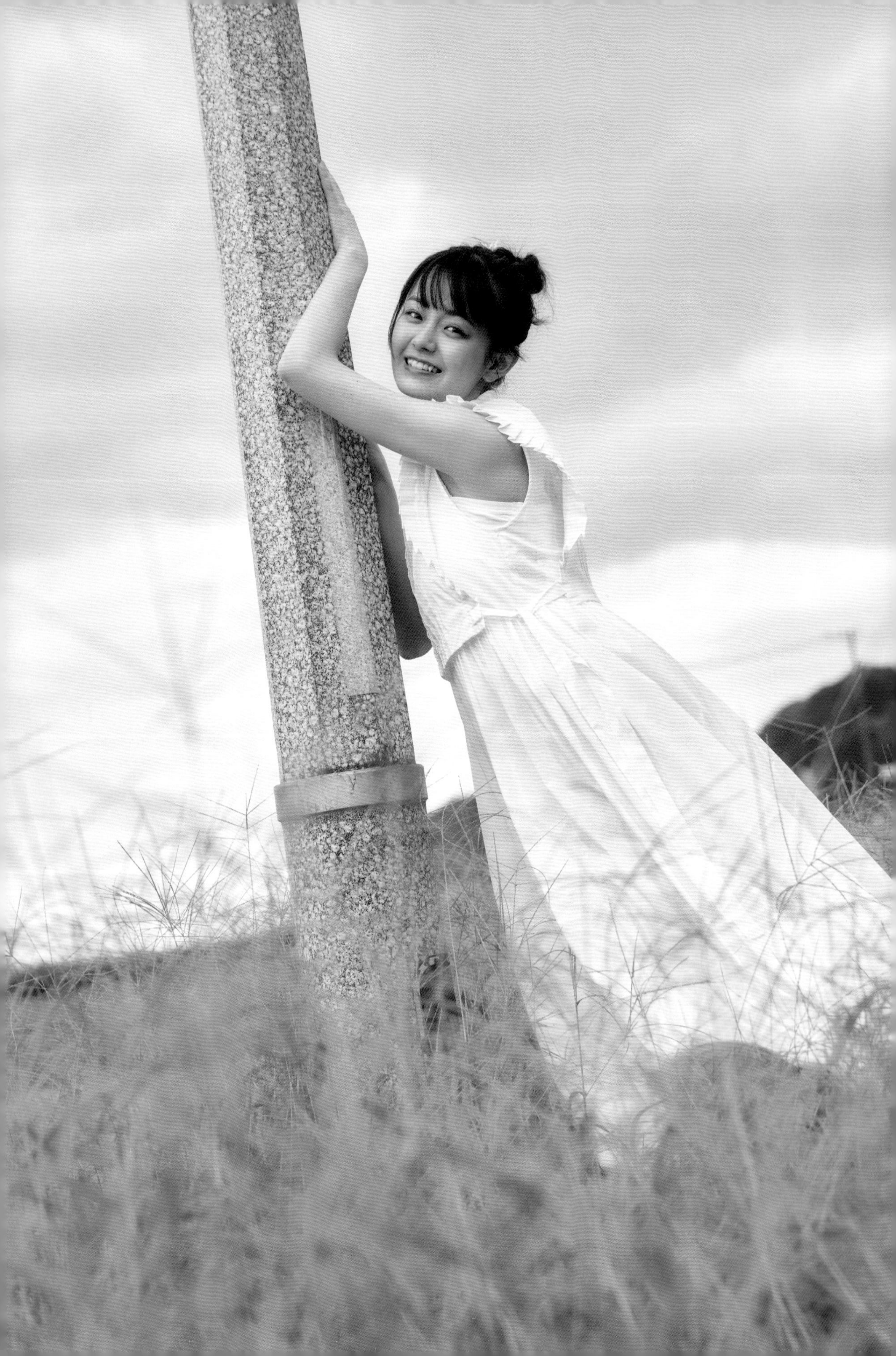

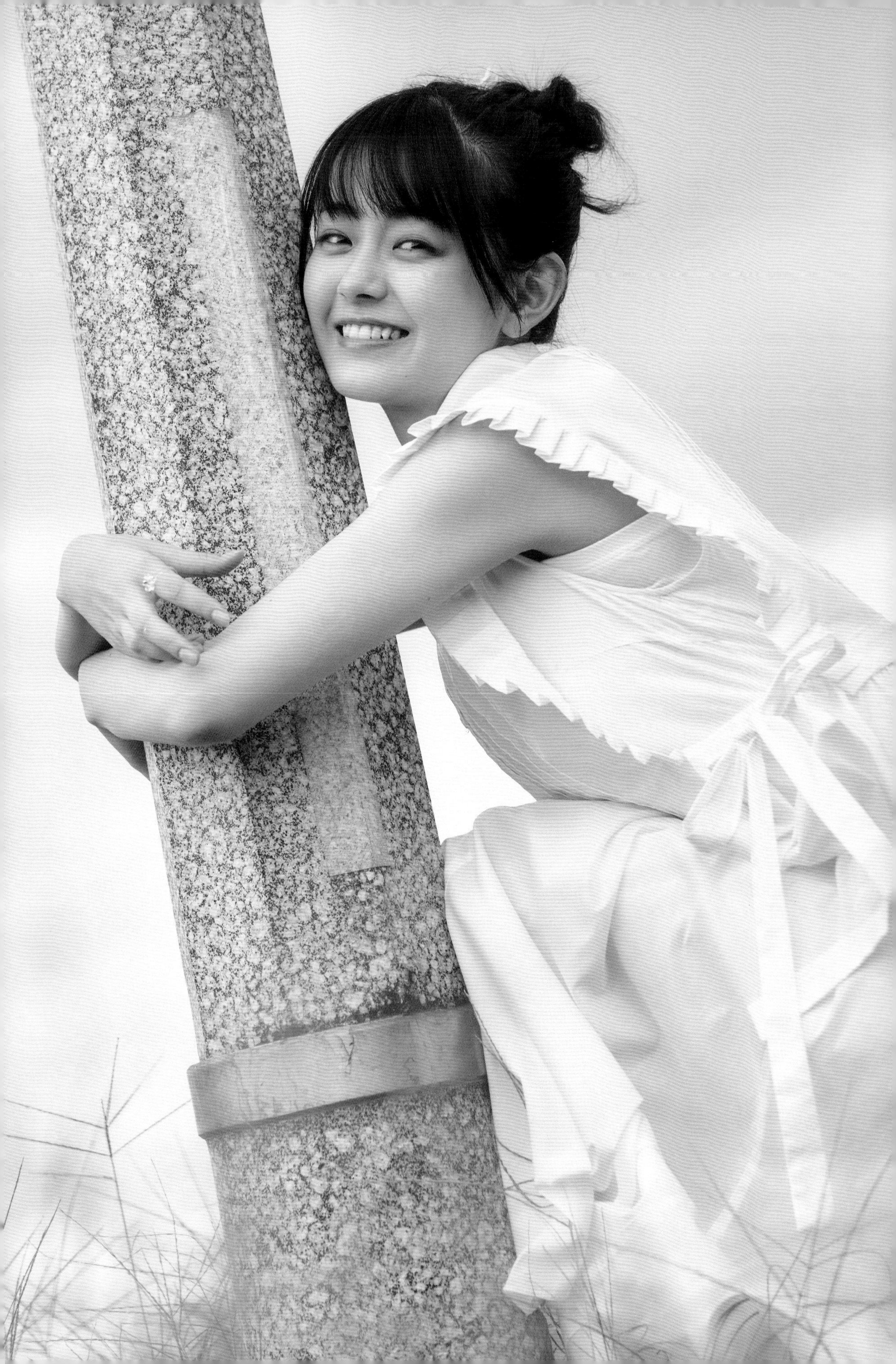

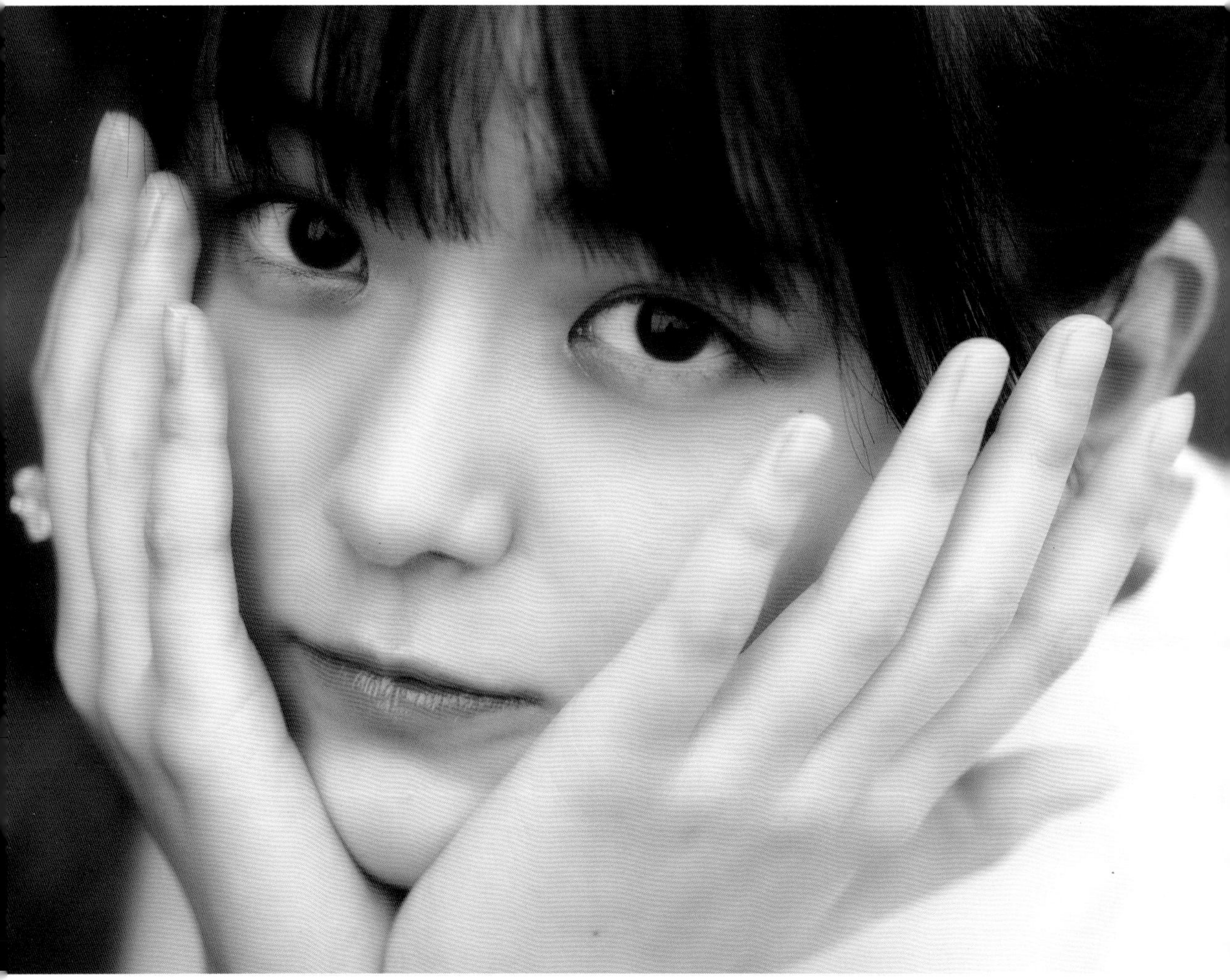